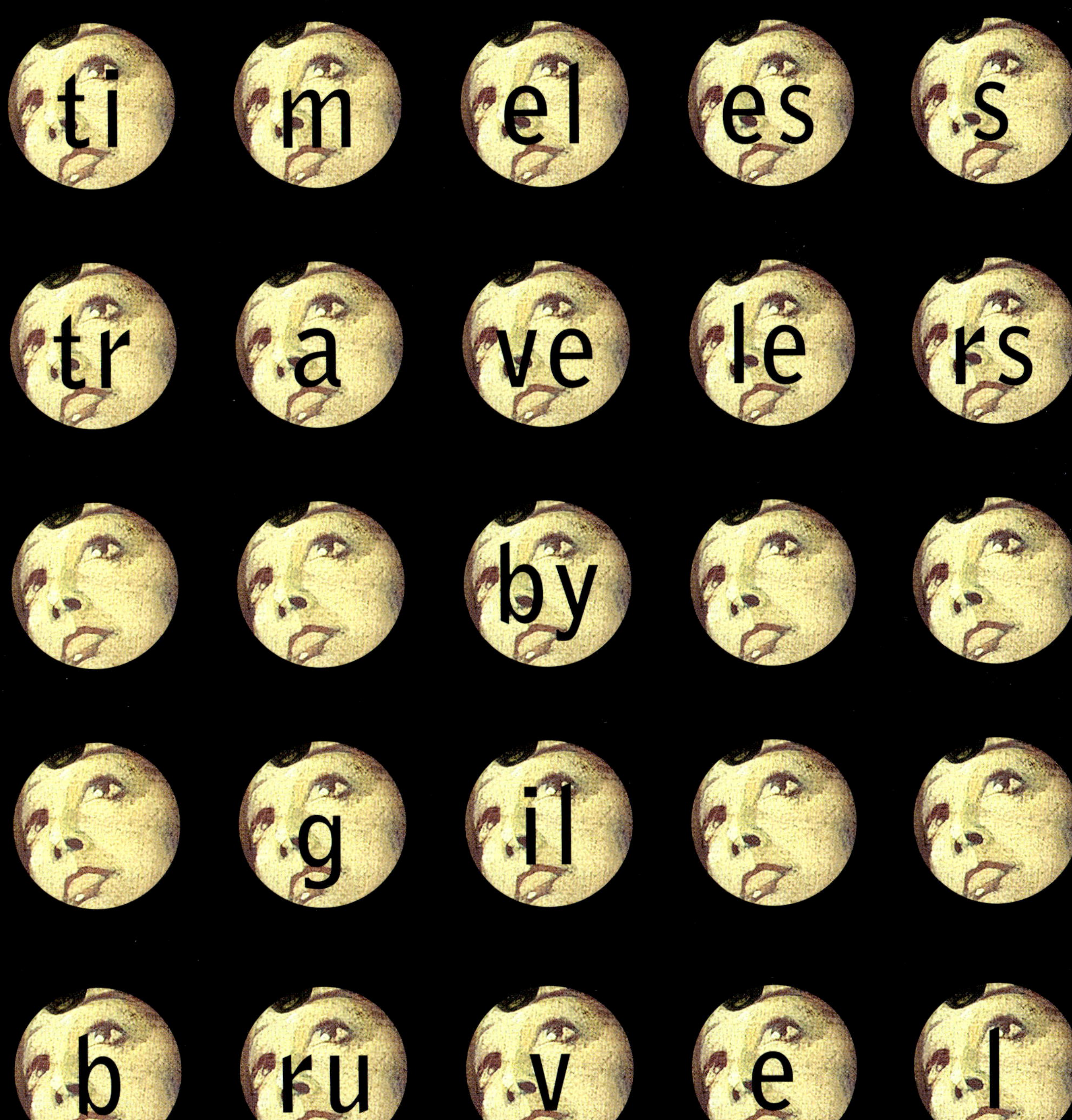
ti m el es s
tr a ve le rs
by
g il
b ru v e l

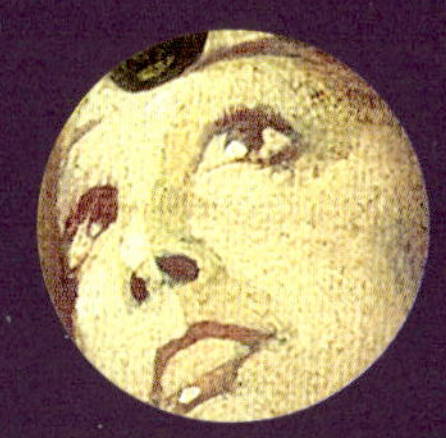

timeless travelers
portraiture by gil bruvel

Published by Bruvel Press
a subsidiary of Bruvel, Inc.

Artwork by Gil Bruvel
Artwork created in: aquatint, oil, gouache, tempera, watercolor, pastel, oil pastel, ink, graphite, colored pencil.

Produced by Marianne Bruvel

Introduction written by
Karen Auvinen

Book Design by Pamela Beverly
Art & Design SLC, Utah
www.pamelabeverly.com

Photography by:
Thomas R. DuBrock
Rob Ratkowski
Steven Minkowski

ISBN
0-9673388-3-2

Printed by
Midas Printing Limited,
Hong Kong
First Edition - 2002

For more information
about the artist please visit:
www.bruvel.com
or contact the artist at:
bruvel@aol.com

Bruvel, Inc.
50 Briar Hollow Lane,
7th Floor-West,
Houston, Texas 77027 USA

www.bruvel.com

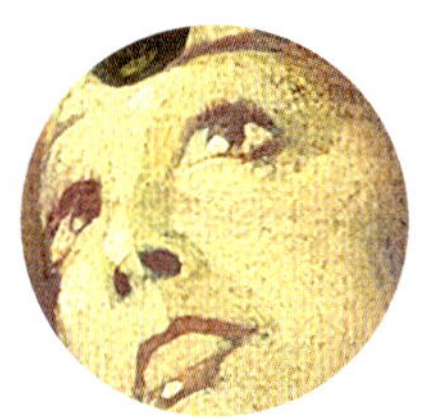

table of contents

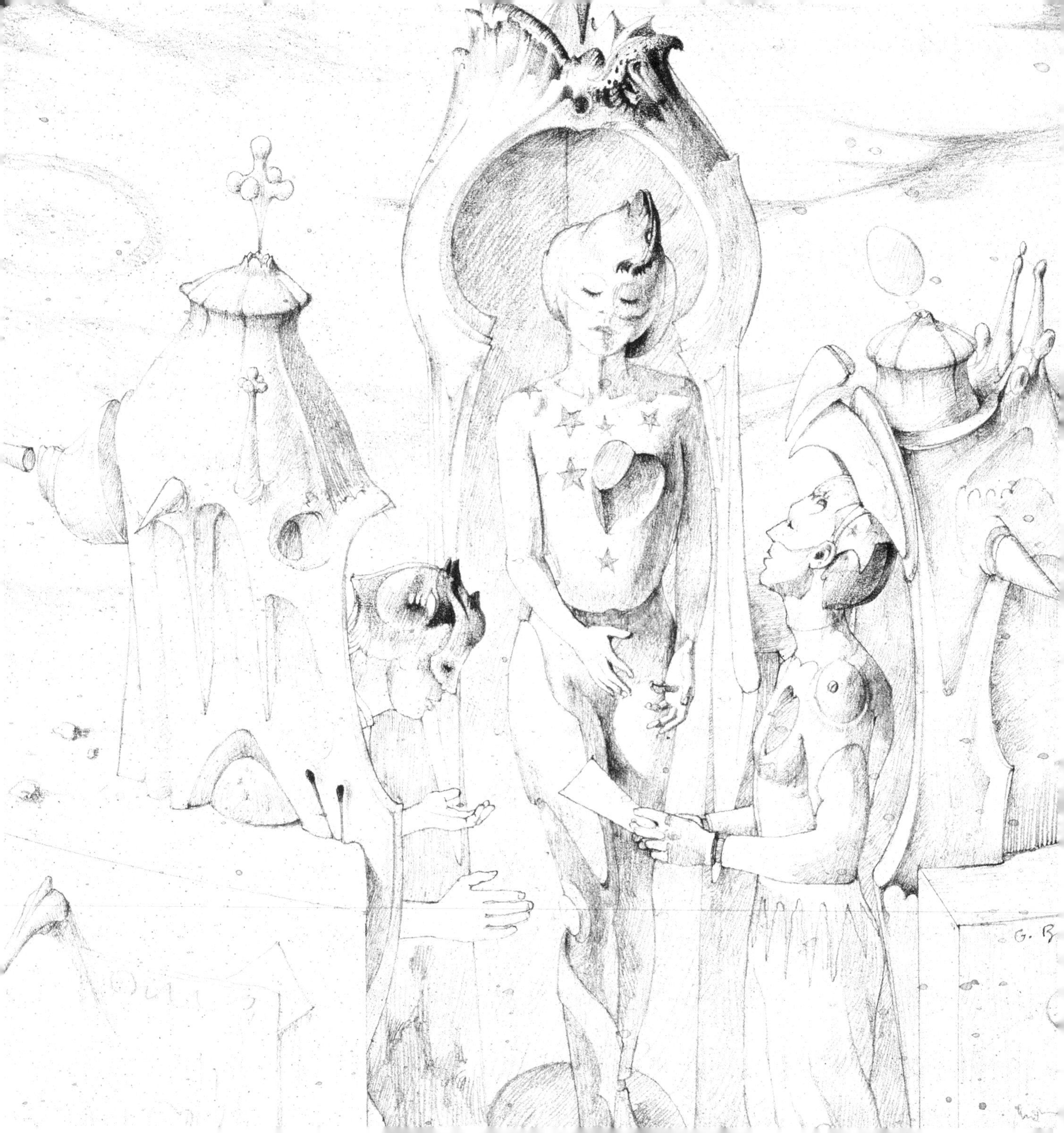

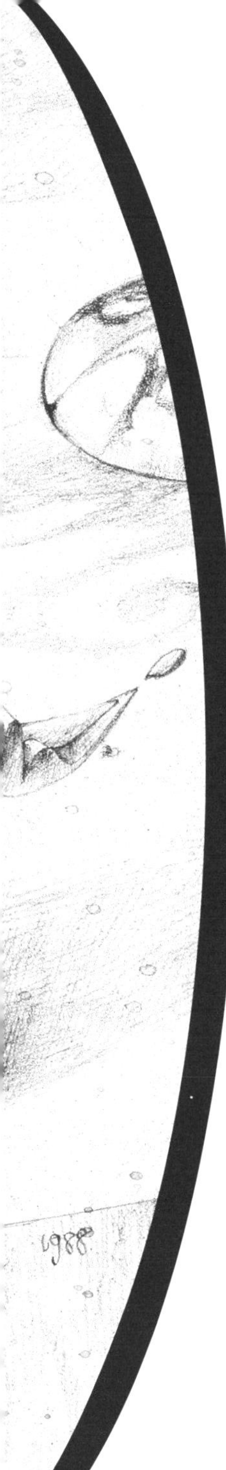

A Universe Within Itself:
The Visionary Art of Gil Bruvel

This book is about portraiture. In it you will find human instruments, masks, the winged face of a woman, figures with no faces at all, a building built from the bust of a man, the serene face of the sleeping moon, marionettes gamboling on hidden strings, and even a giraffe. You will be struck by color—a sense of movement and imagination—and in the end, something deeply human. You will be surprised. And then you will know you have stepped into an extraordinary realm of experience and art, a place of archetype and symbol, a place of intuition—evocative of meditation or a vivid dream: Welcome to the Visionary Art of Gil Bruvel.

"I have no interest in recreating reality."

Gil Bruvel's Visionary style grew out of the dream of making intuitive art. "I have no interest in recreating reality," he says; instead his work emphasizes the imaginative aspects of the mind and body, along with intuition and what he calls "flow—the notion of not knowing, which creates interesting dimensions in art." After a childhood spent making art and studying at Laurent de Montcassin's Restoration Workshop in Chateaurenard, France, the classically trained Bruvel has emerged as a defining force in the Visionary Art Movement. The result is canvasses alive with color, animated by whimsy and archetypal vision.

Bruvel cites Metaphysical painter Giorgio de Chirico, whose paintings used unrelated objects to create brooding dreamscapes, as an early influence in terms of thinking and style. Indeed, his aesthetic grows out of the Modern Art Movement of the late 19th and early 20th Centuries with its resistance to traditional subject and composition, and can be traced to other important artists, including Dadaist Max Ernst, one of the founders of

Surrealism, and Umberto Boccioni of the Italian Futurist Movement. While Bruvel is influenced by the Modernists' experimentation, his work has developed a Visionary aesthetic: Bruvel's art seeks to deepen the human spiritual connection between self and psyche, between intuition and dream, in new and startling ways.

"A universe within itself..."

From the beginning, Bruvel's inspiration for *Timeless Travelers* has been to move closer to the canvas. To this end, he chose close-up details of larger works as the organizing metaphor for the book's portraits. "I wanted to take pieces of my paintings," says Bruvel, "and show the viewer a whole other way of looking at my work." Smaller details, like the smile of a woman or the intricate scrolling along a cheek—details that might have been overlooked in a larger work—*blossom*, specifically and unexpectedly, says Bruvel, inside the borders of the newly created portrait. Opening the pages of *Timeless Travelers* is like opening up a window to a sky full of stars: Each portrait sparkles in its own unique light, each "creates a universe within itself."

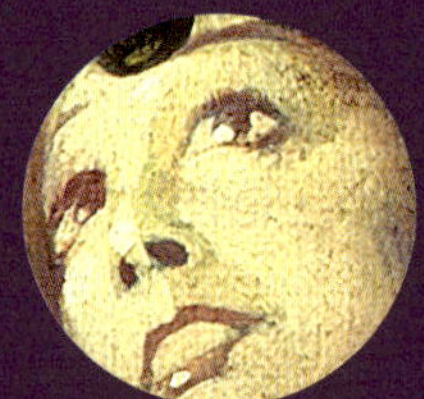

And these tiny universes shine a curious light onto Bruvel's artistic process: He works on the portraits one by one before they are refined and brought into focus in the larger work. Bruvellian canvasses are full of the kind of individually detailed work depicted on these pages. And in this way, *Timeless Travelers* is a book of artistic journey and creative process, one that examines the details of Bruvel's oeuvre to reveal surprising insights.

"The ever-changing flux... of our own Identity."

Even though Bruvel's paintings may summon dreamscapes and futuristic visions, his concern is essentially human. "By exploring portraiture," says Bruvel, "I can explore, in detail, each facet of what we are made of–what we are composed of." Following in the tradition of de Chirico and others, Bruvel's work studies construct–the idea that humans build arbitrary perceptions of themselves to present to the world–in order to examine the underlying truth of human nature and existence. Bruvel's examination of these perceptions manifests in his work in the unusual and often surprising shapes and structures on human bodies. *Timeless Travelers* is a pageant of figures with elaborately constructed masks, beaks, hats (or "hairdos," as Bruvel calls them); some with detailed contours shadowing their cheeks or metallic looking projections spiraling from their eyebrows; others with hinge-like limbs and architectural shapes encasing their bodies. These figures represent Bruvel's fascination with perception. He sees a tension or "ambivalence" between what he calls "constraint and freedom," that the individual human perception of self and psyche can either limit or liberate. And this is a powerful force for Bruvel; "We have," he warns, "the ability to make ourselves our own prisoners—but we can *also* free ourselves as well." His work seeks to examine the mutable nature of identity (as manifested in masks, faces, costumes, shapes etc.) in order to understand the ways in which individuals perceive and represent themselves to the world. To this end, portraiture works perfectly with Bruvel's own vision. "For me," he says, "the portrait is the ideal medium to represent the ever-changing flux of our own *representation* of our own identity." Thus, the figures in *Timeless Travelers* appear obscured or masked, emerging or transmogrified depending on where their individual balance—the flux of their identity—lies. In the end, Bruvel's work is to understand that this process of being is not static, but evolutionary.

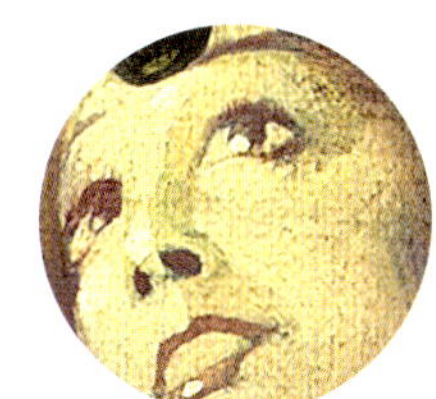

"[The Mask] is definitely not costuming ...it is definitely very real."

One of the most interesting and unusual motifs to permeate *Timeless Travelers* is the Mask. Masks emerge almost organically from the faces of the subjects here, pointing to a critical departure from traditional portraiture. Bruvel is fascinated with the Mask, which has been used for centuries in theater and in ritual to represent an *assumed* personality or trait, one not normally associated with the Mask bearer. However, in Bruvel's portraits, the Masks represent interiority—"the things that we assimilate from the outside world and turn into ourselves." He continues:

> I don't value so much the Mask for its costuming use. My personal exploration over the years brought me to the realization that masks have a very strong power. In relation to the psyche, they represent *and* signify reality. To me, the mask is where the social distinctions are blurred and obliterated, where "masking" is a condition *sine qua non* of participating in our own personal truth. Masks are representations of ourselves that forces us to unify our past and our present in a solidified representation of our inner self. Sometimes, for me, masks represent rebirth and renewal—dramatized through symbolic portrayals of sex and destruction. The mask itself draws its own strength from the myth it creates. The visage/mask is a mythical facade through which much of the world will embrace us. This concept of the visage is based on a Neo-platonic belief that artwork, beauty, and grandeur reflects an inner stability, social order, and virtue. The mask can be a way to revert to the past as the most concrete, secure and uncontested source of its identity. It is definitely not costuming for me at all—

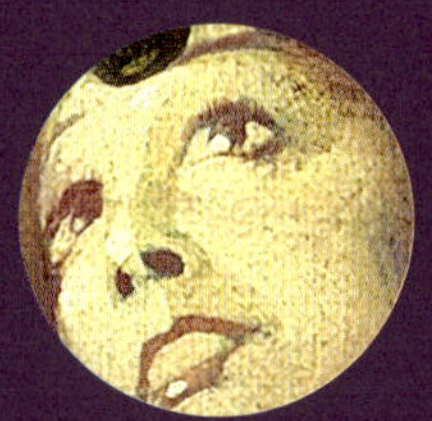

It is definitely very real....

By placing Mask within portraiture, Bruvel is able to explore not only construct and perceptions, but emotions as well. Most viewers are immediately attracted to Bruvel's use of color, but Bruvel resists the use of words like *vivid* to describe his work; insisting "colors are more like vibrations." He traces this idea to the work of 19th Century physicist Michel- Eugene Chevreul, whose Law of Simultaneous Contrast explains optical response to vibrant color. According to Chevreul, an optical sensation is produced when intense hues are juxtaposed, resulting in a "halo" of complementary color. This complementary "glow" quite literally invades the other colors on the canvas so that weaker colors actually appear changed. A gray, for example, would appear yellowish against violet, reddish against green. The result is a canvas alive—quite literally *vibrant*—with color; one that creates an illusion of volume, space, light and movement, but also reflects a specific emotional world. Bruvel says colors "only make sense in correlation with what [he's] trying to express in combination with other colors" and "it is exactly the same on an emotional level." Bruvel's color emanates from an emotional world: It resonates a kind of experience and seeing articulated by an individual portrait or perception.

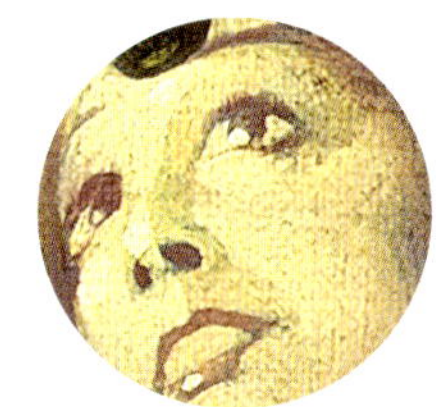

"Each of us creates our own myth..."

The combined elements of Bruvel's work—color, Masks, emotional bodies, shapes and unusual landscapes—result in the Visionary dreamscapes found in *Timeless Travelers.* There's a real sense of emergence among these portraits, as well as a sense of movement and journey. The obscured faces in "Inner Visions" give rise to a meditation on the interiority of self, an examination of how one thinks about and sees oneself in the world. From here, Bruvel works playfully with masks in "Almost Human," a section which reveals perceptions as constructs—the Vision or Ideal manifest in human flesh. Traveling through "Beaks" and "Gatherings," you will arrive at "Emerging," where human faces really begin to take shape among structure, and more realistic faces come startling into focus. Finally, after "Timeless Travelers"—an homage to the universal aspect of our collective humanity—the portraits turn the tables in "Gazed Upon," a section in which the mirror reflects more than just study and the faces seem to look back—reminding us that portraiture is an imaginative transaction between artist, subject and audience.

It's difficult to experience the figures that animate these pages and remain unchanged. While this may be the function of all art, it seems the special province of Visionary Art. Inside *Timeless Travelers*, you will find unexpected mirrors and surprising personal insights. Perhaps, you will be curiously attracted to a sudden figure—the movement of its hand or the tilt of its head, the dark angle of an eye cast upward. And in the same way, you might be disturbed by another—strangely familiar—a figure that tugs at the trappings of self. Traveling these pages, you will enter into your own mythological terrain, the one that crowds your dreams at night and has the ability to change the face of the day. Perhaps you will begin to imagine new stories or different futures inside these faces. Whatever your response, it will be deeply personal and profound. "Each of us creates our own myth," says Gil Bruvel—each a tiny universe full of stars—and the myths and visions of *Timeless Travelers* are as plentiful and bright as the whole wide world.

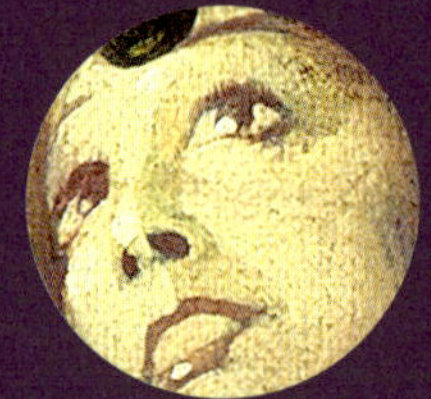

—Karen Auvinen

nner visions / visions intérieures

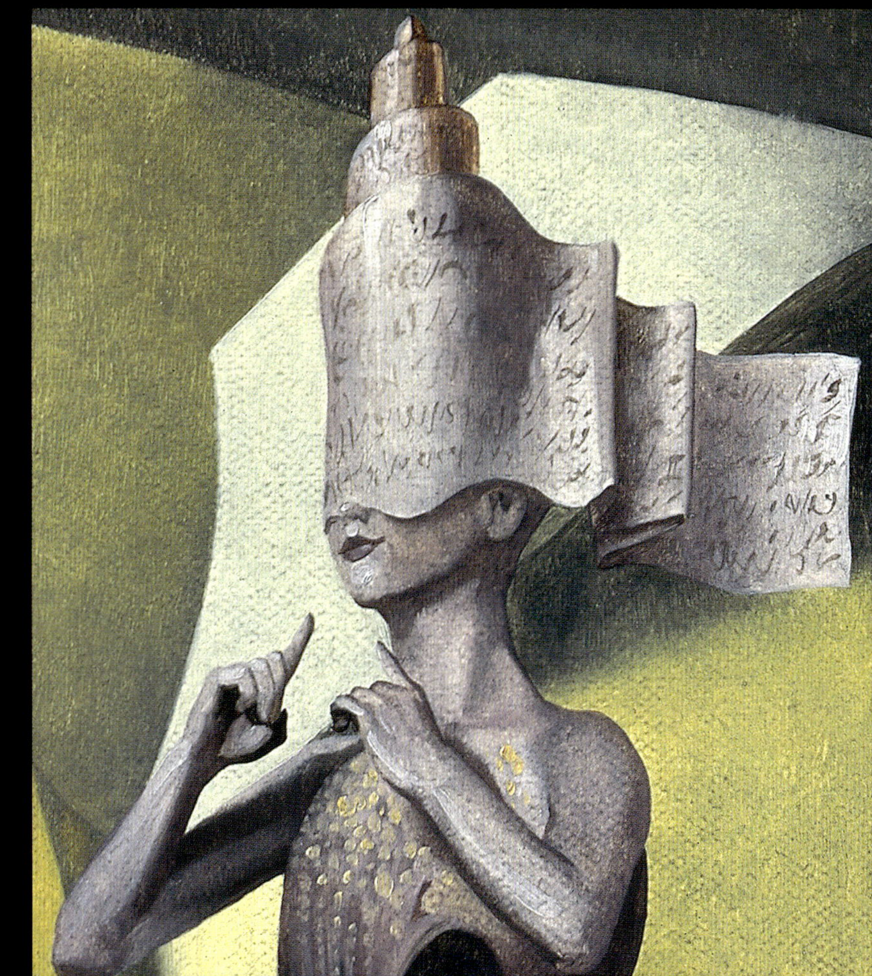

◄ LA CONVERSATION

JUSTICE - study ►

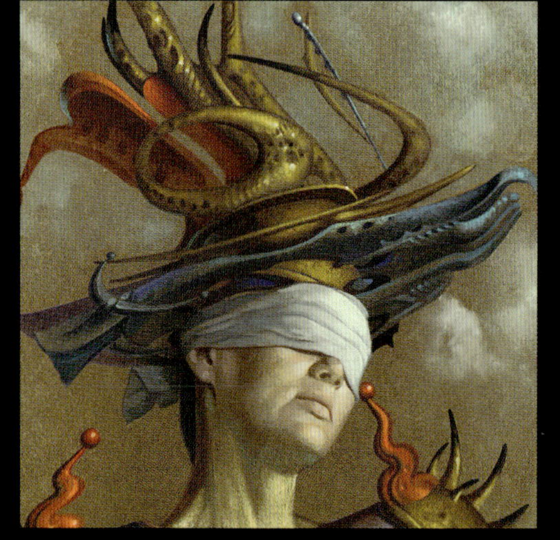

HOW AN ANGEL CAN MAKE A PORTRAIT ►

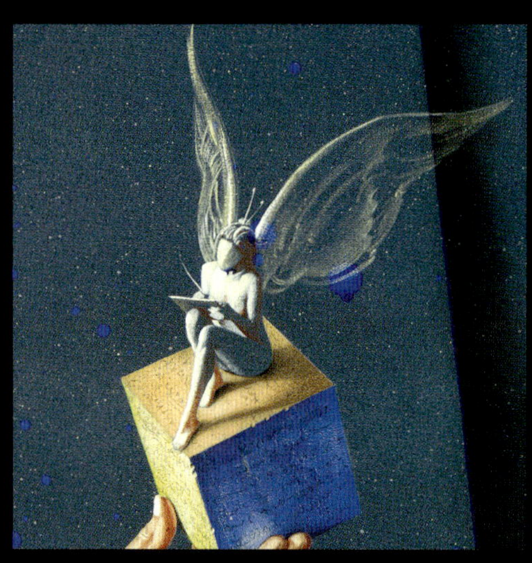

HOW A FISH CAN MAKE A PORTRAIT ►

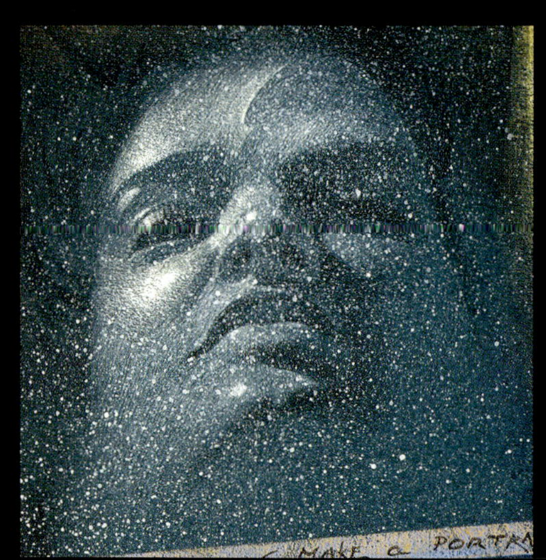

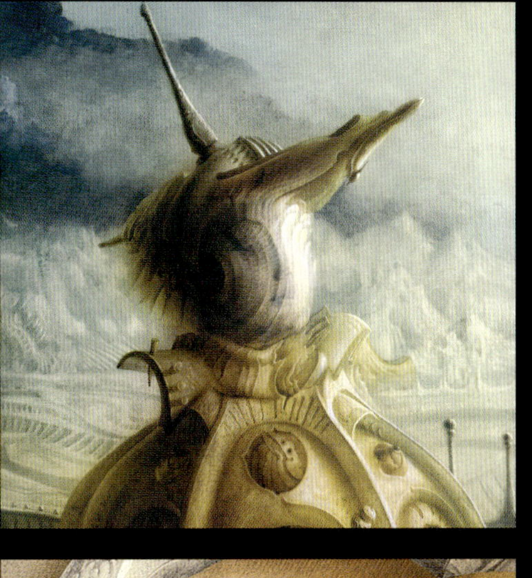

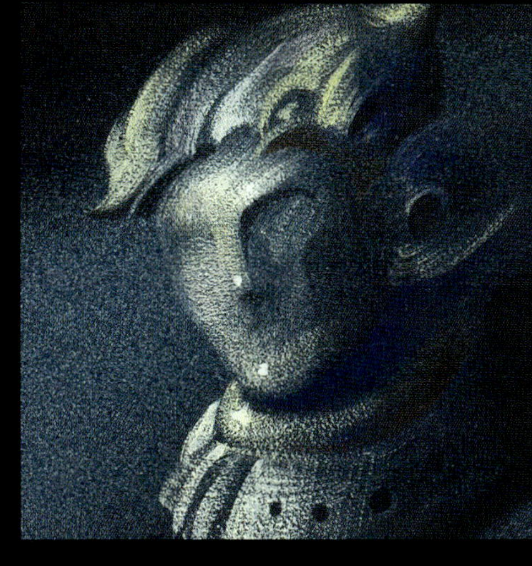

◄ THE GUARDIAN

◄ HALLUCINATED CITY

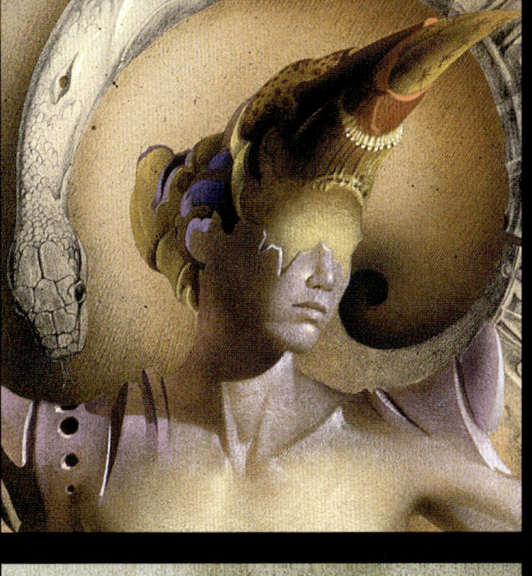

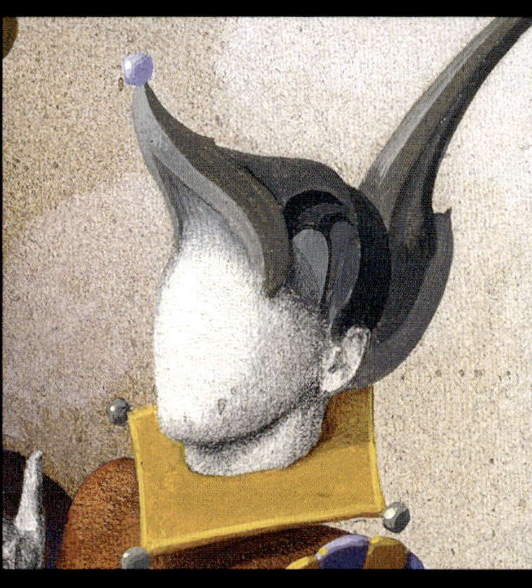

◄ THE FORGOTENESS

◄ THE JUGGLER

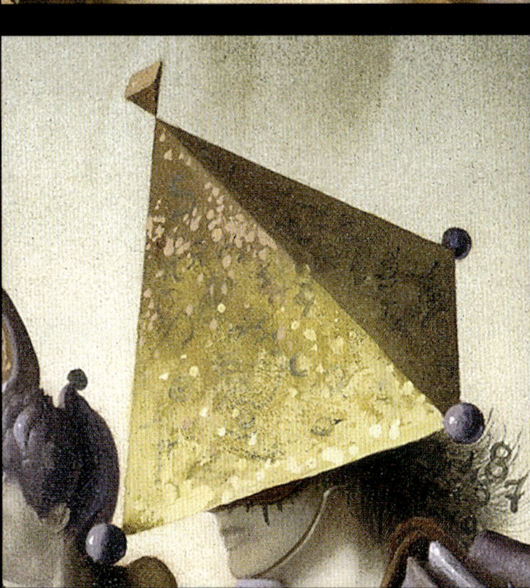

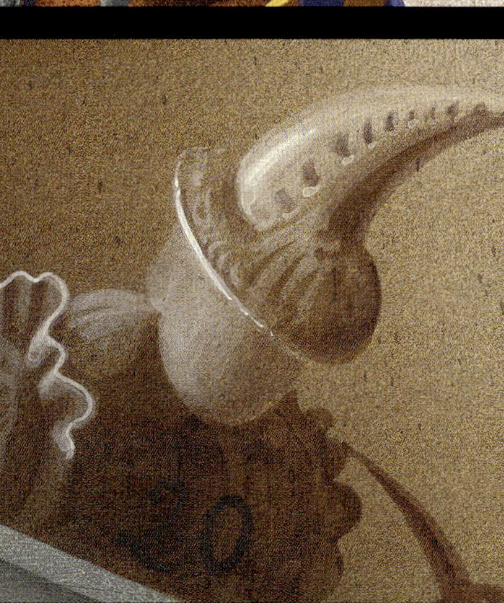

◄ LIMIT OF THE VISIBLE

◄ THE JUGGLER

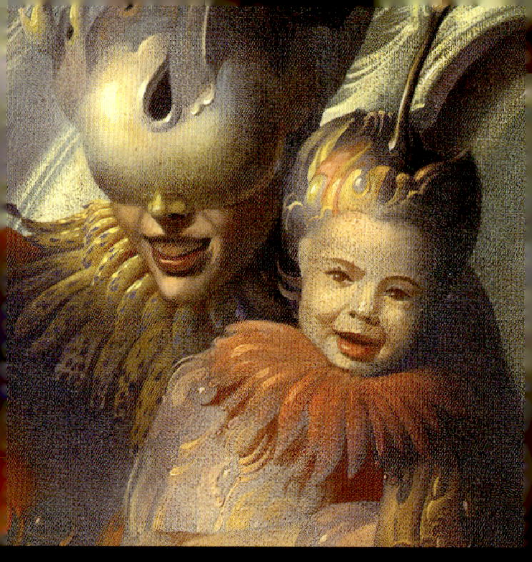

THE INVISIBLE VOYAGE

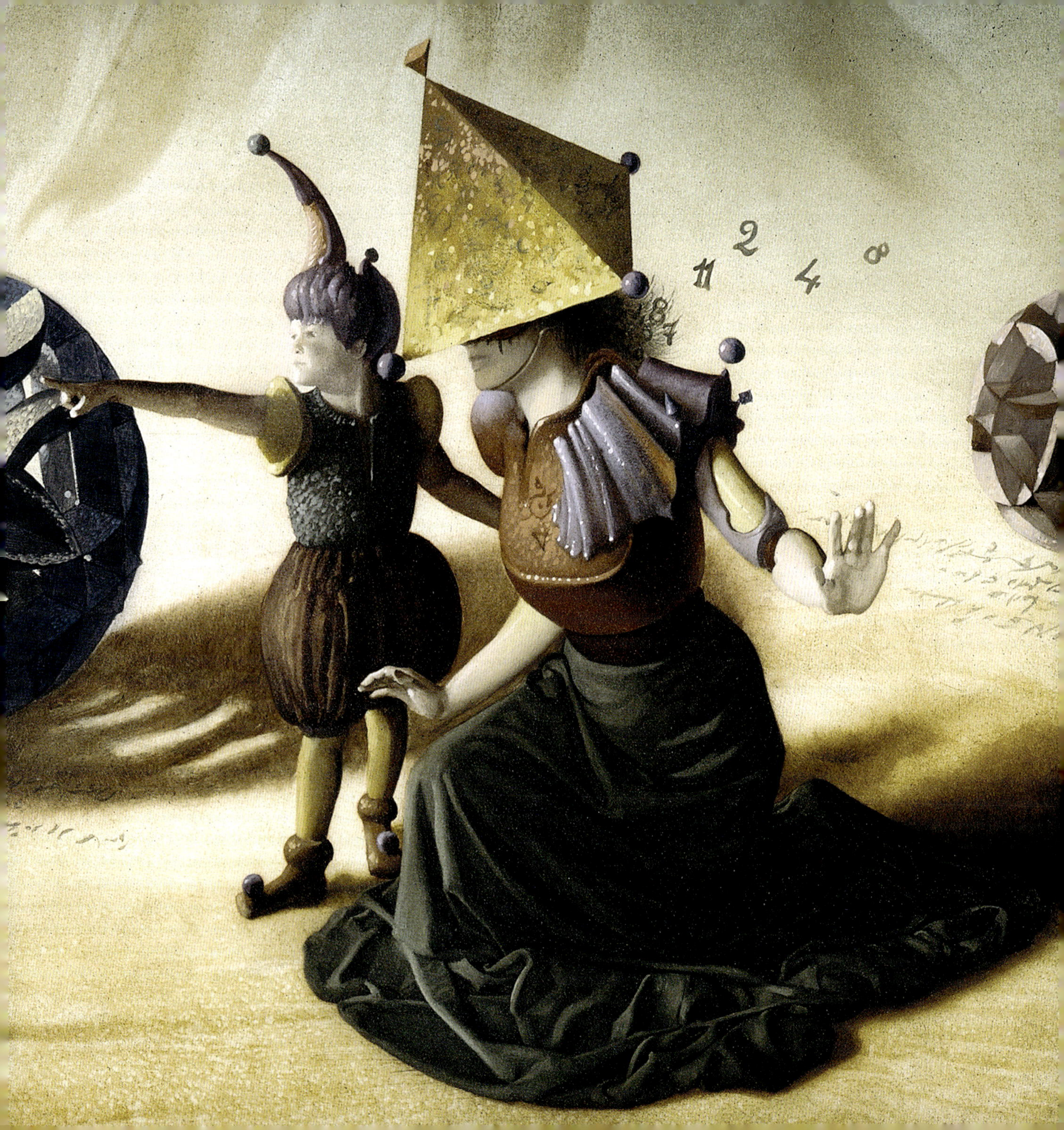

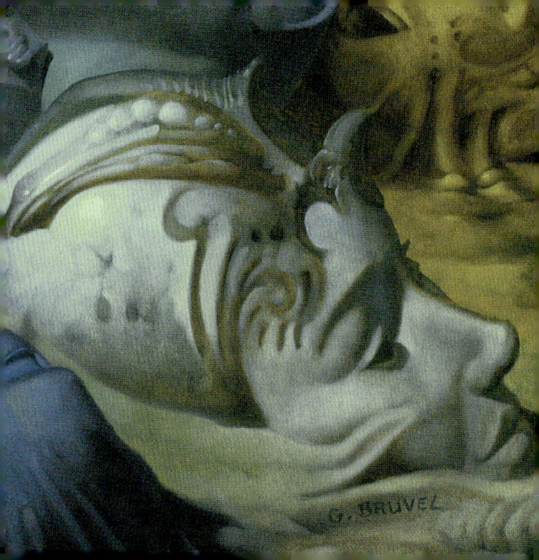
G. BRUVEL

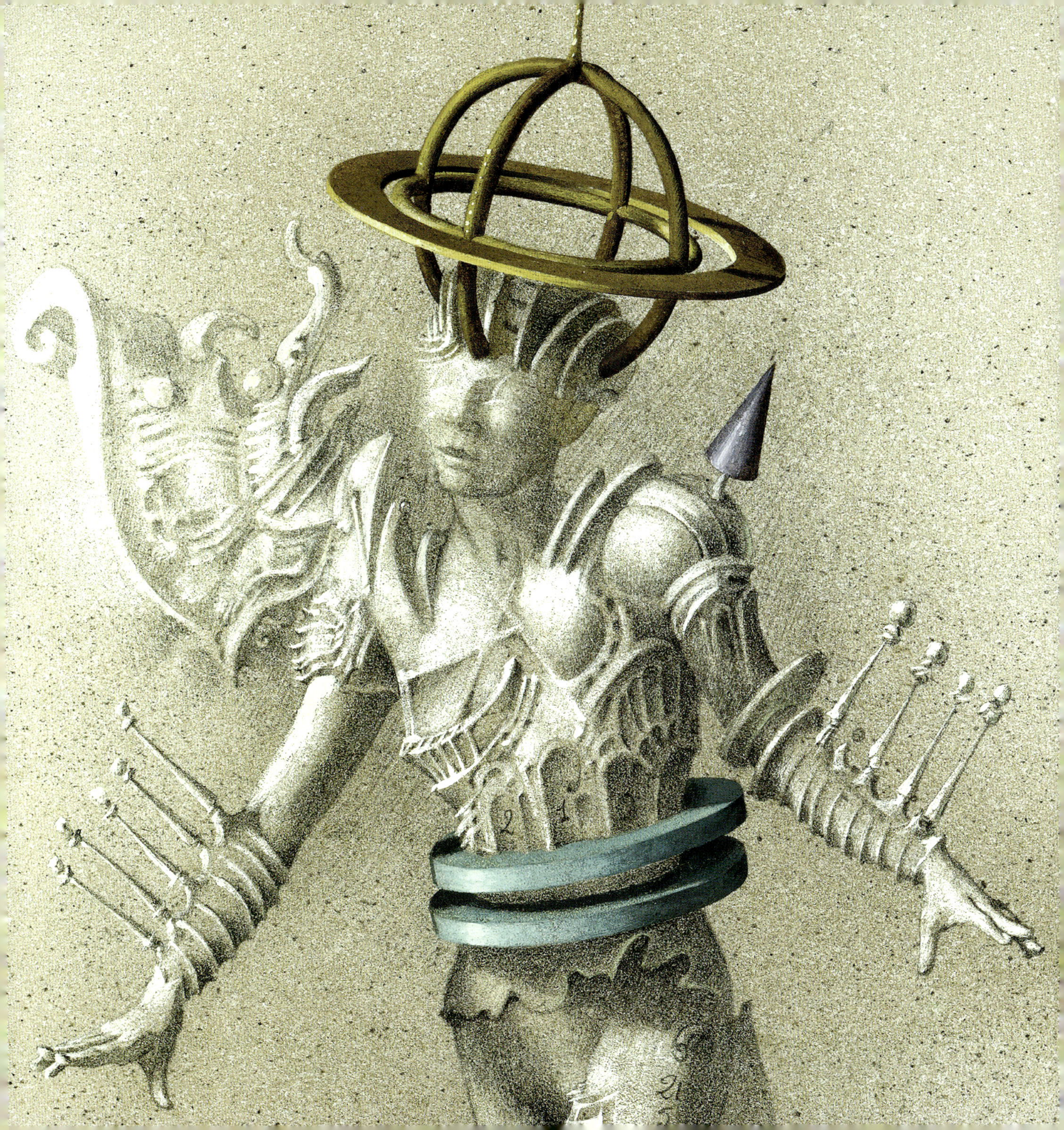

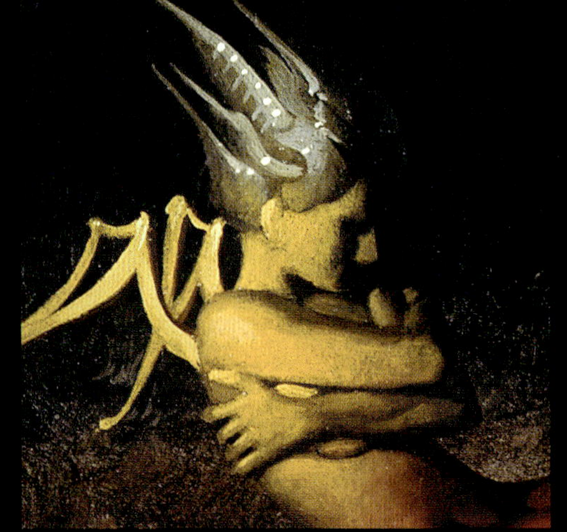

WHISPERS - study

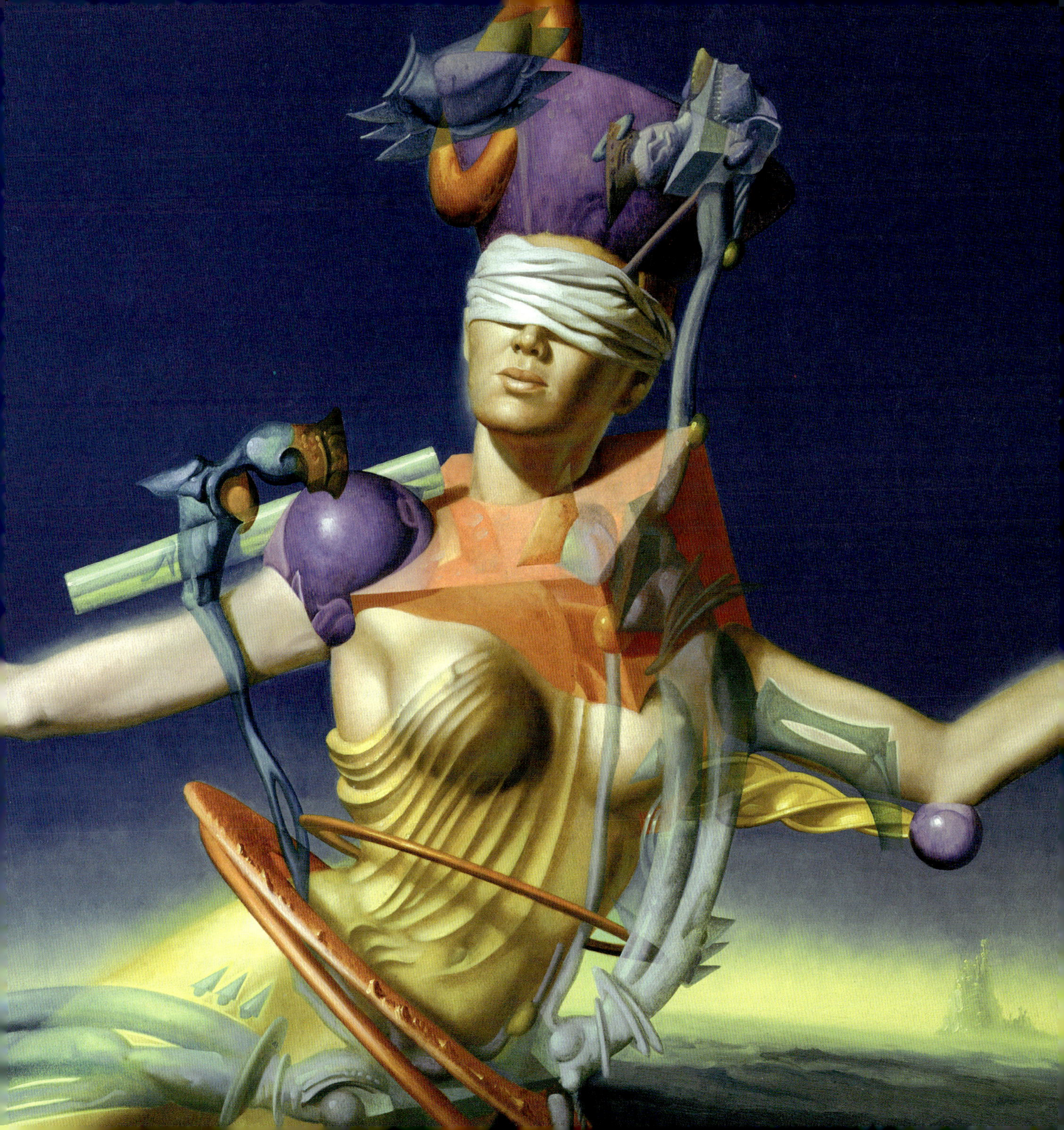

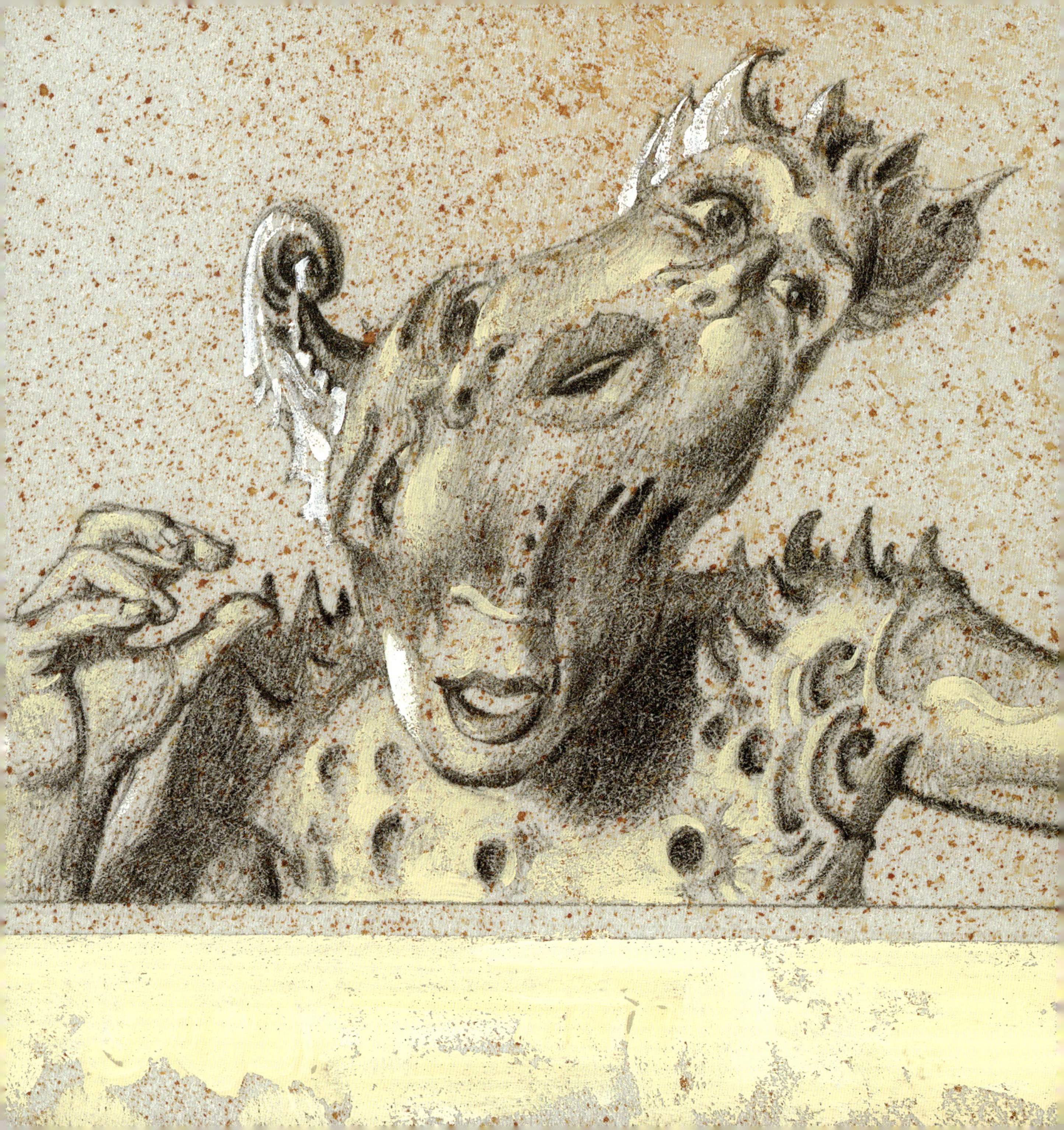

IN SEARCH OF GRAVITY - study

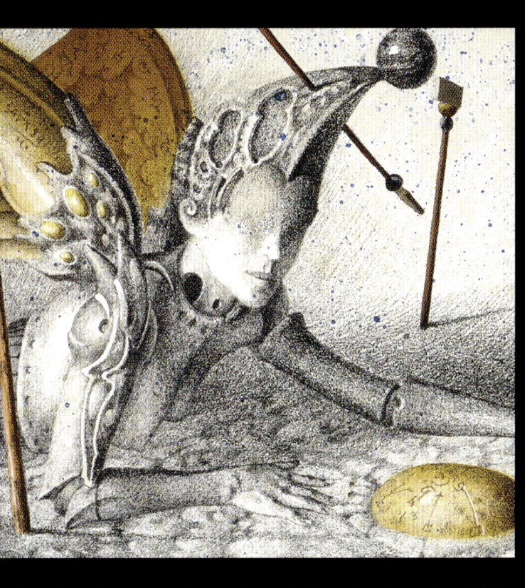

GO IN PEACE

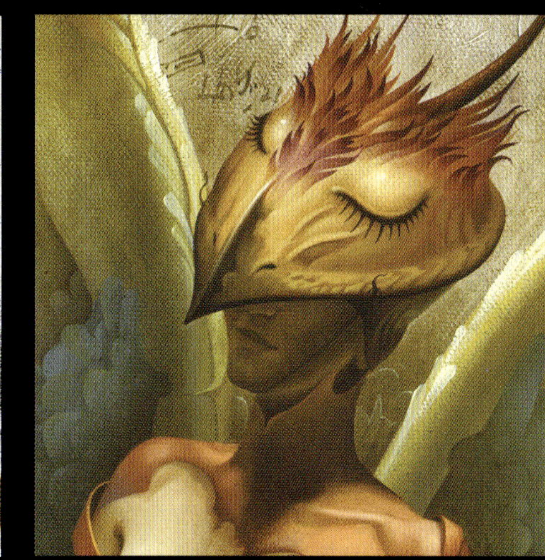

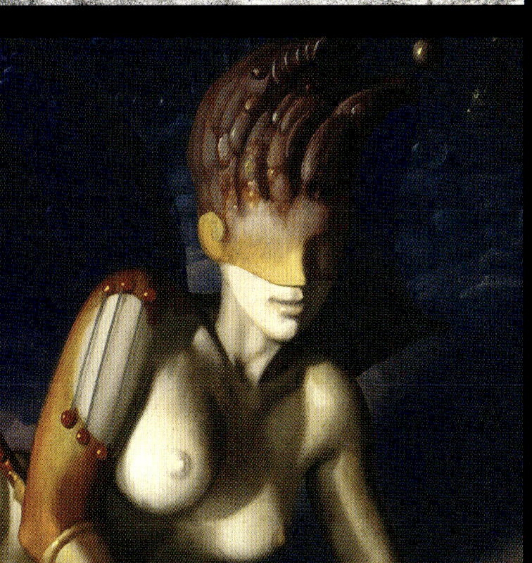

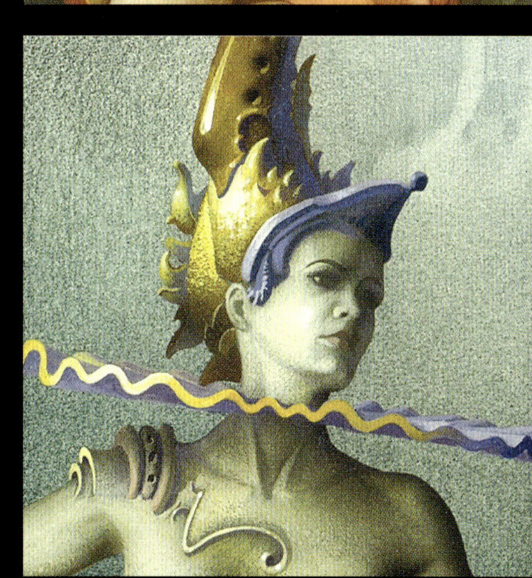

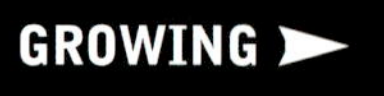

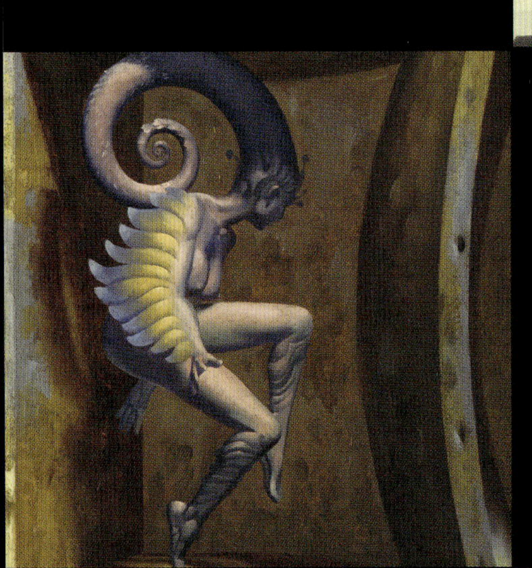

THE PLAYER

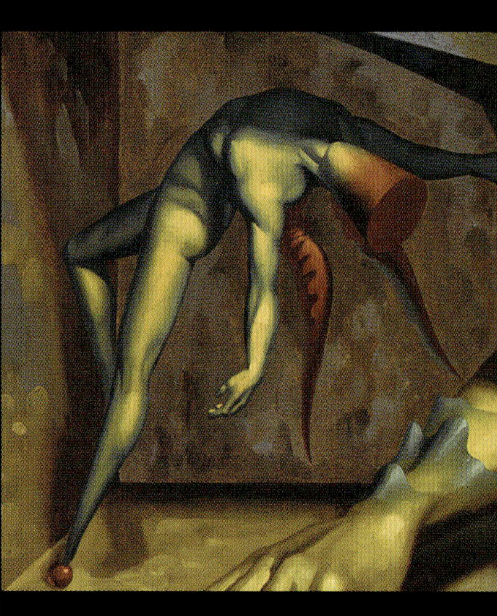

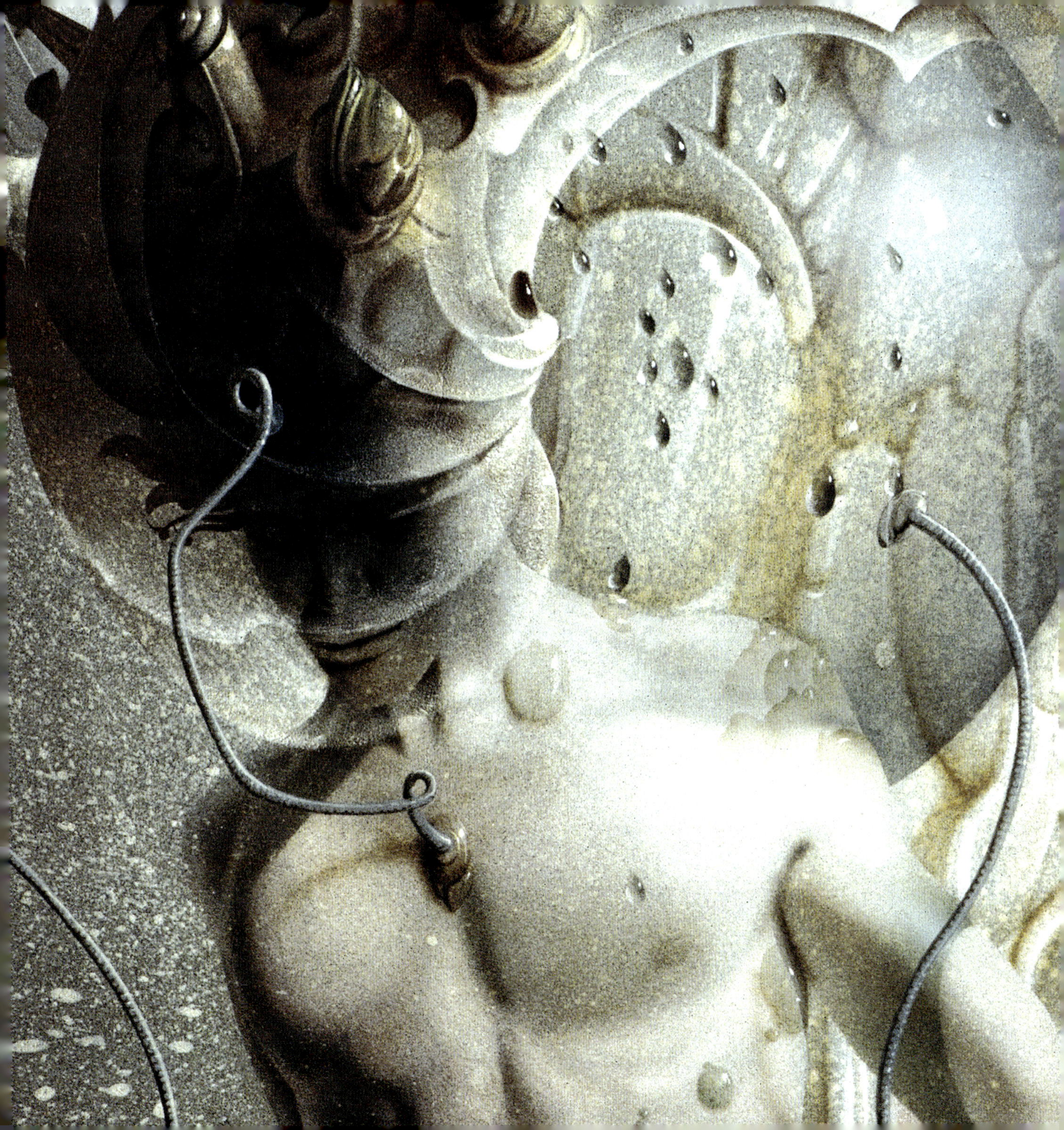

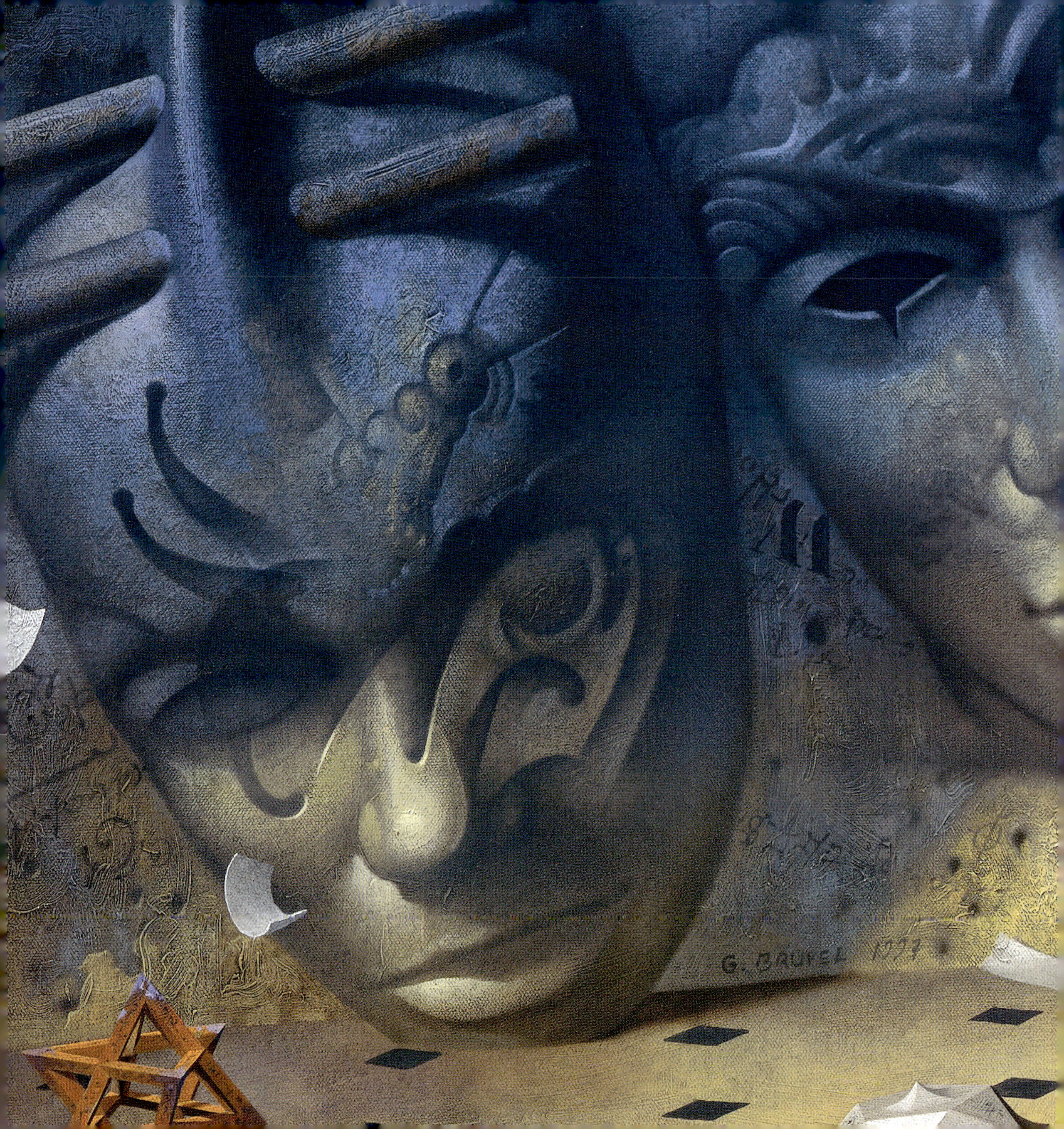

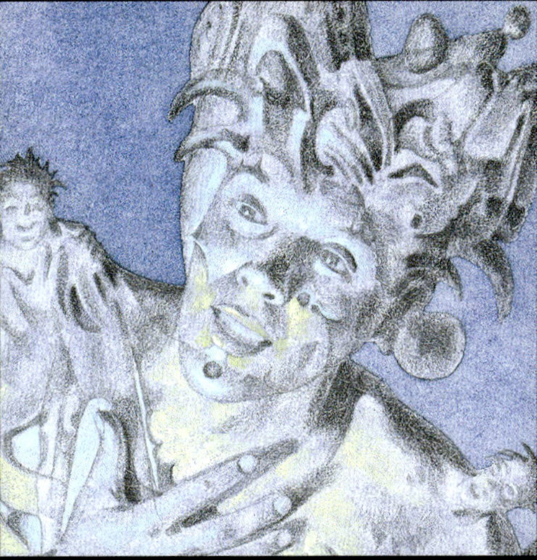

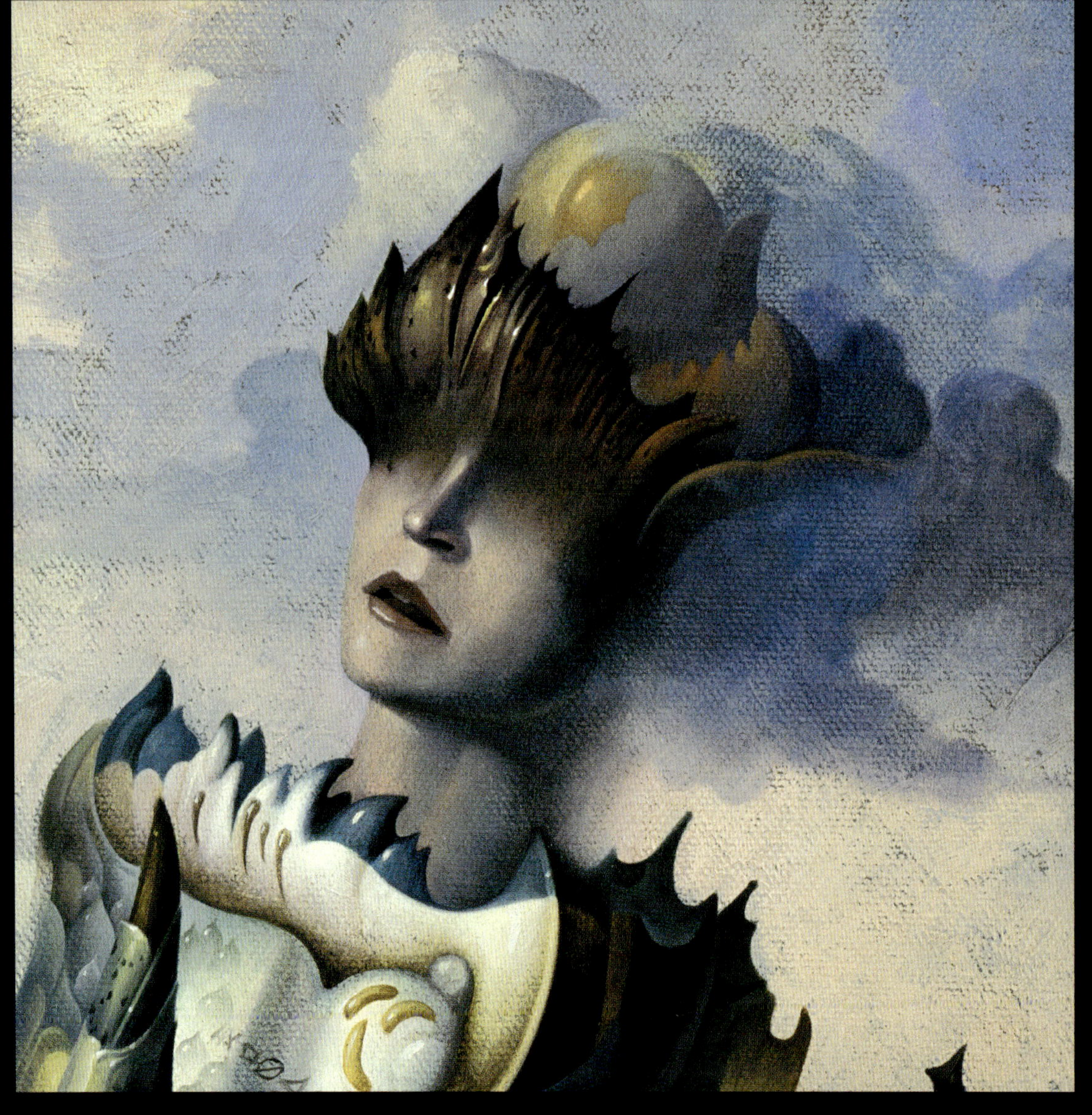

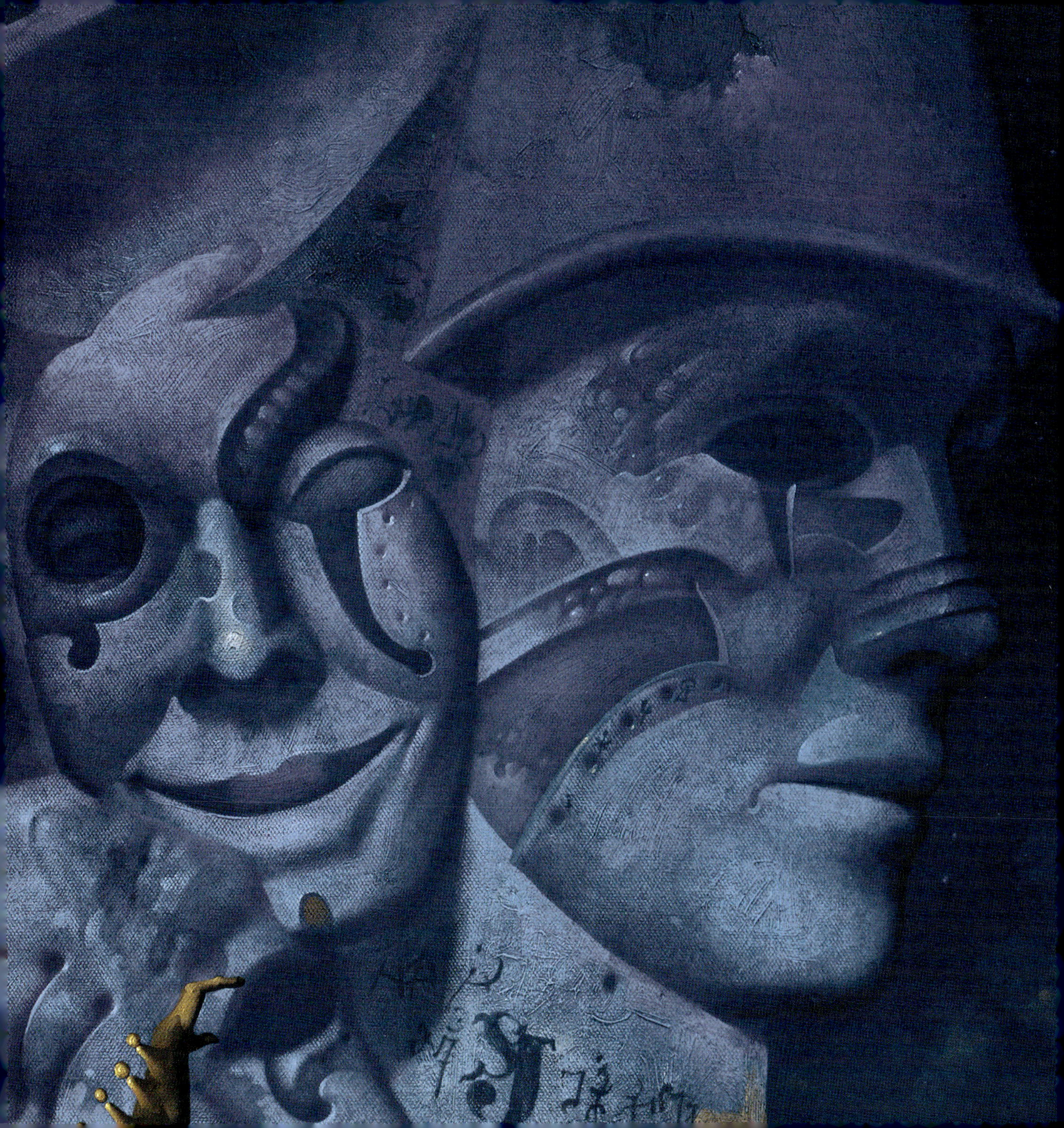

PROFILE OF AN ANGEL ➤

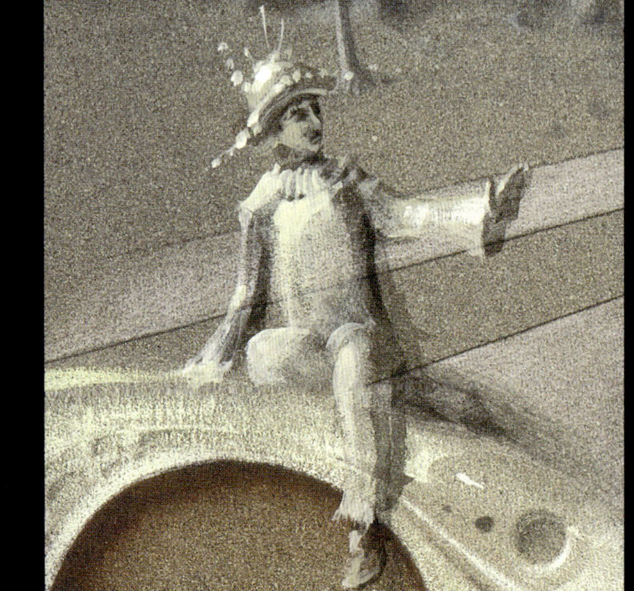

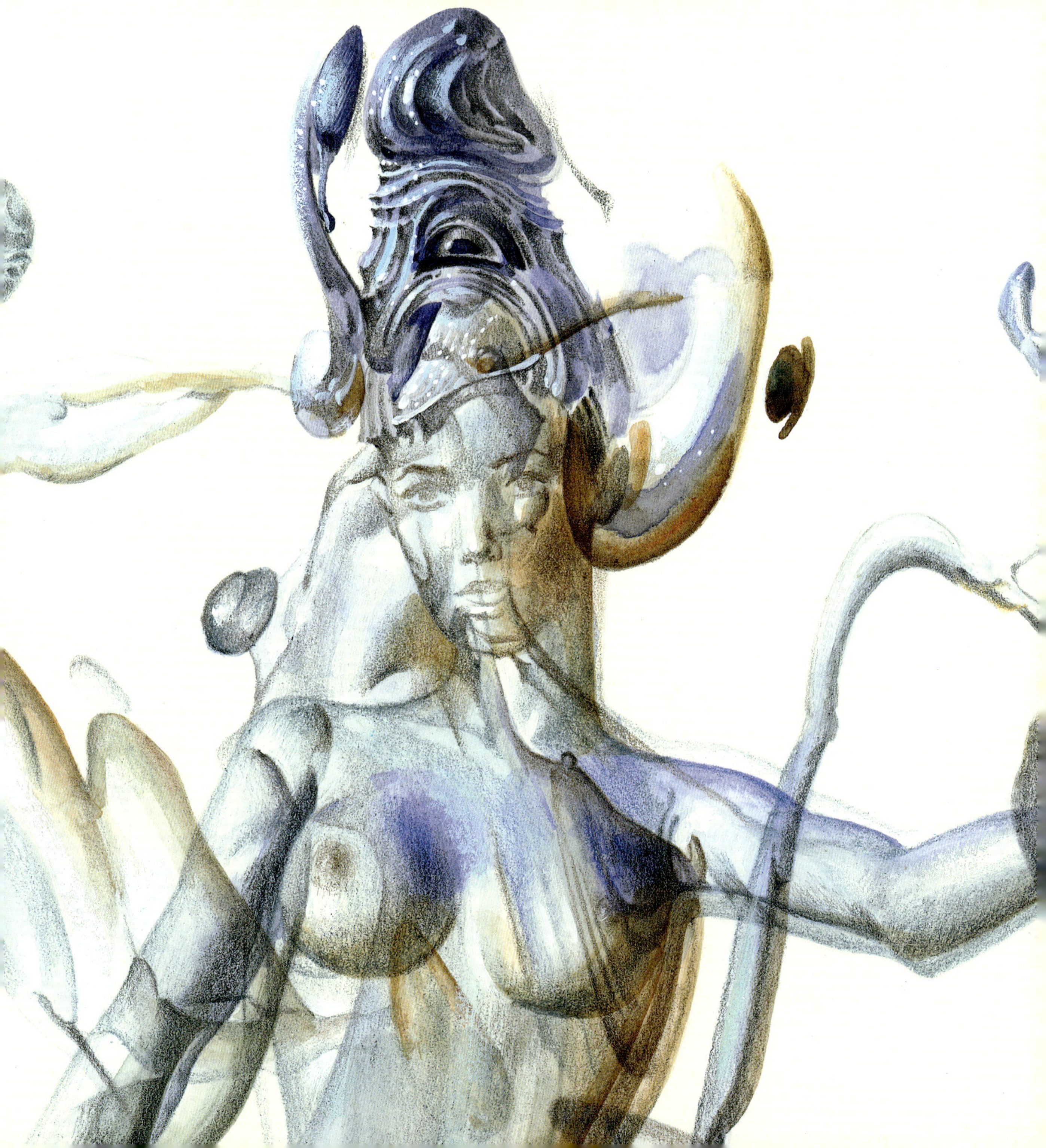

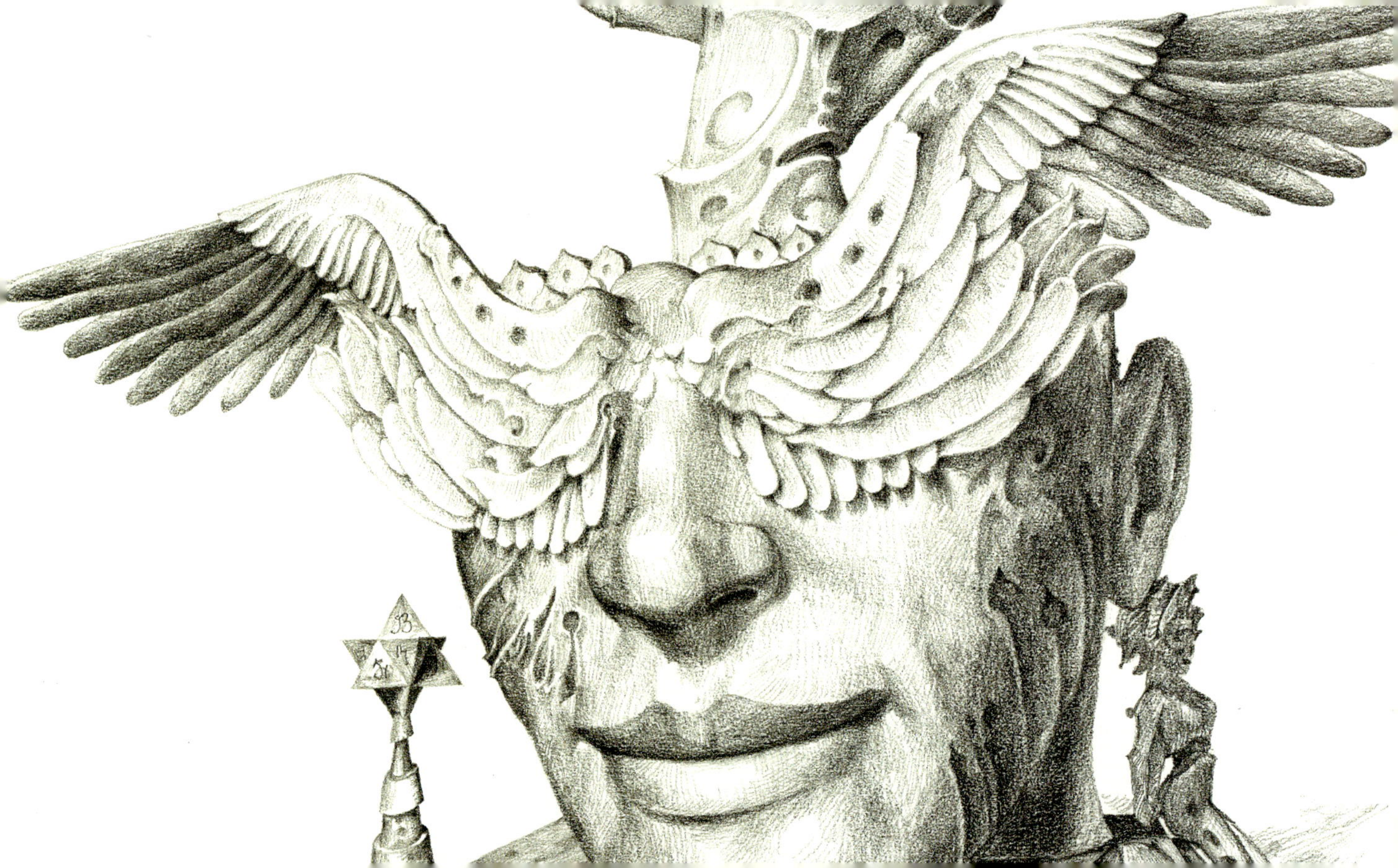

almost human / presque humain

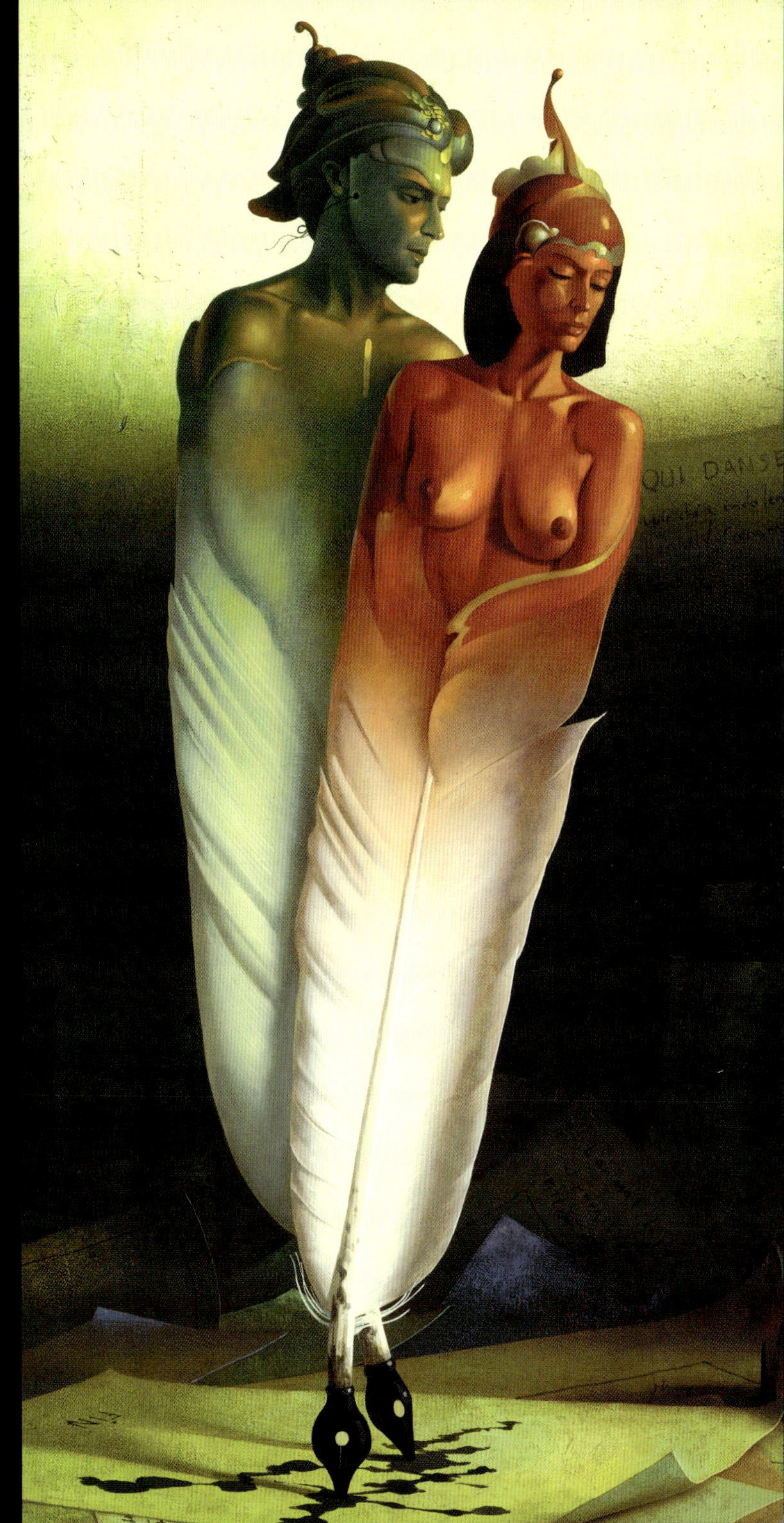

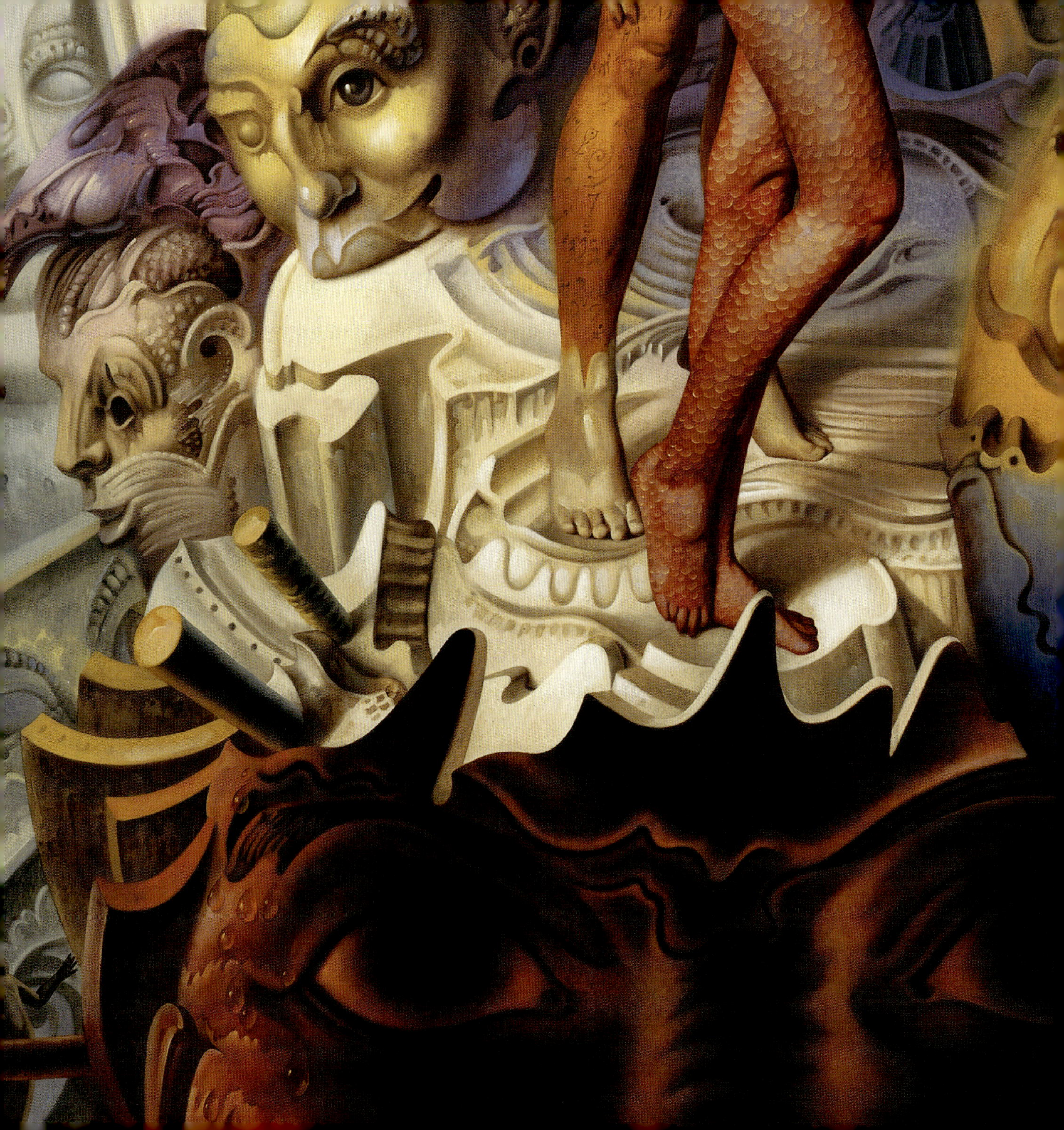

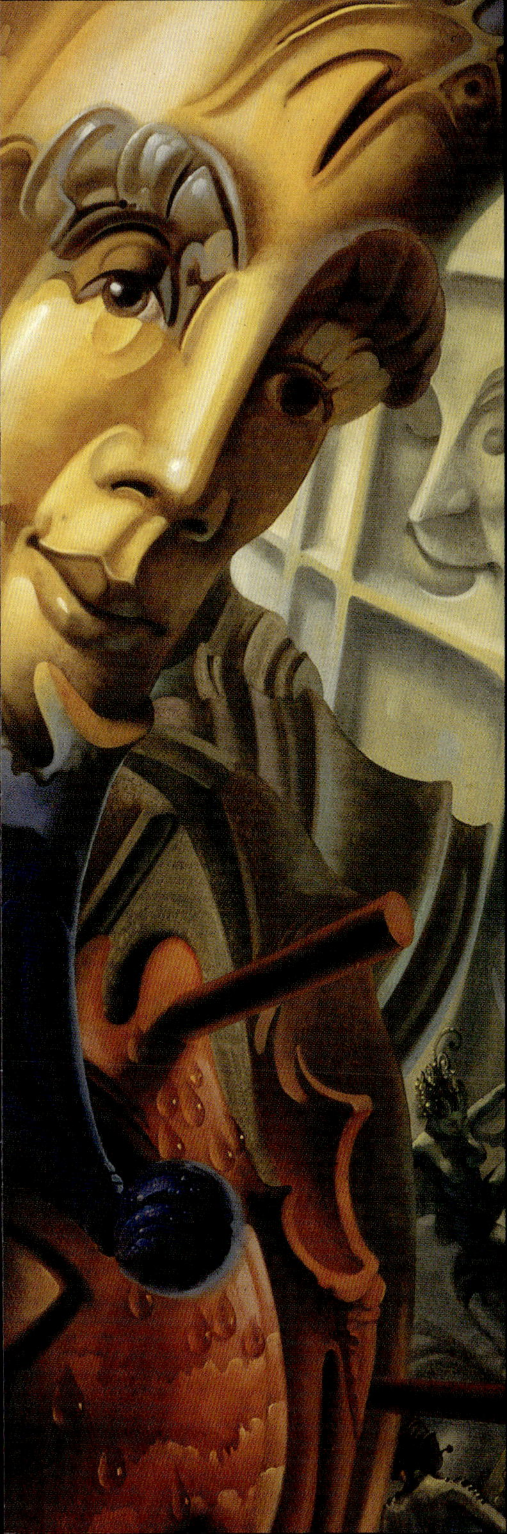

◄◄ THE LITERARY LOVERS

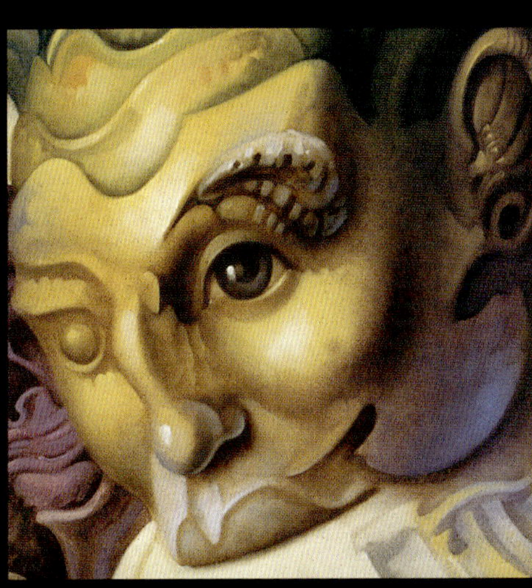

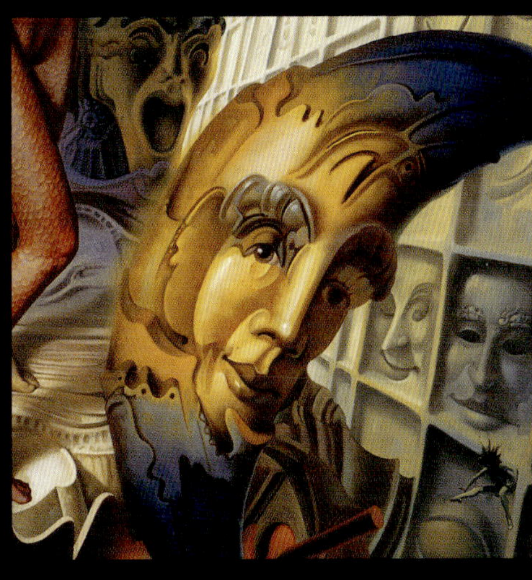

▲
◄ TIMELESS EXISTENCE

SKY AT THE END ➤
OF THE SEA

JUSTICE ➤

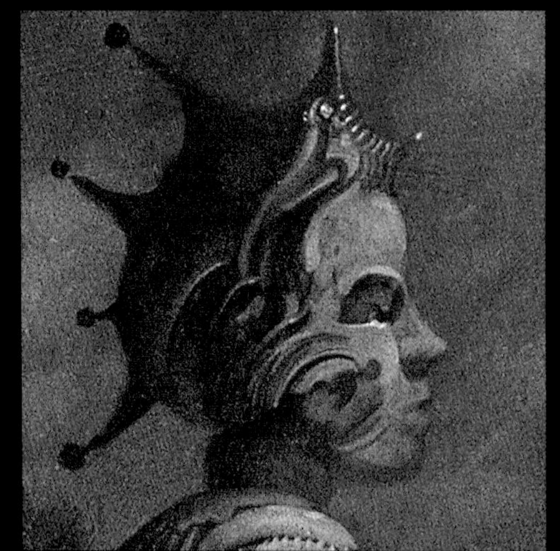

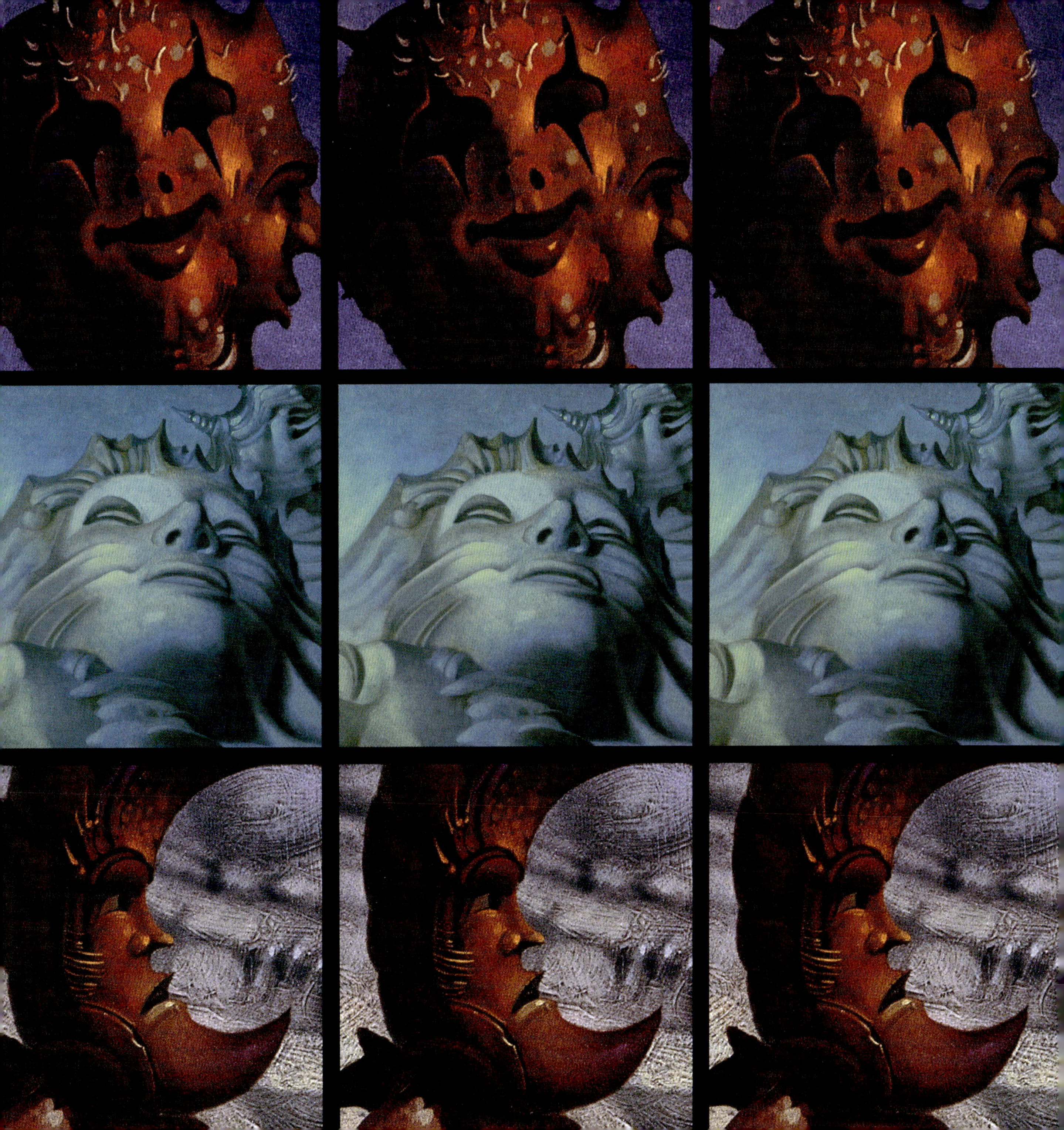

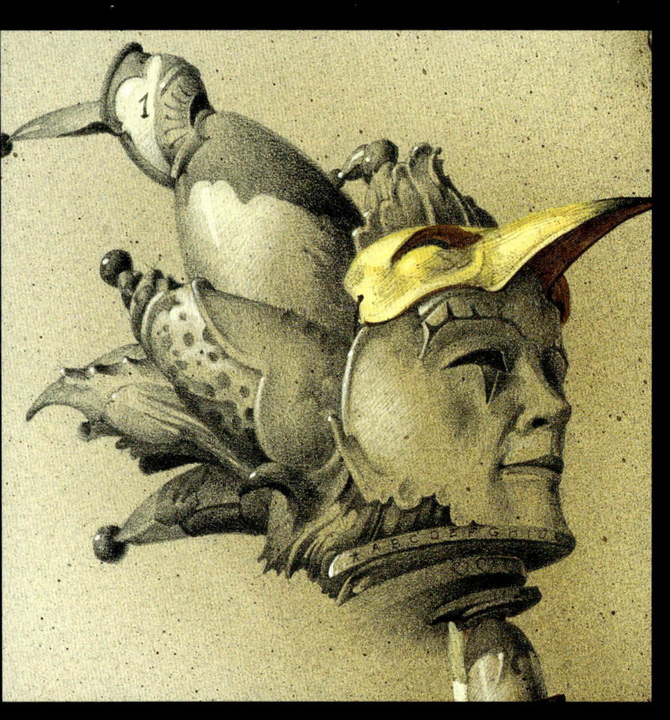

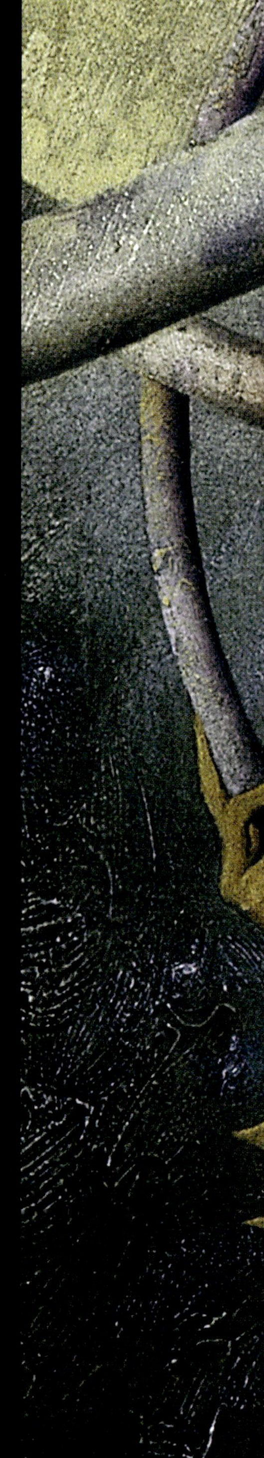

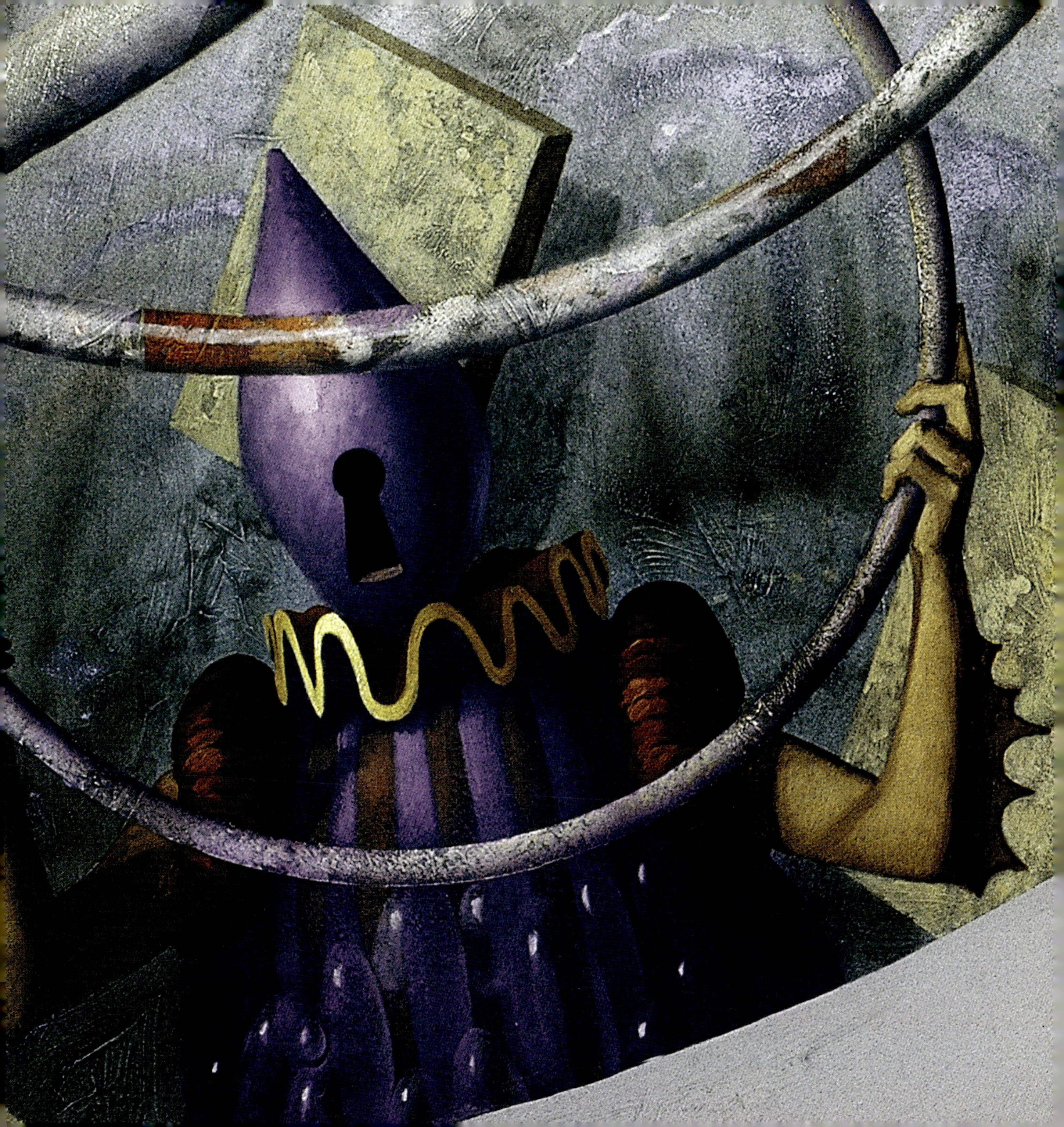

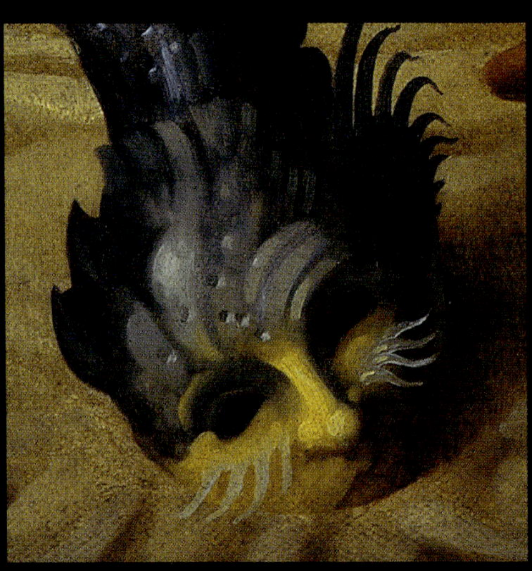

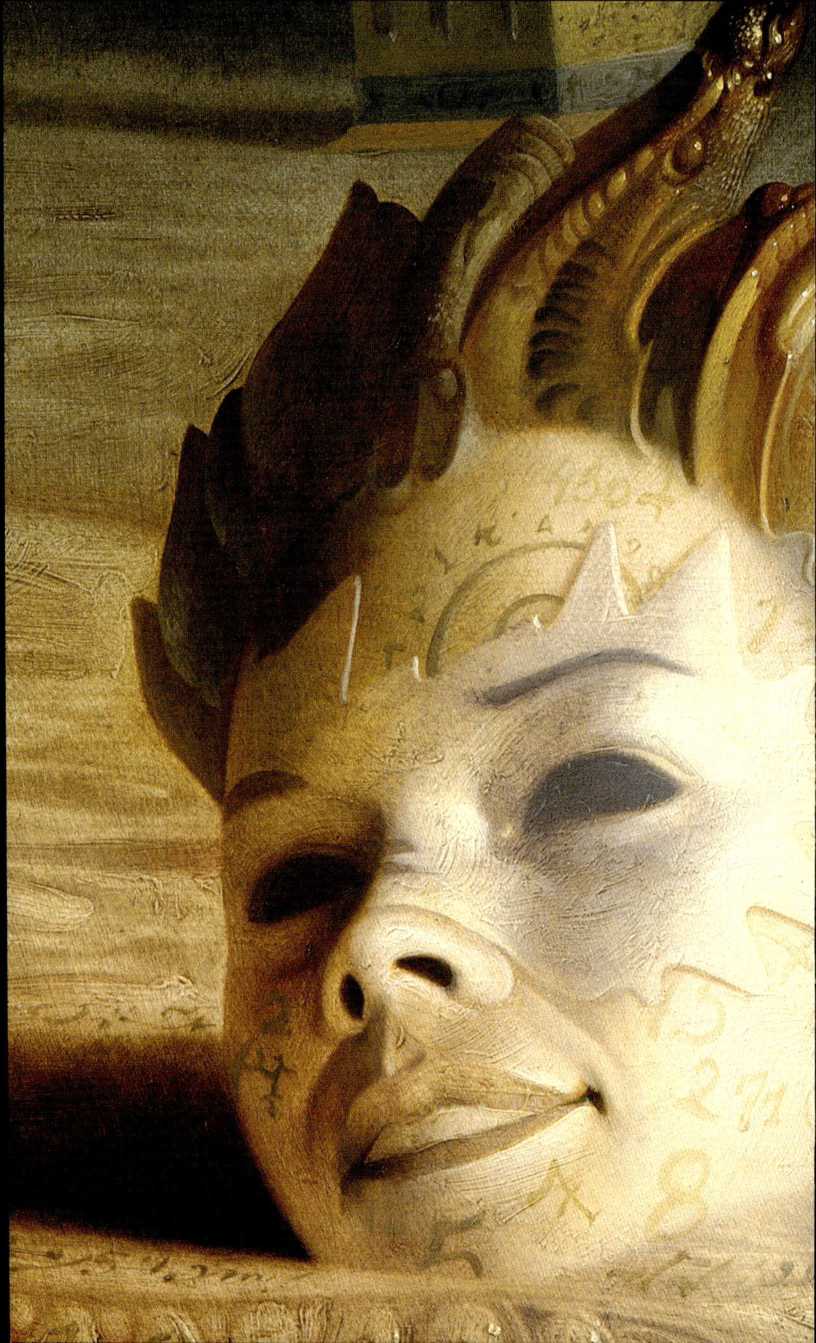

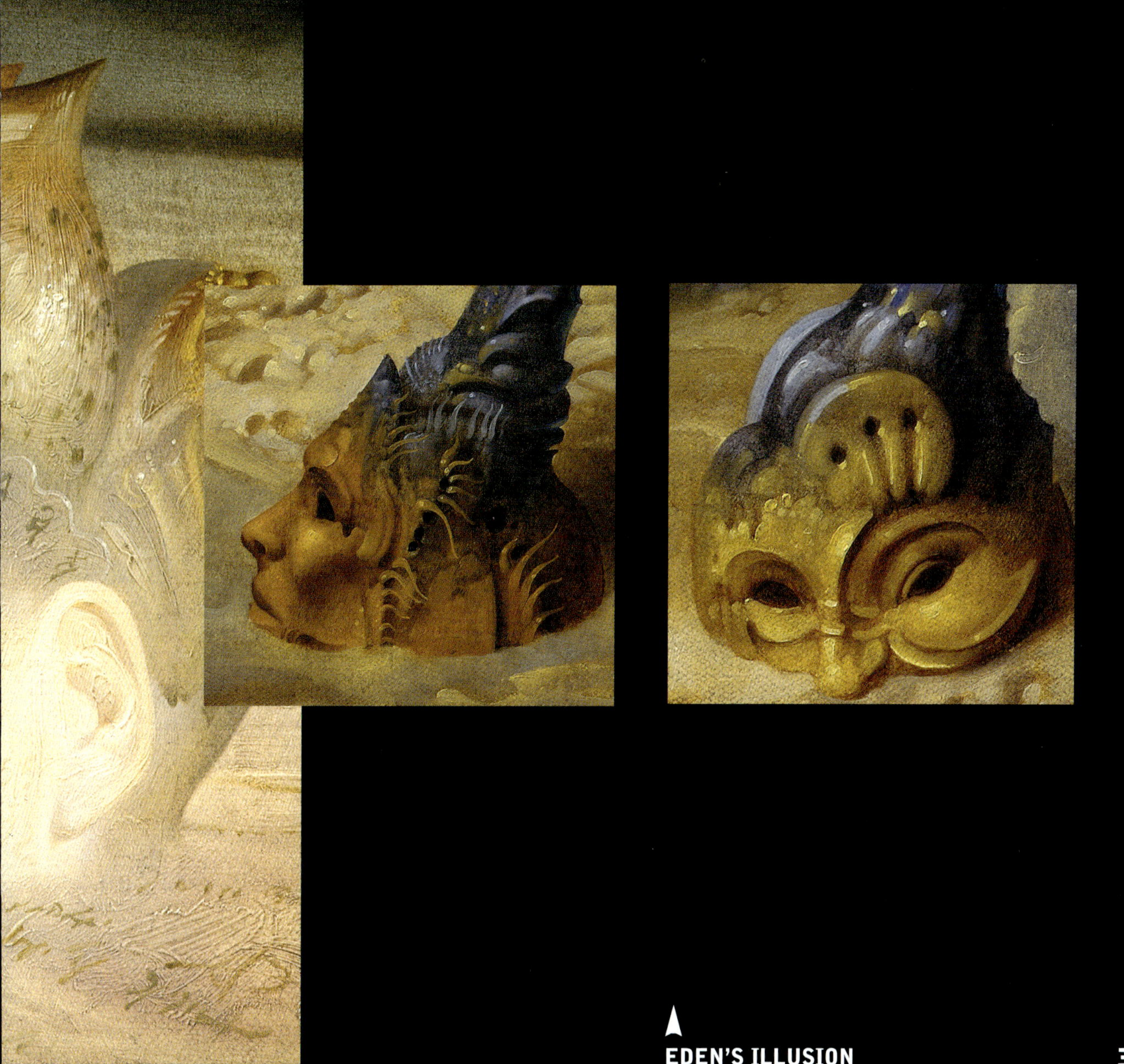

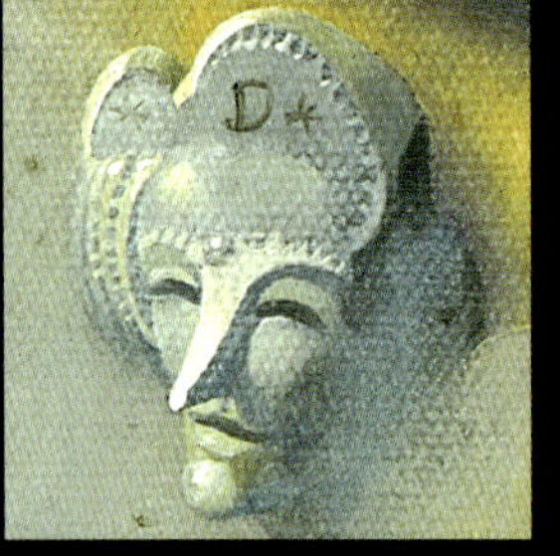

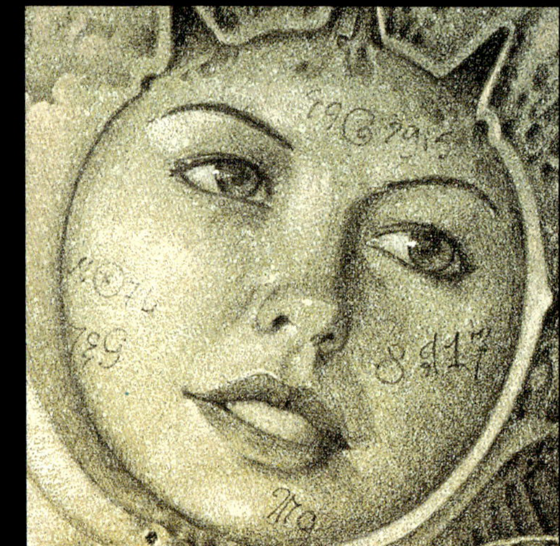

▲
SELF PORTRAIT
ON THE BEACH
WITH THE MOON

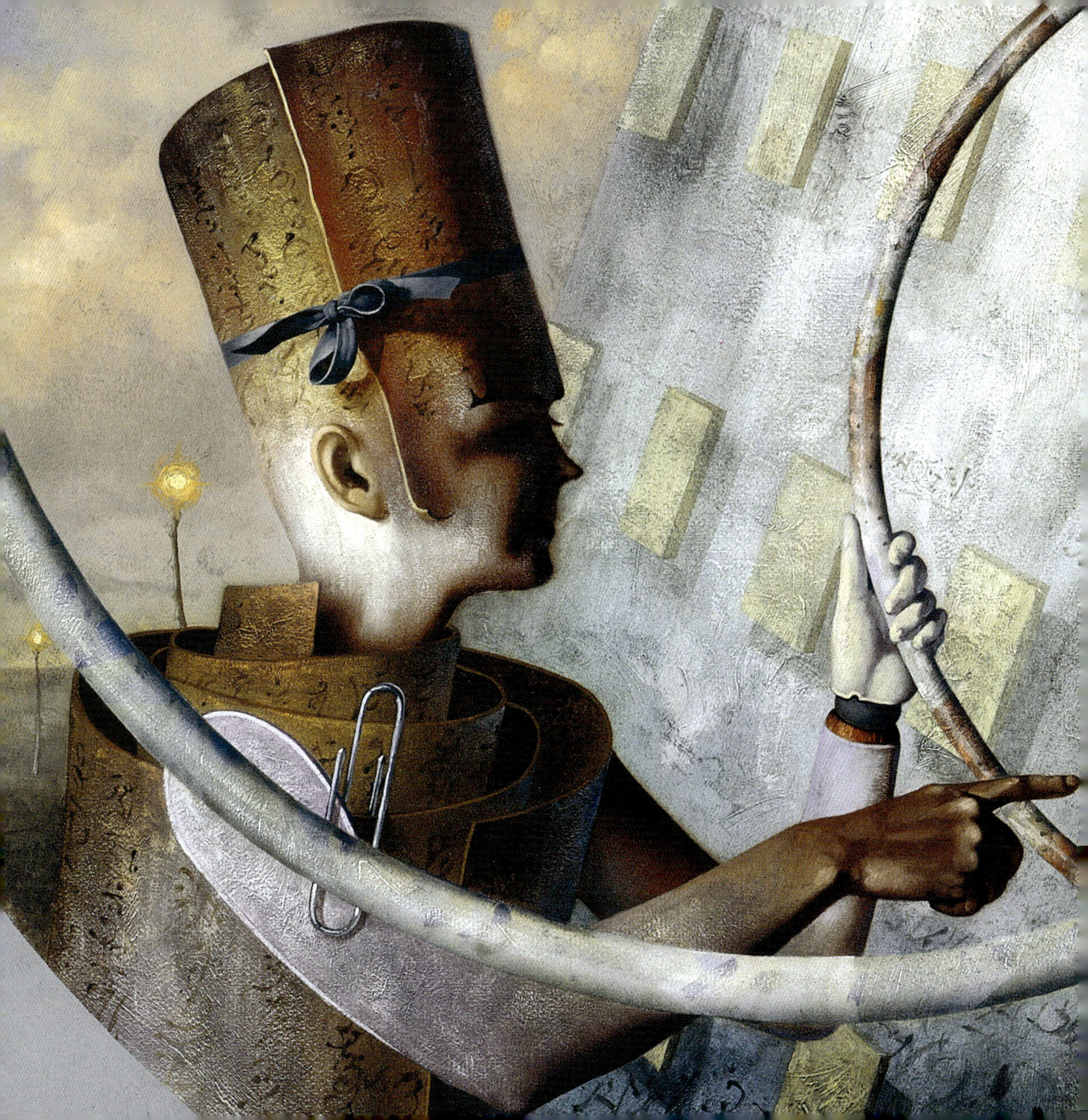

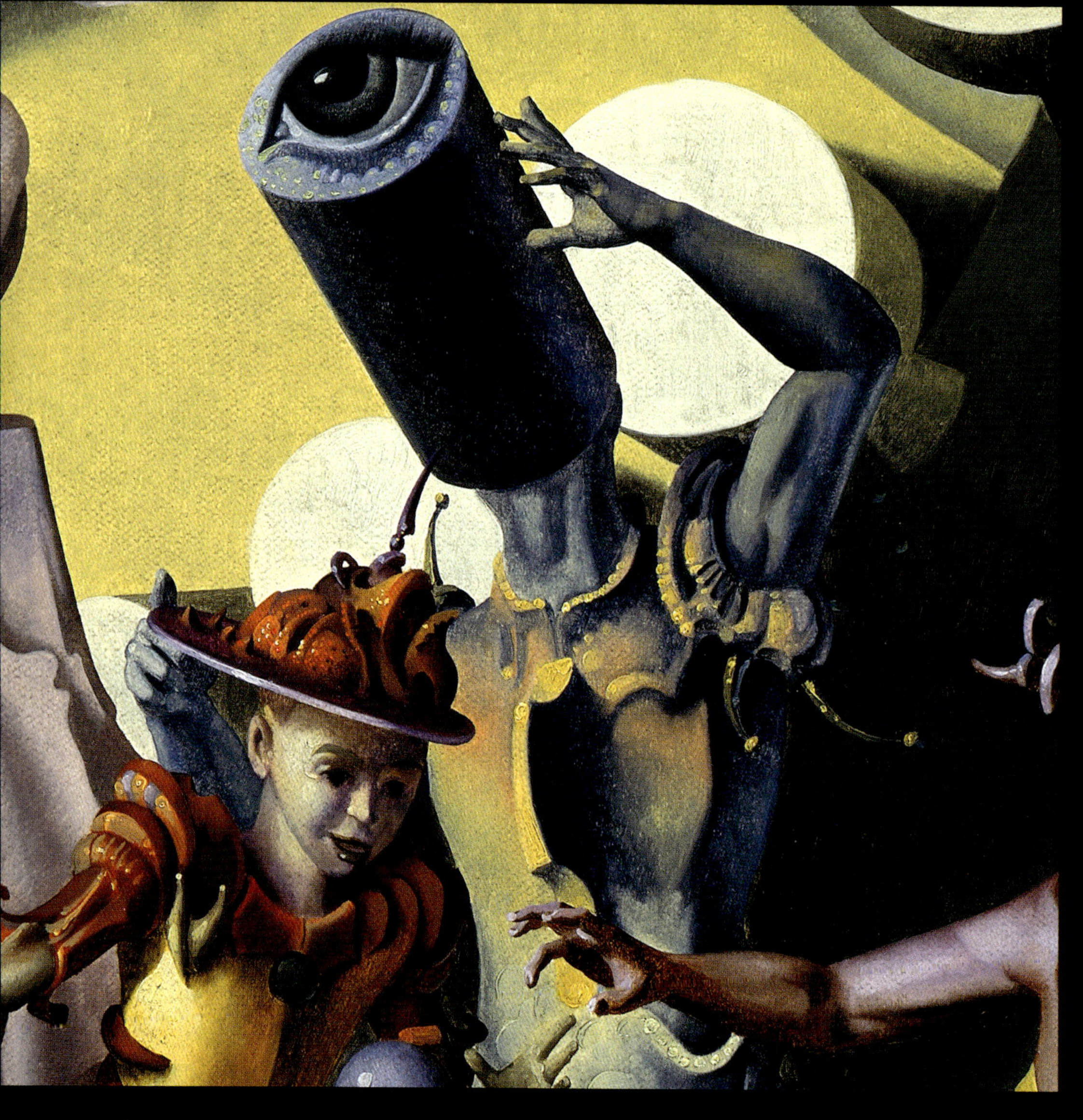

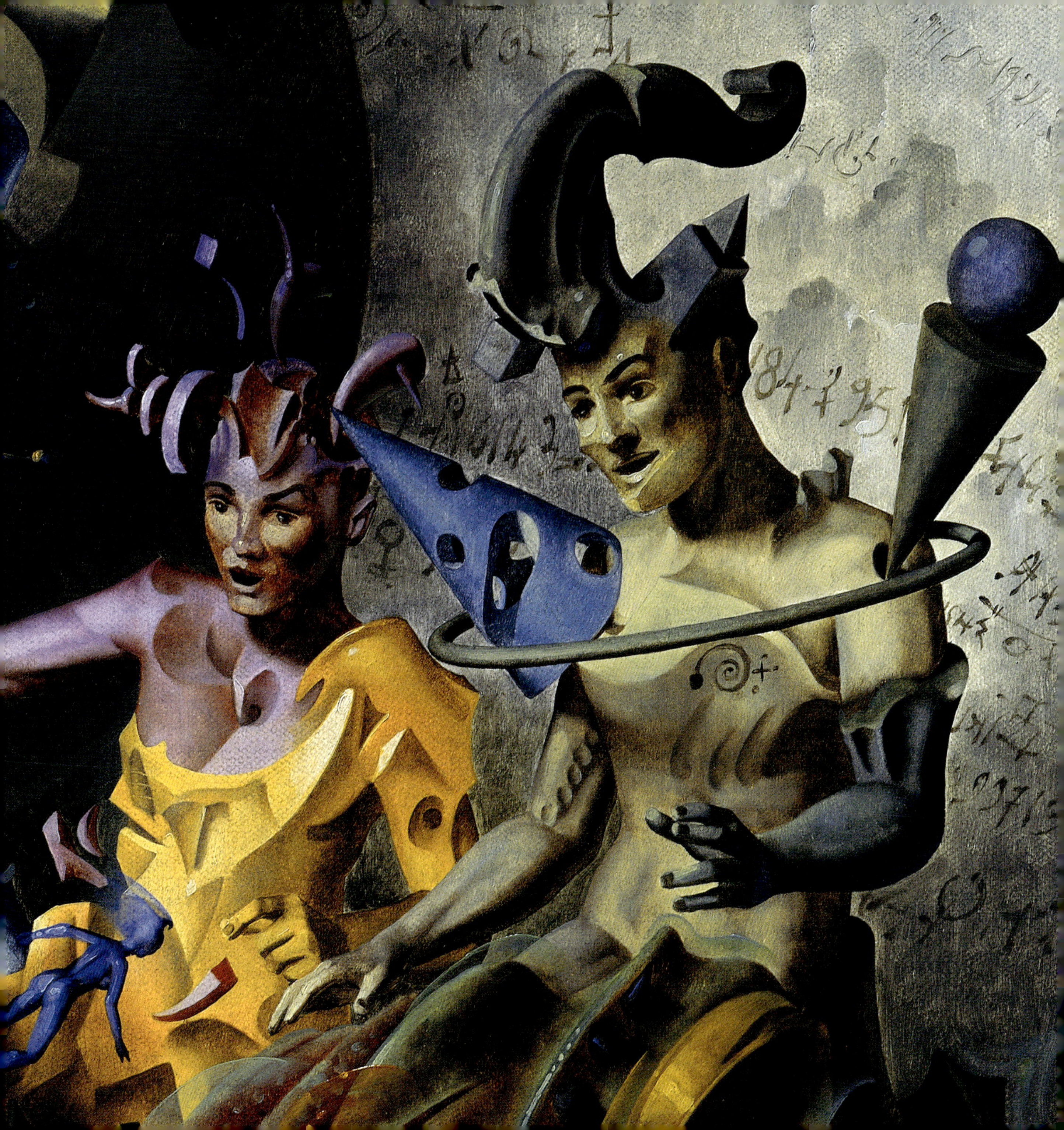

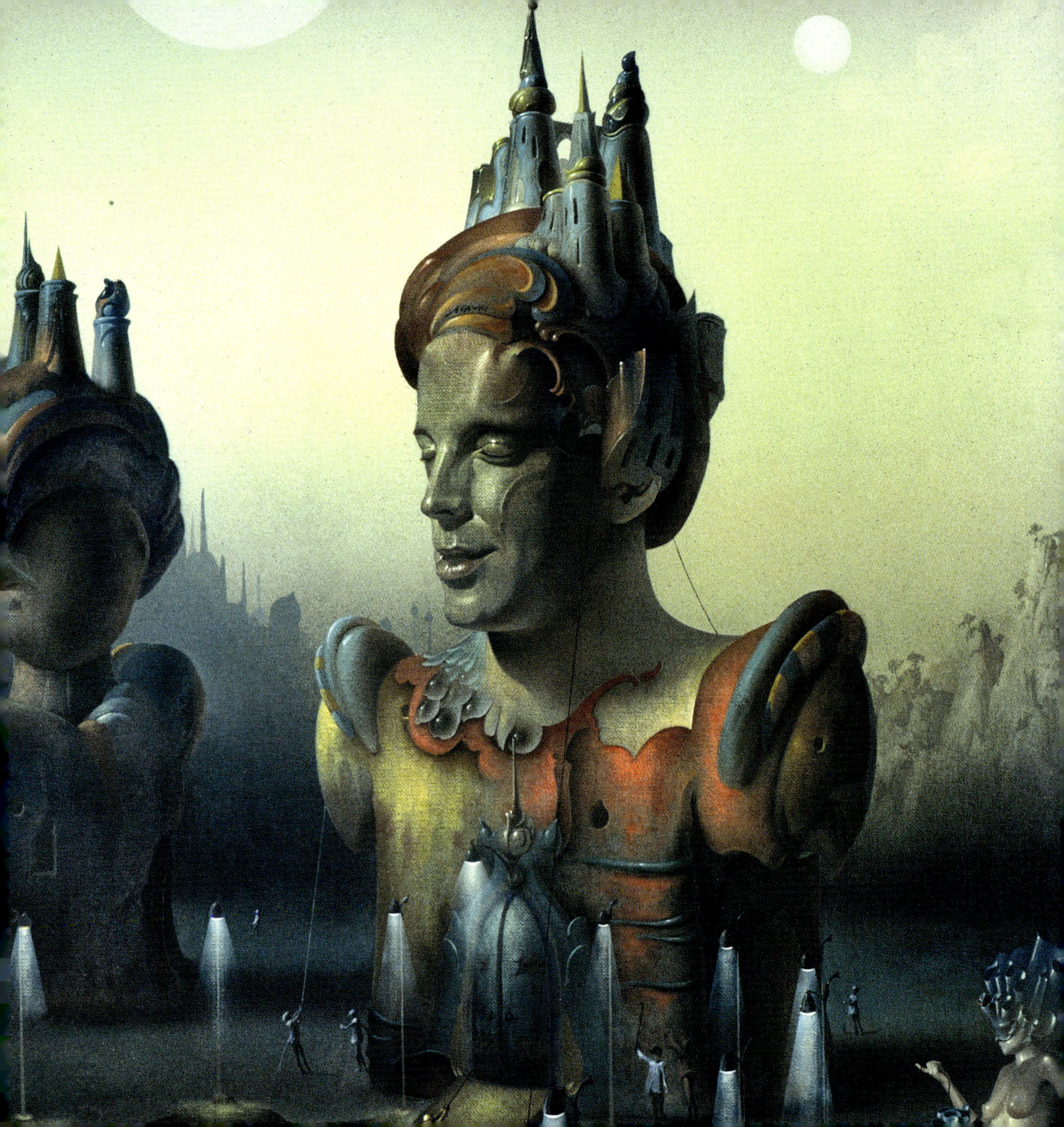

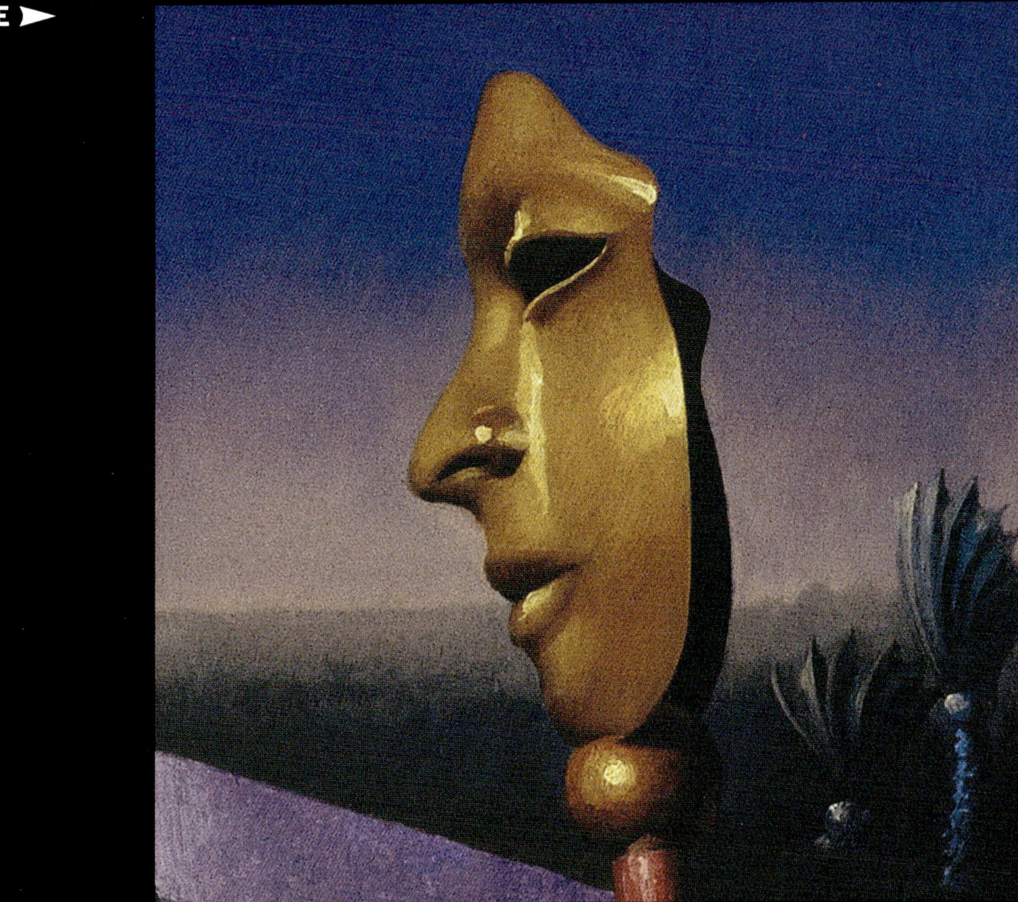

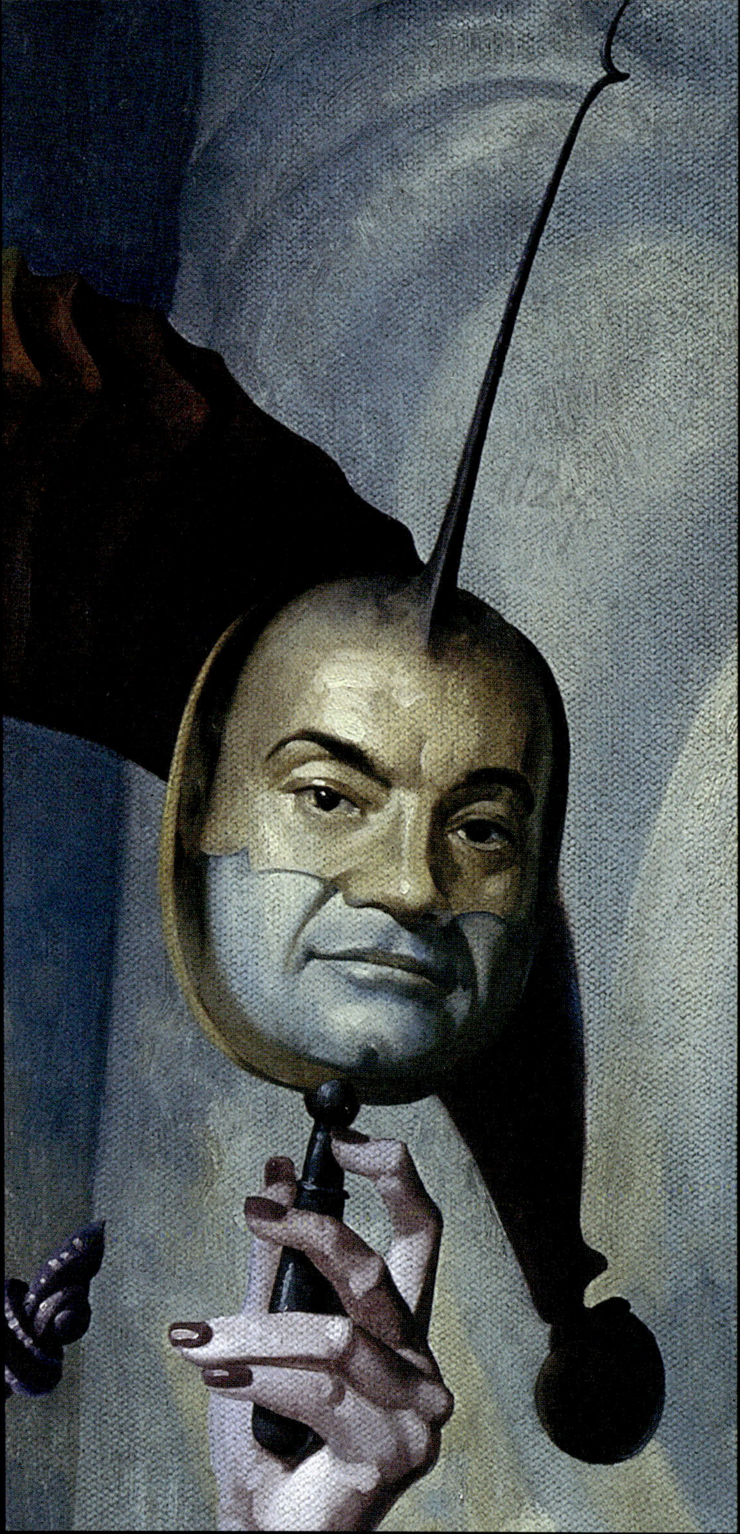

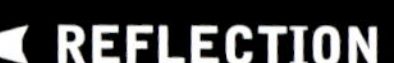

TIMELESS EXISTENCE ►

LA CONVERSATION ►

THE WORLD ►

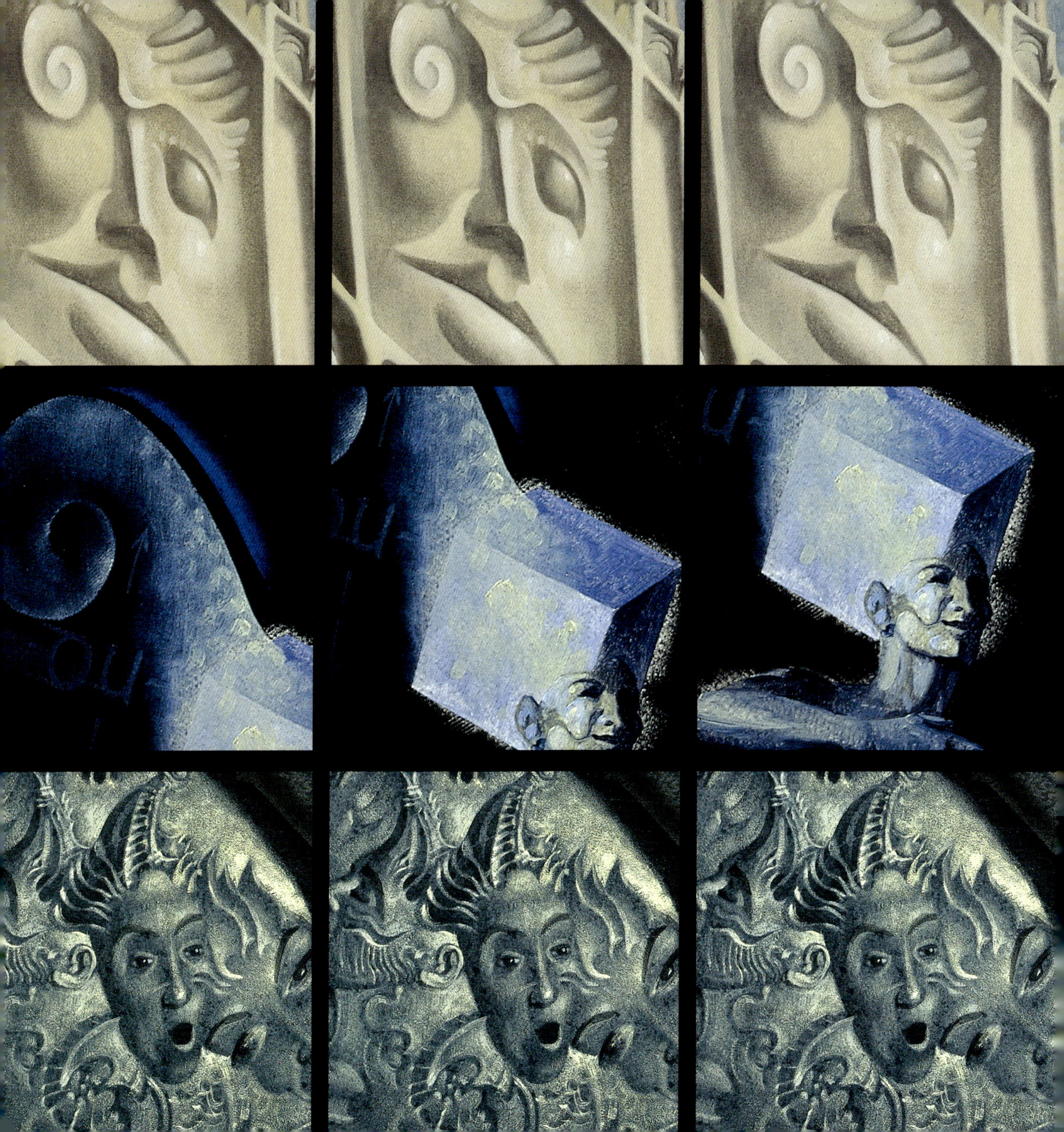

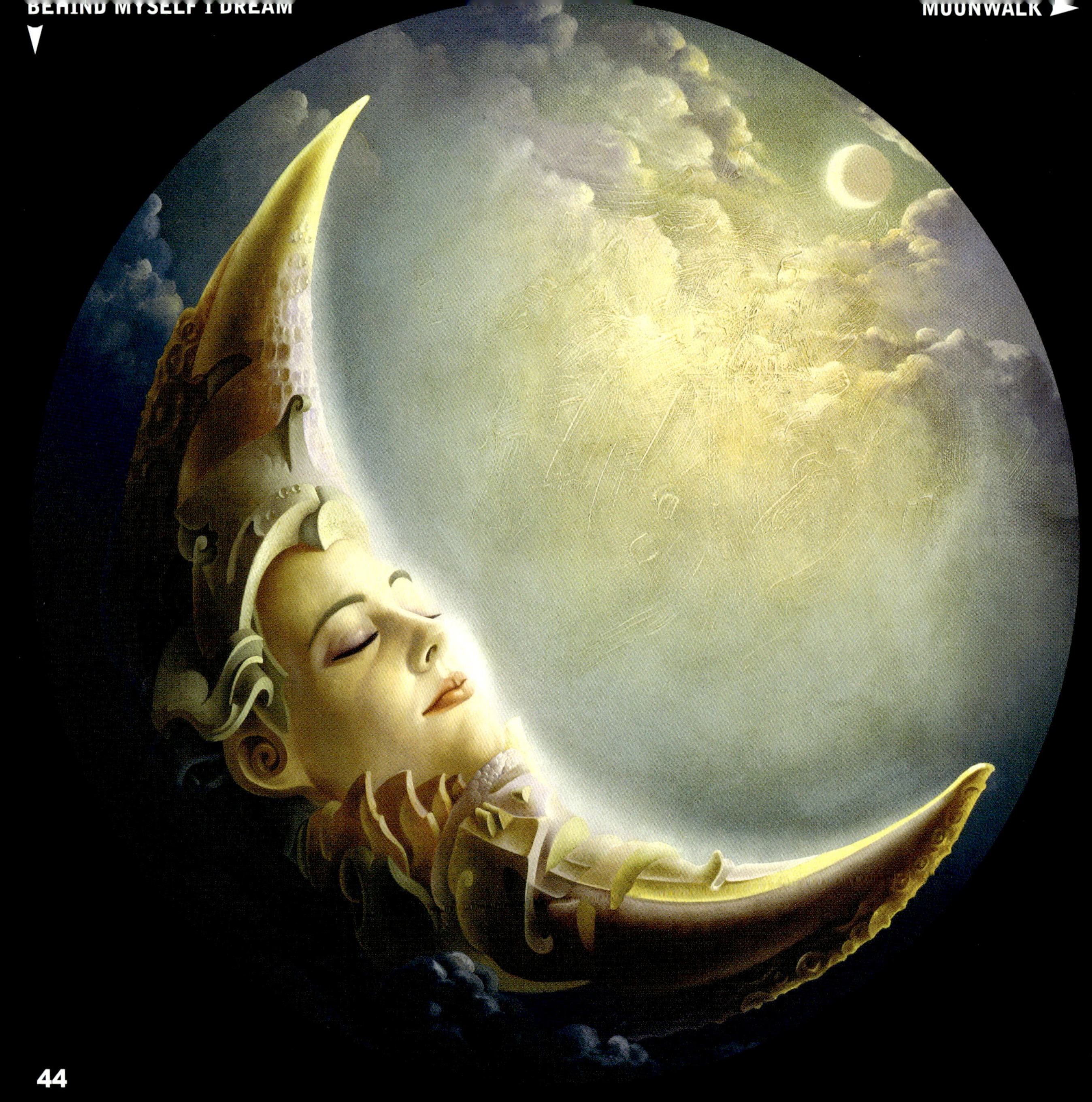

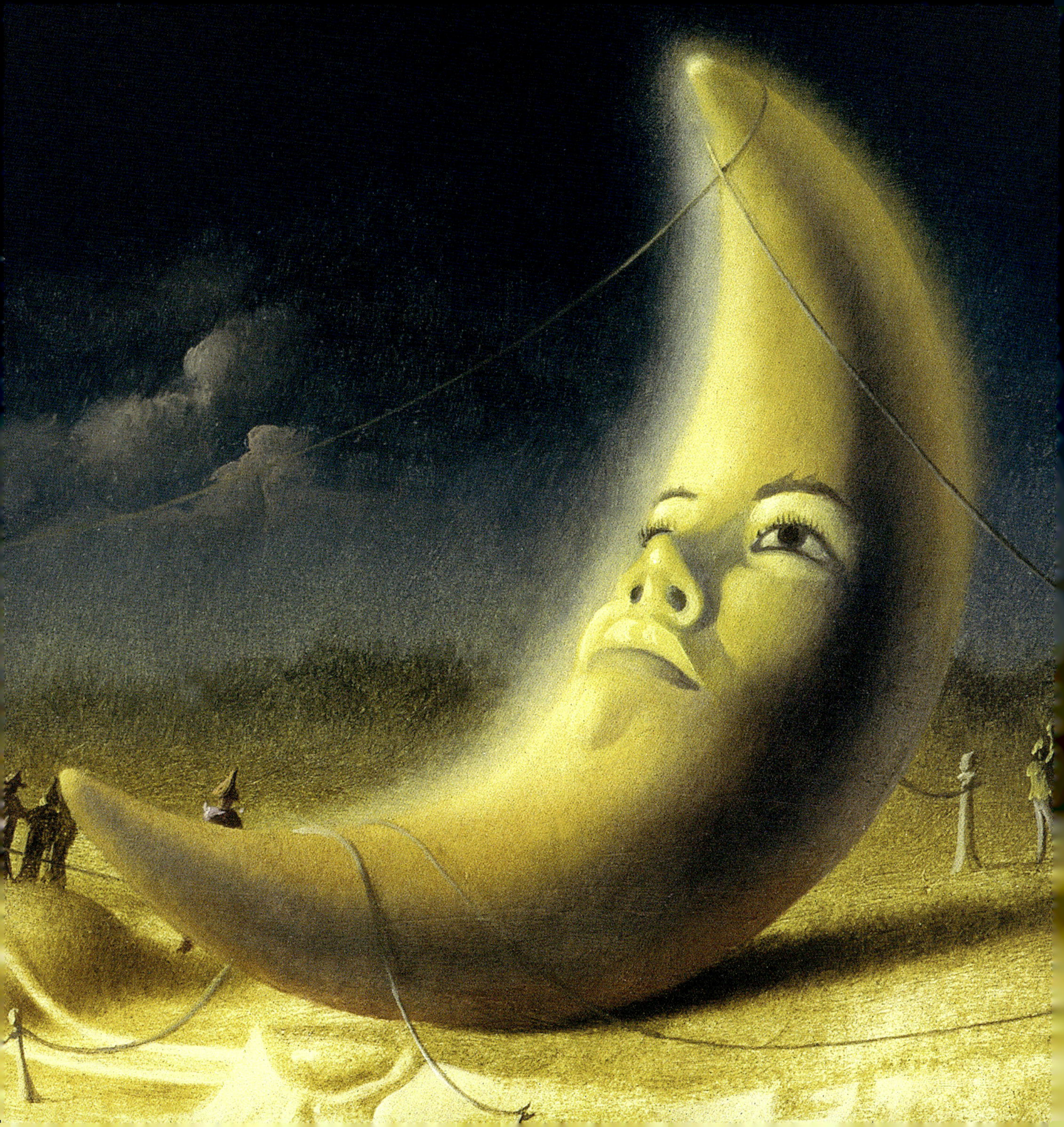

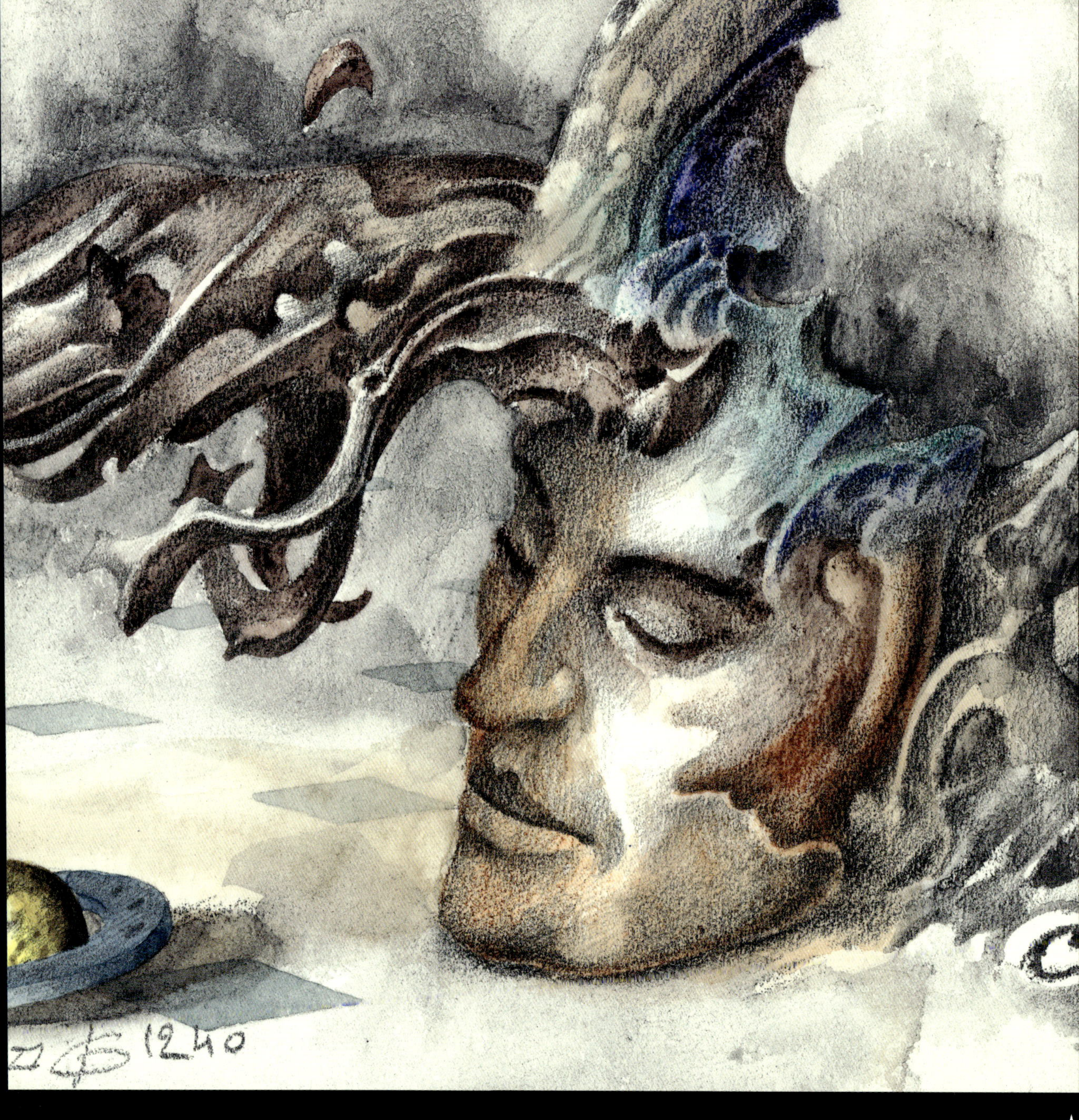

STUDY BASED AROUND THE TASTE OF AN APPLE

beaks / becs

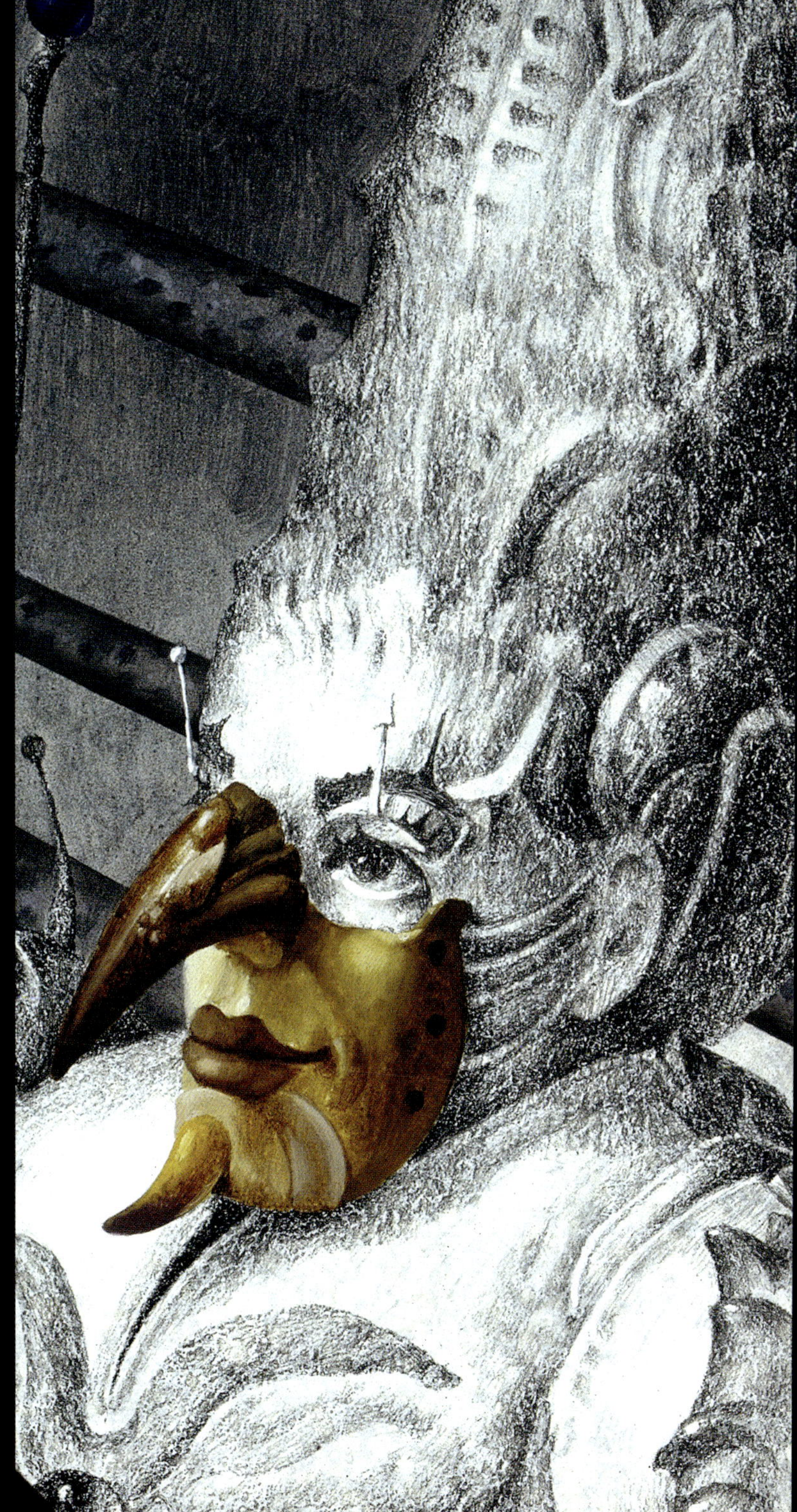

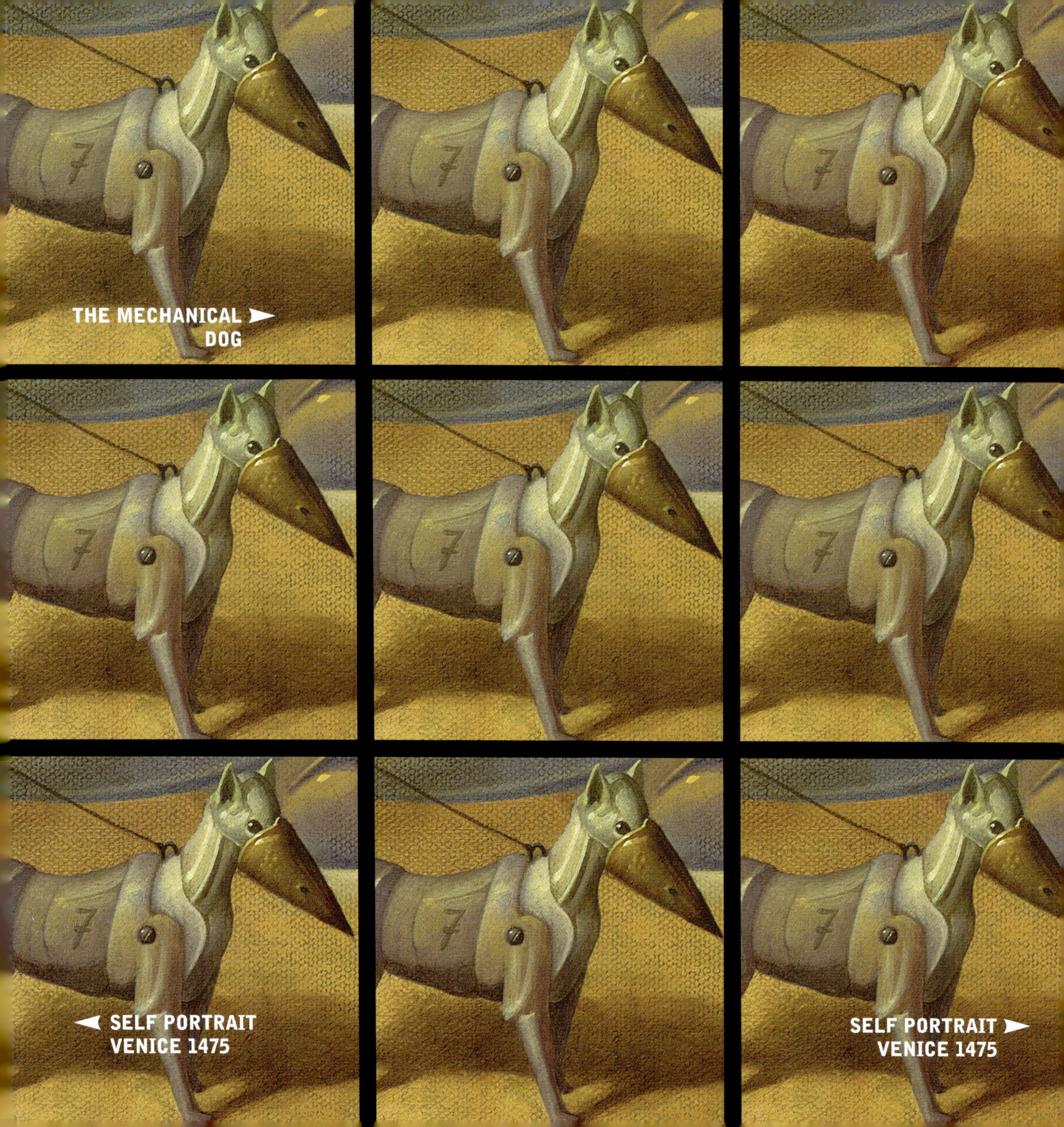
THE MECHANICAL DOG
SELF PORTRAIT
VENICE 1475
SELF PORTRAIT
VENICE 1475

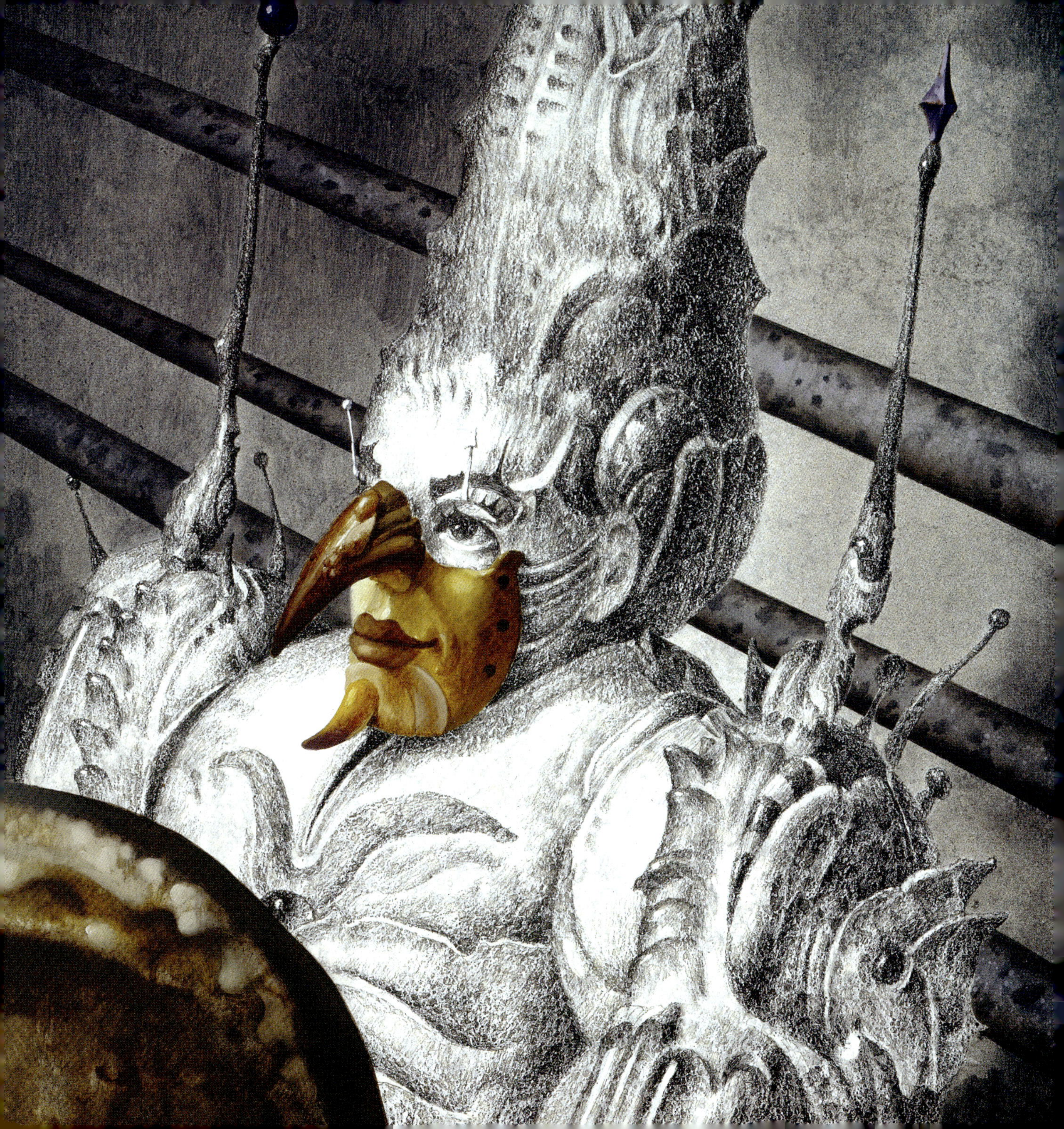

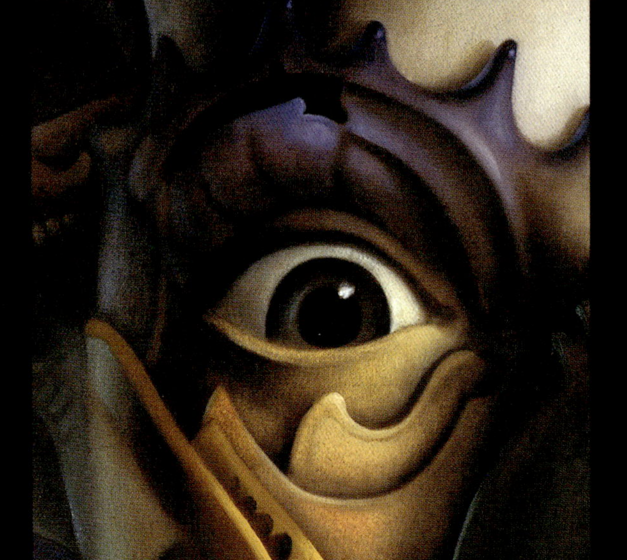

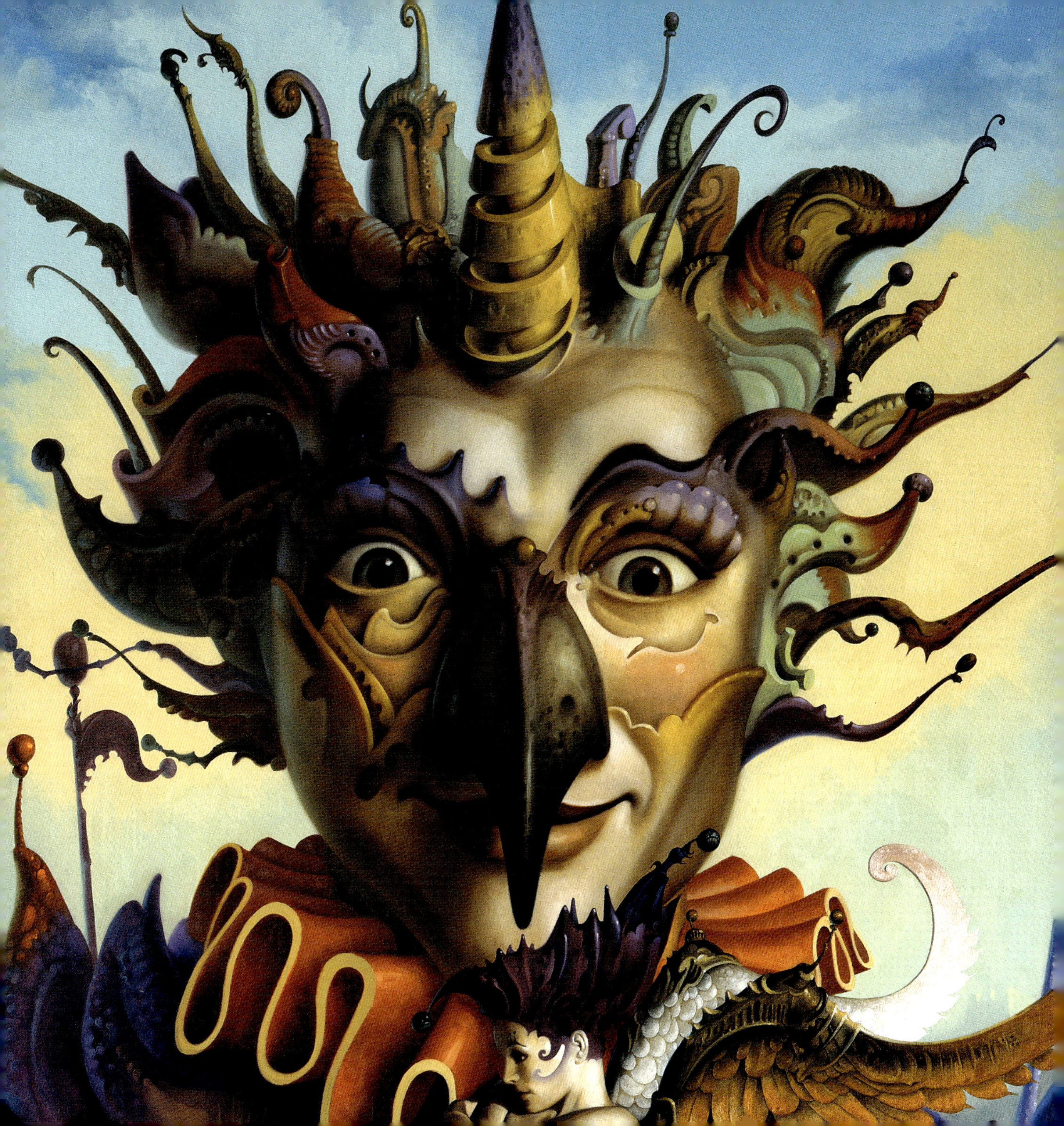

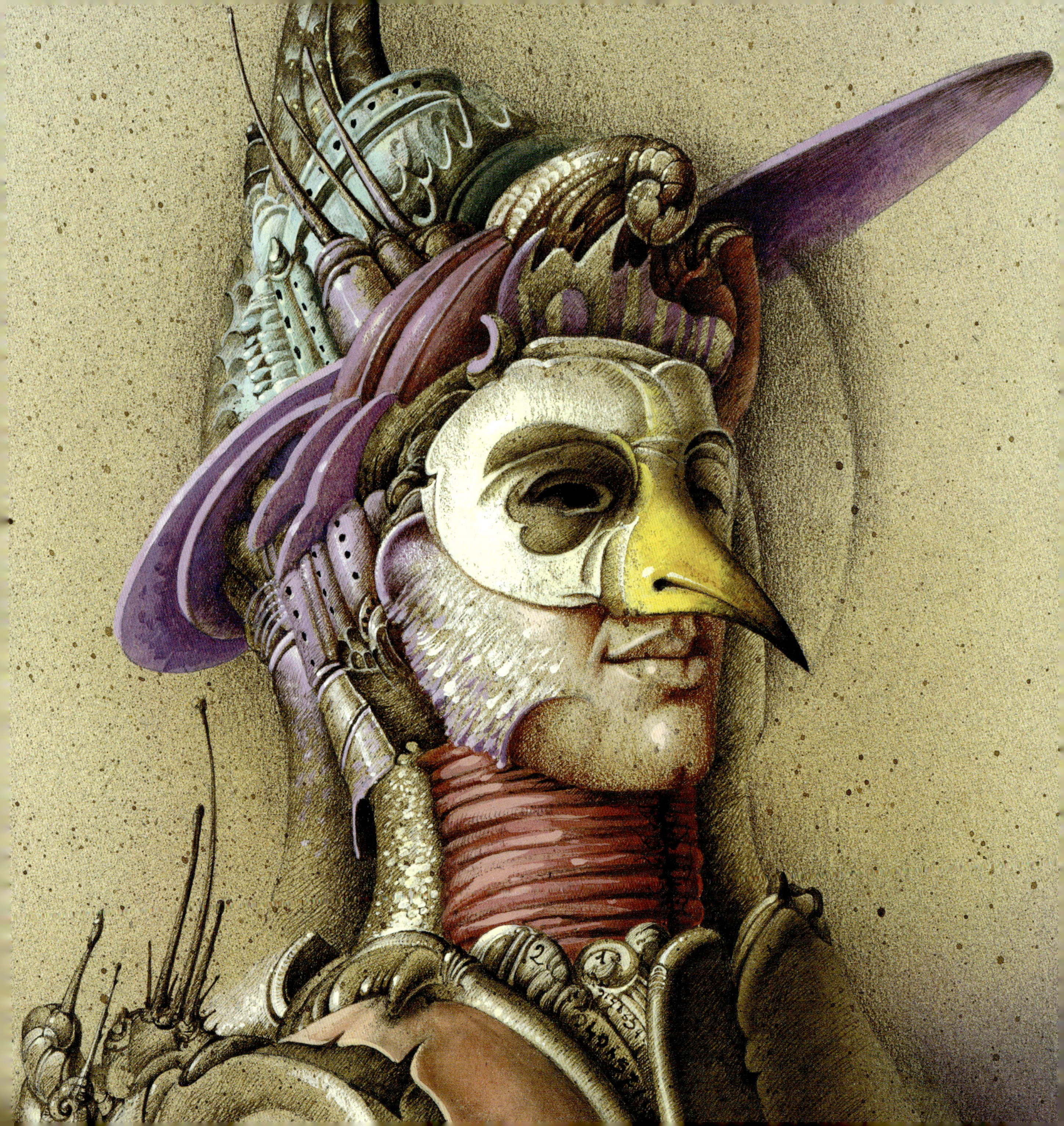

THE PIANO

PORTRAIT OF A BIRD

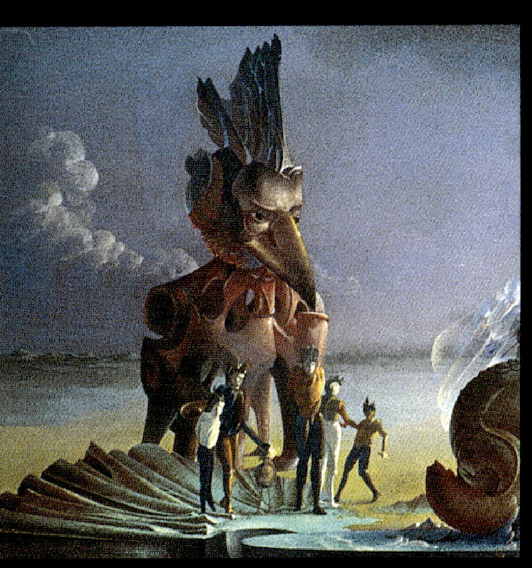

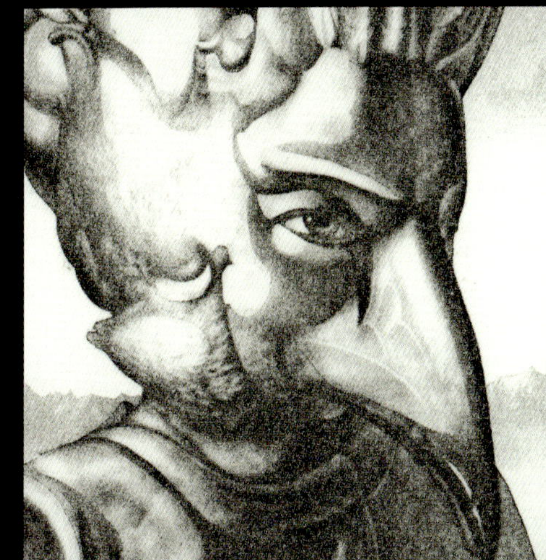

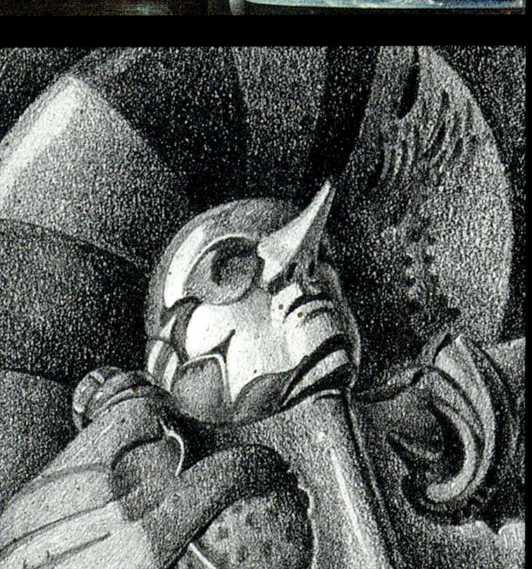

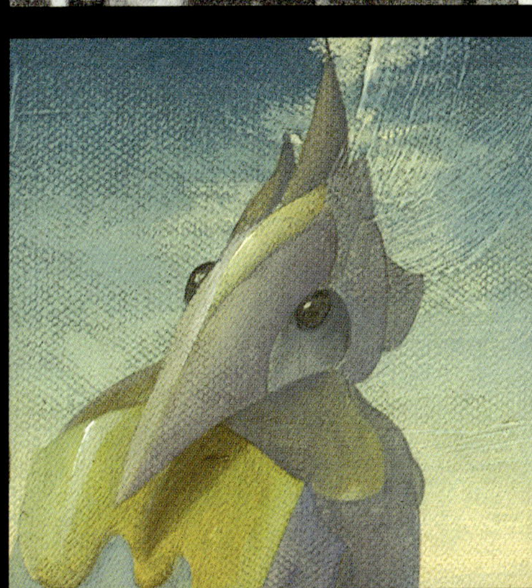

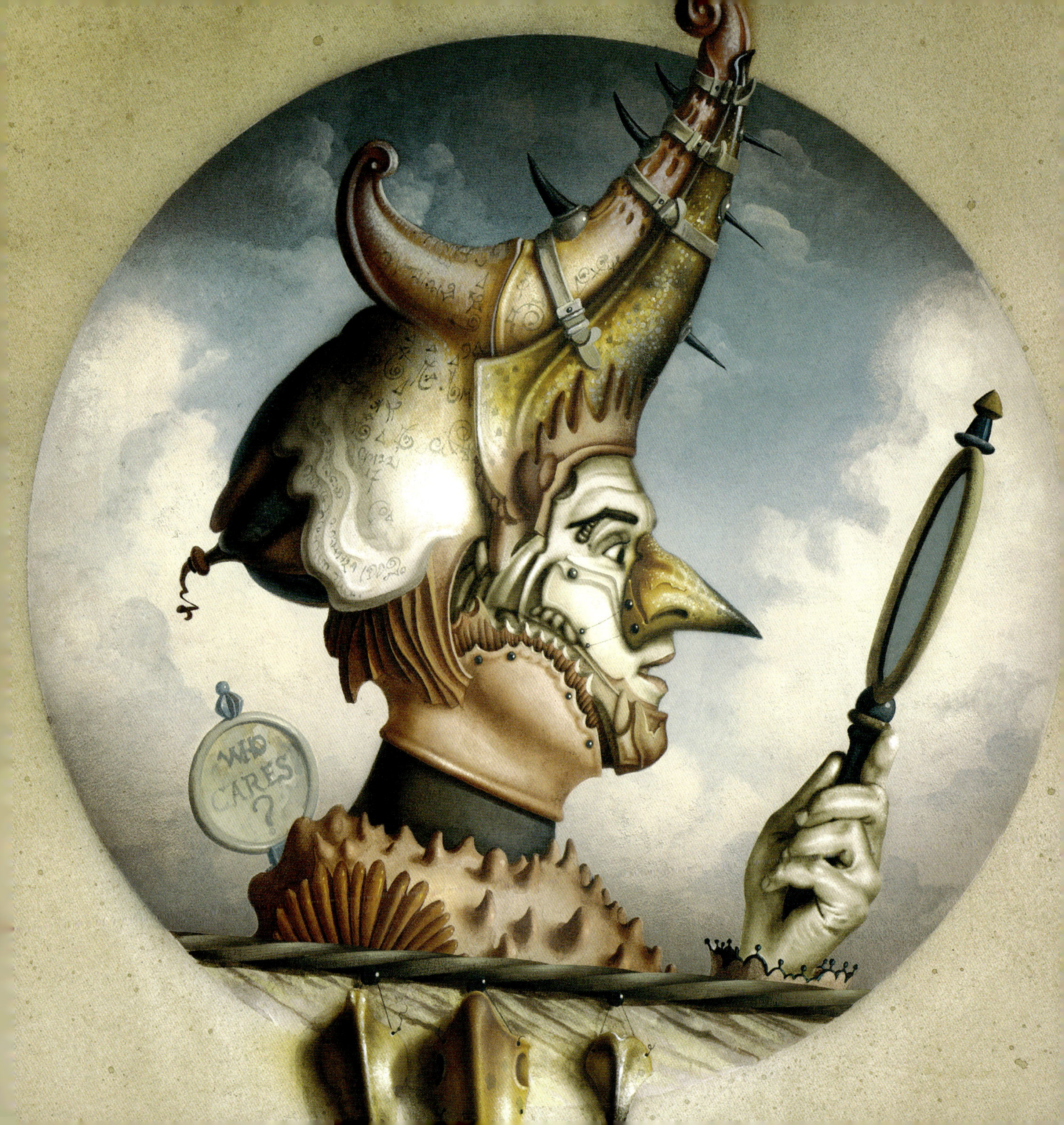
WHO
CARES
?

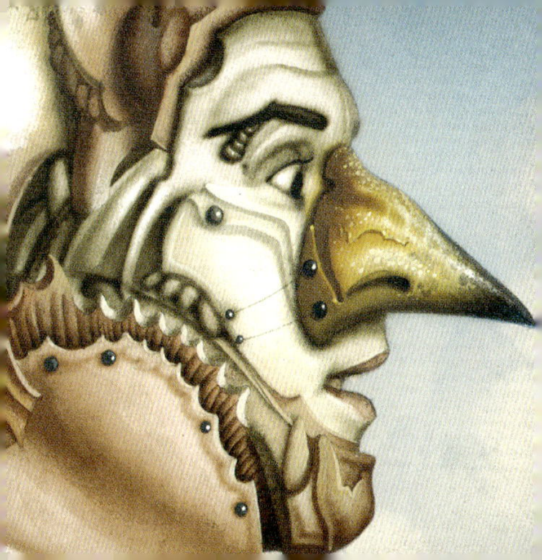

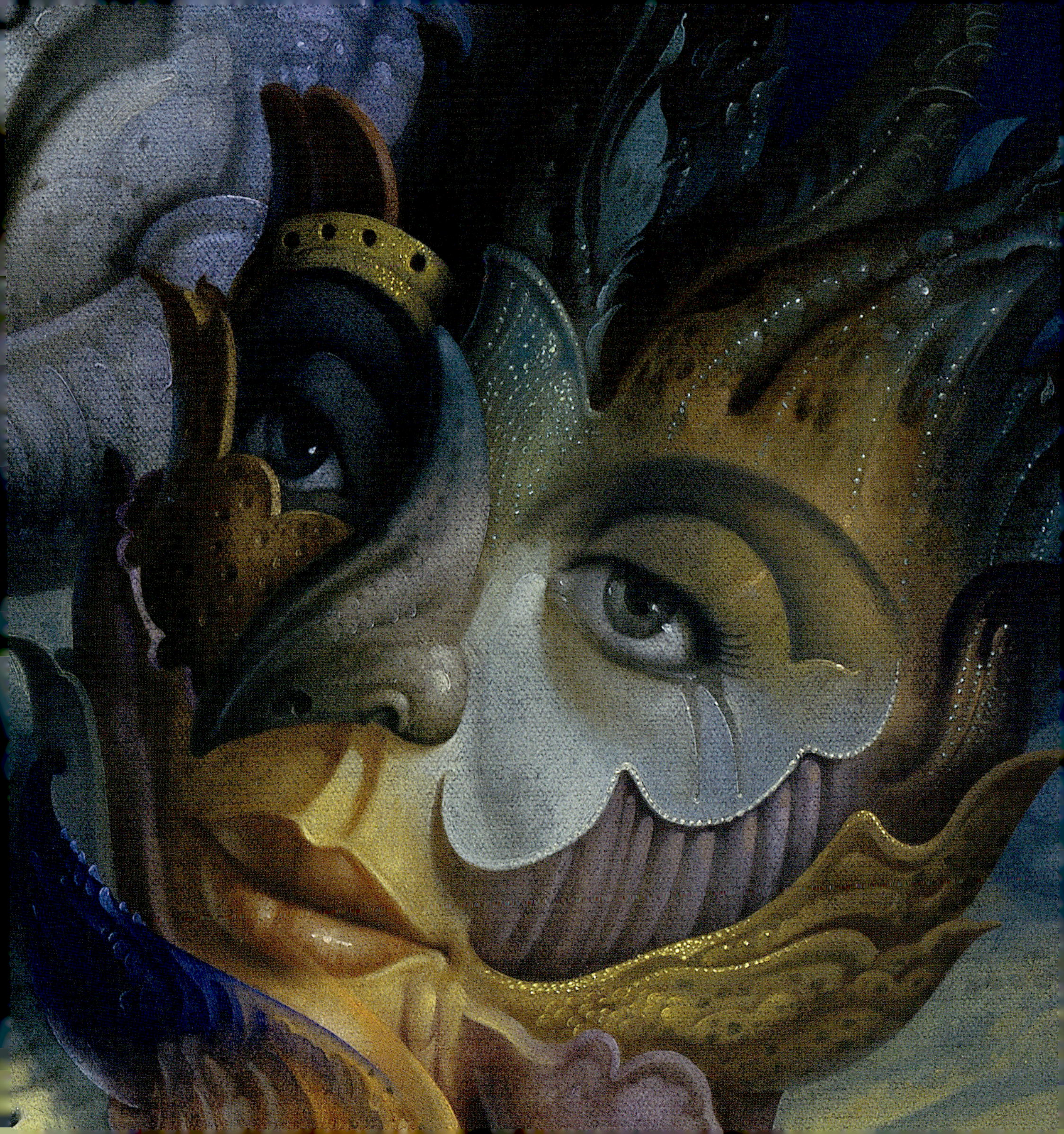

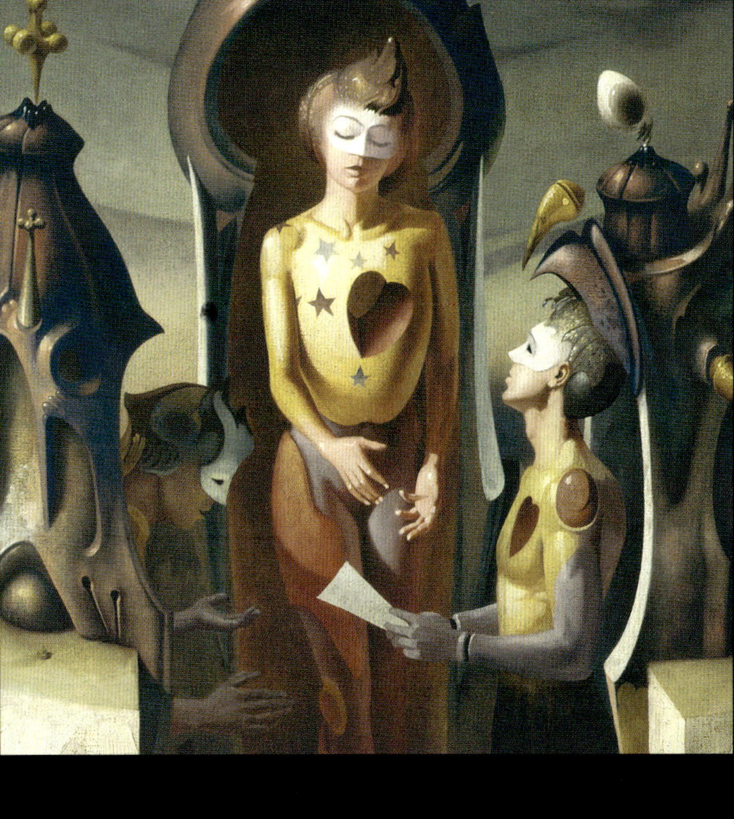

gatherings / ensemble

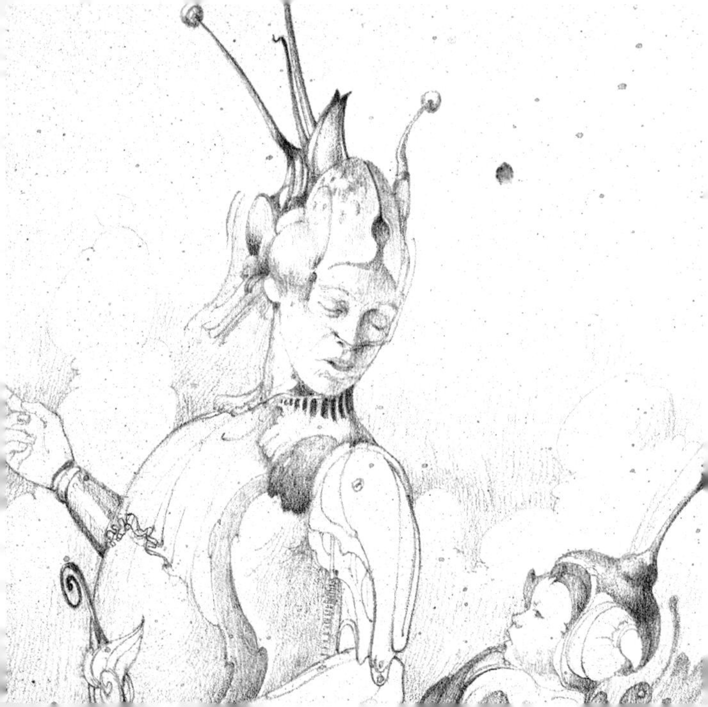

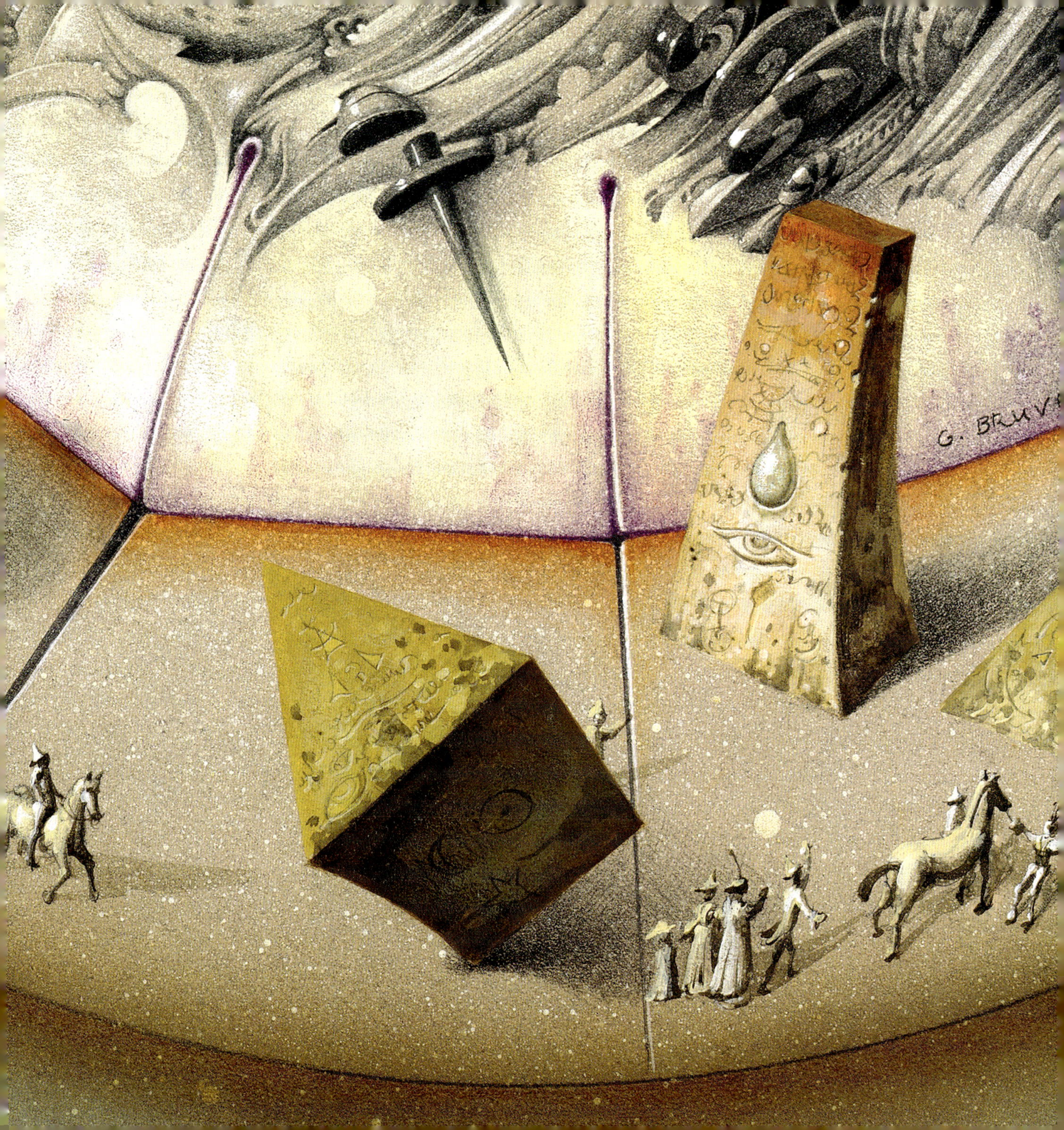

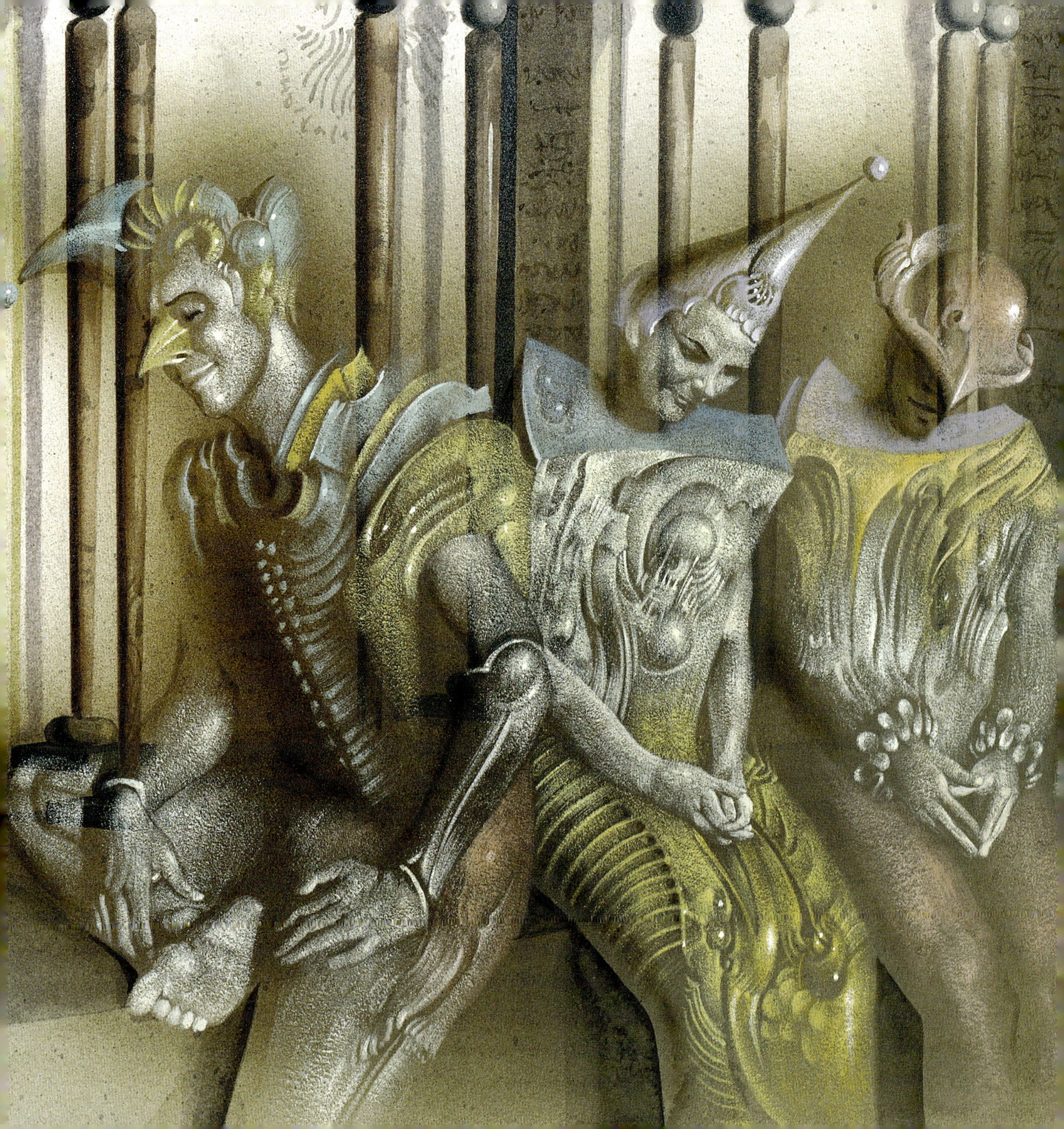

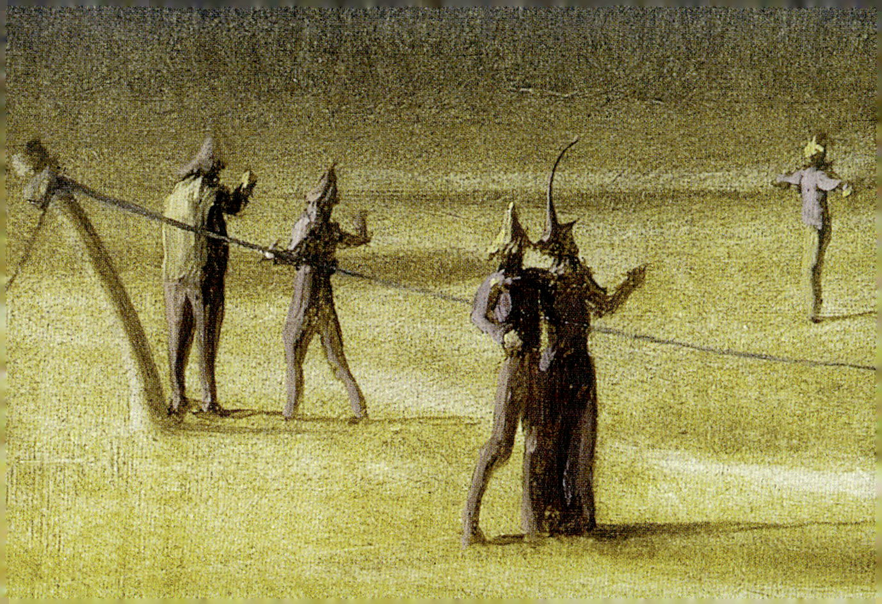

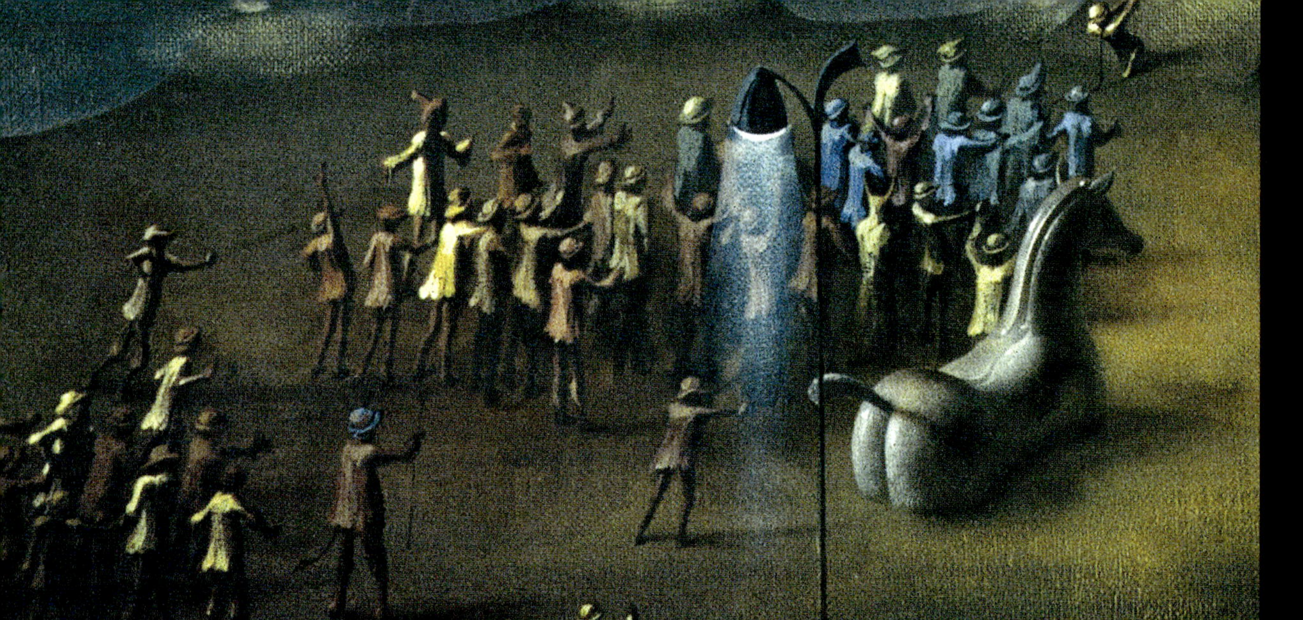

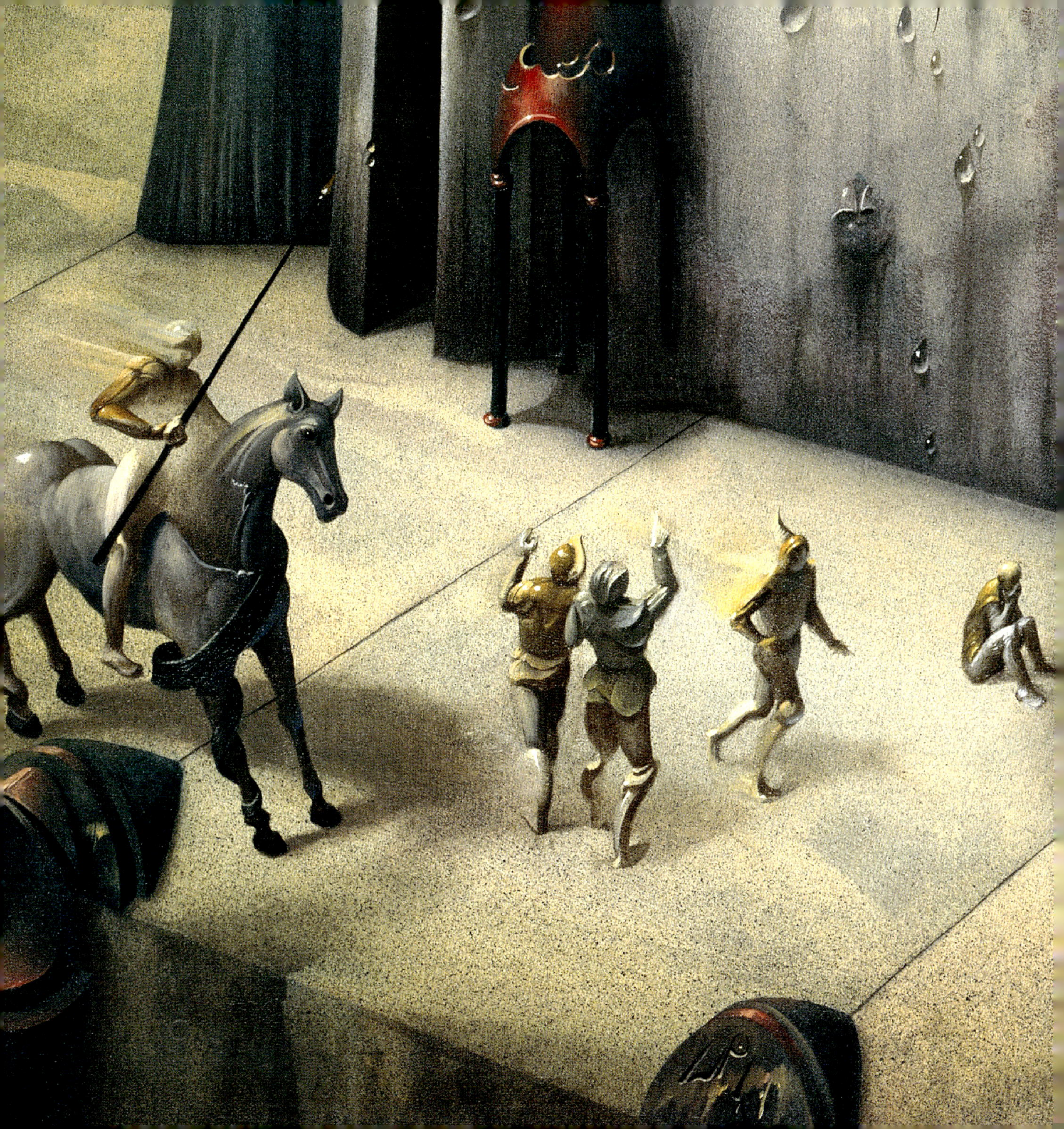

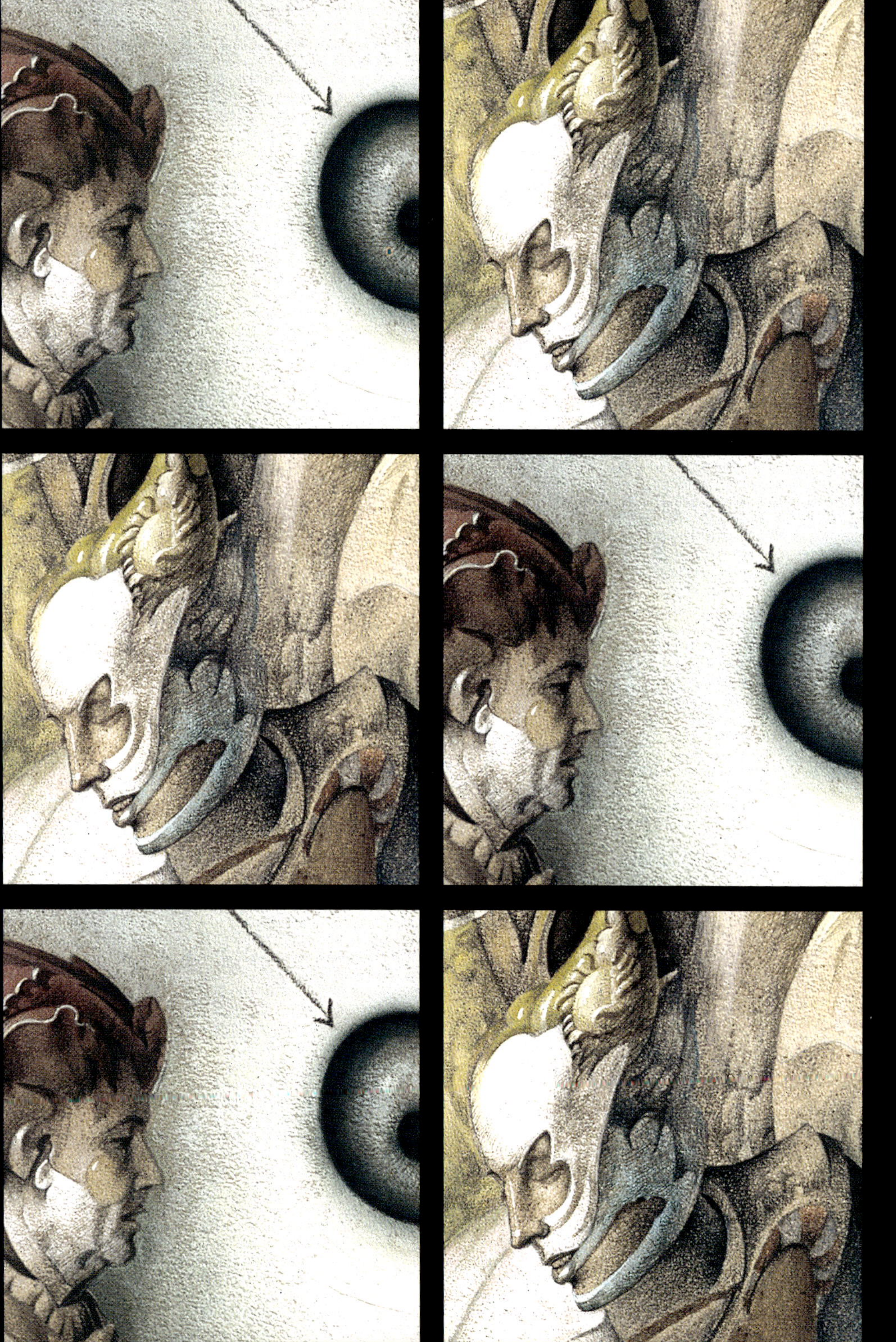

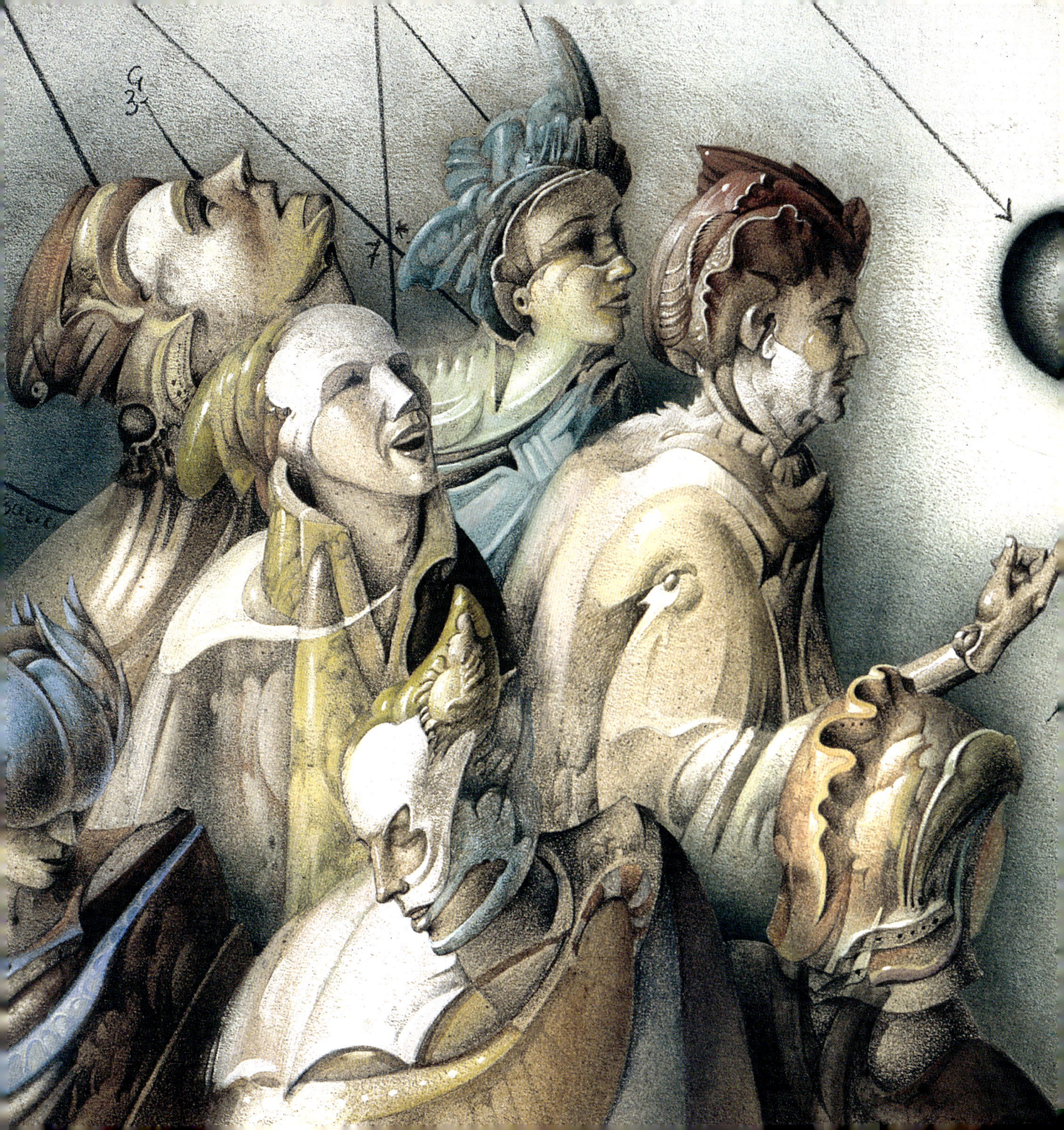

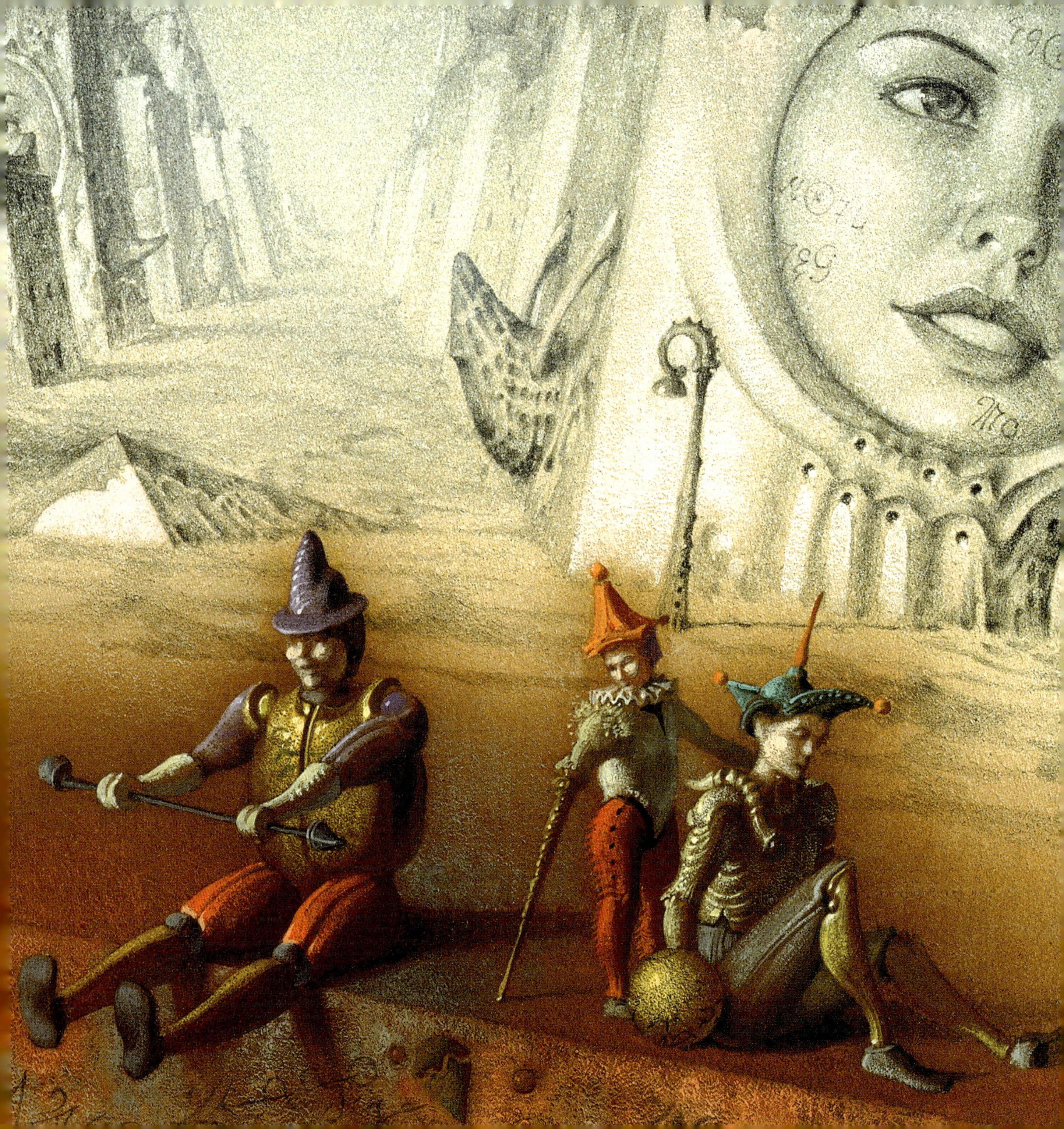

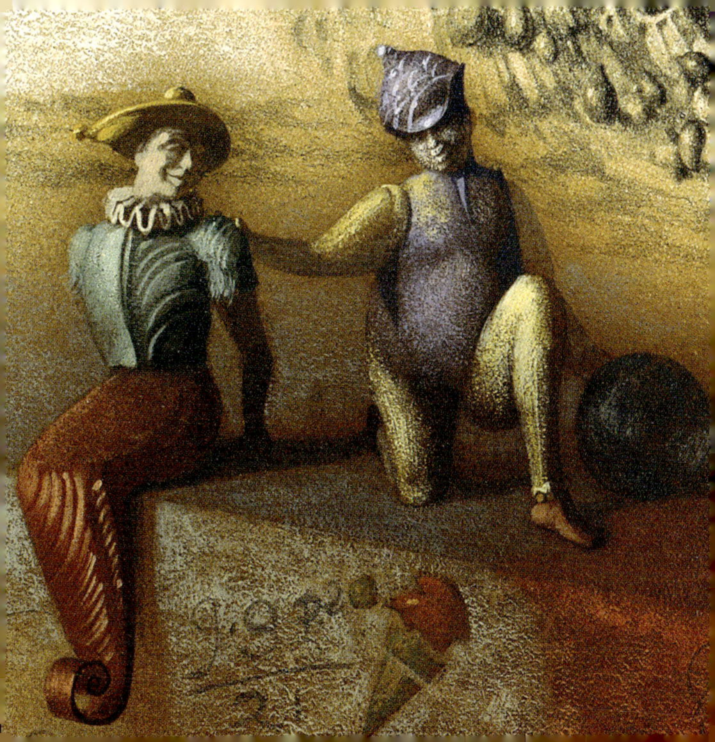

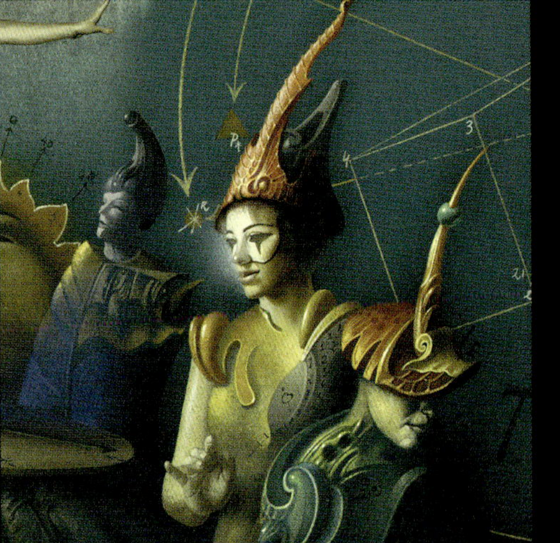

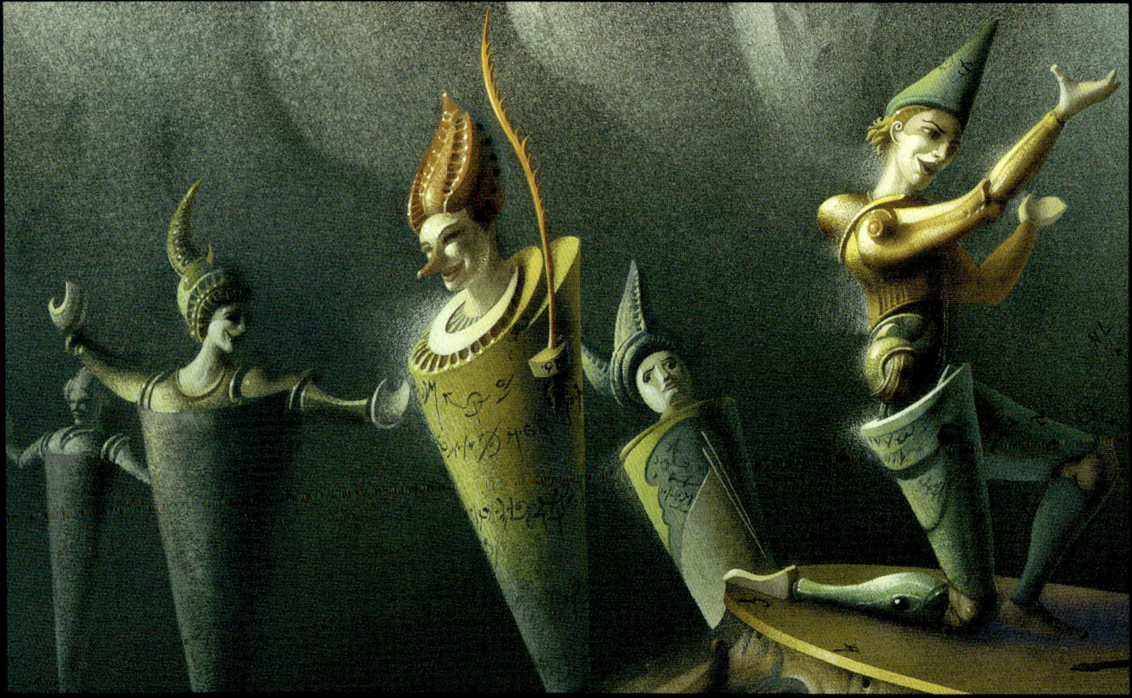

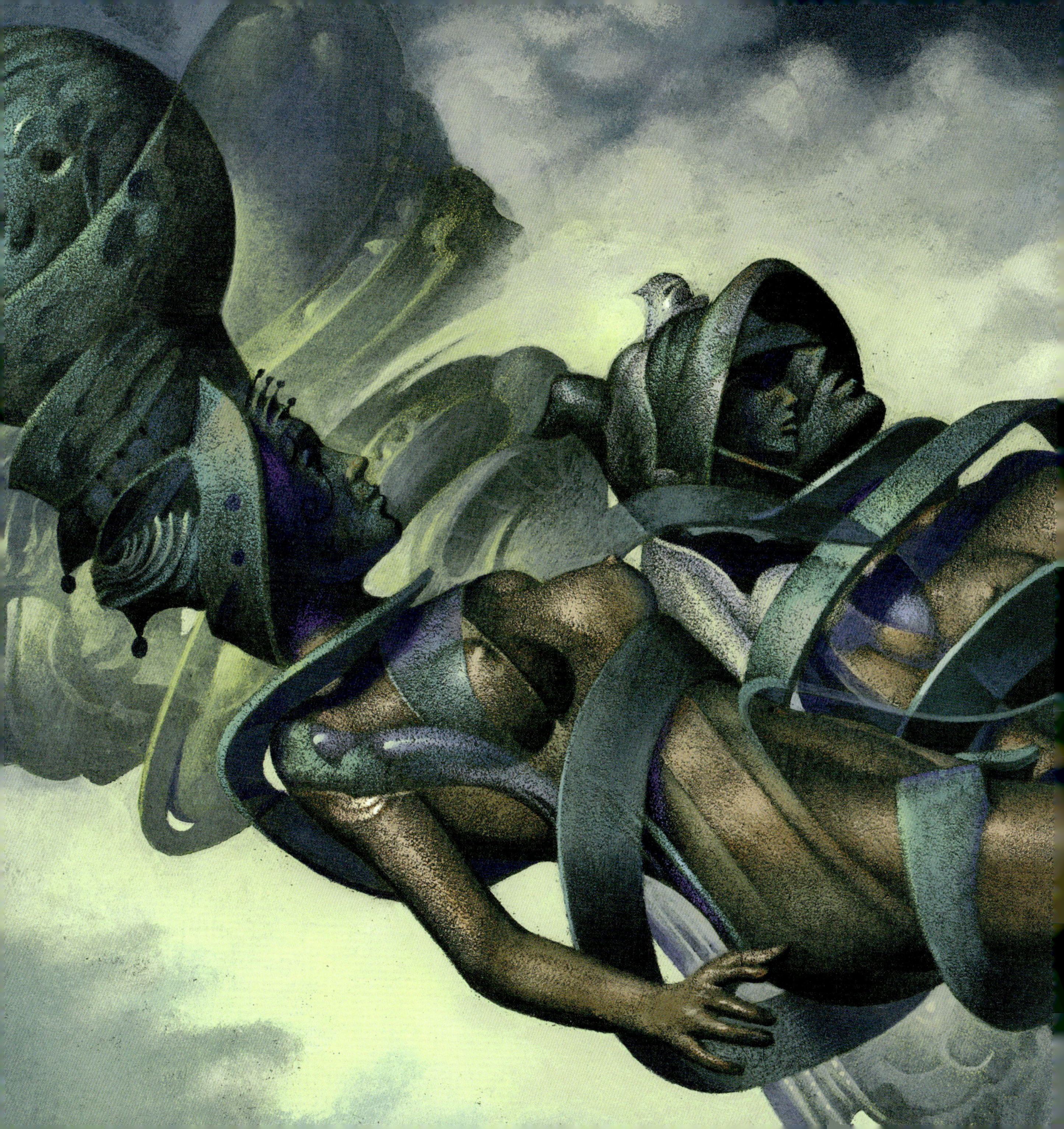

THE PHILOSOPHERS ➤

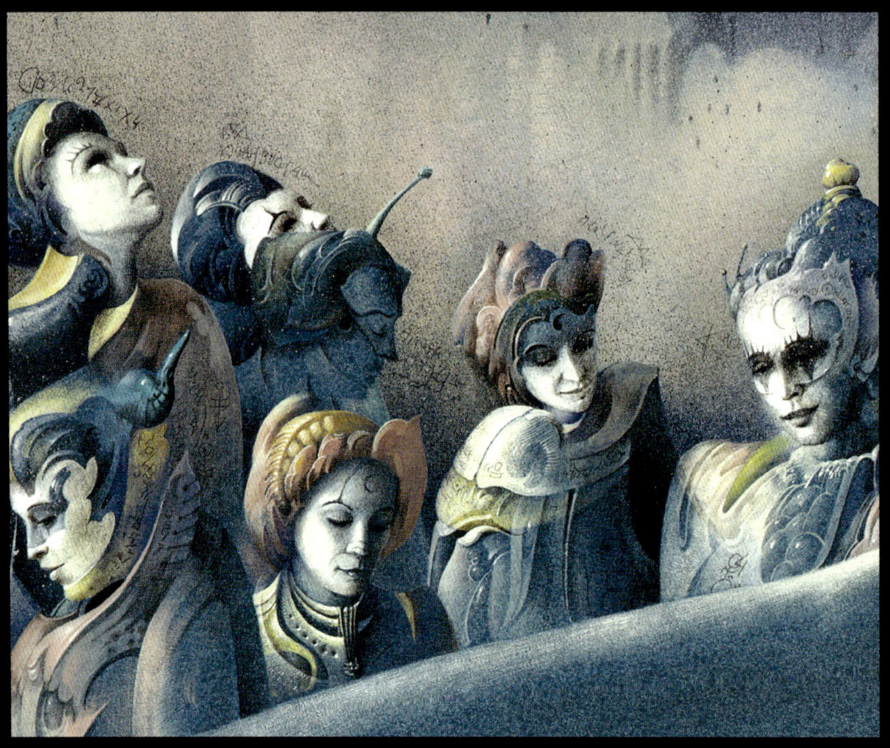

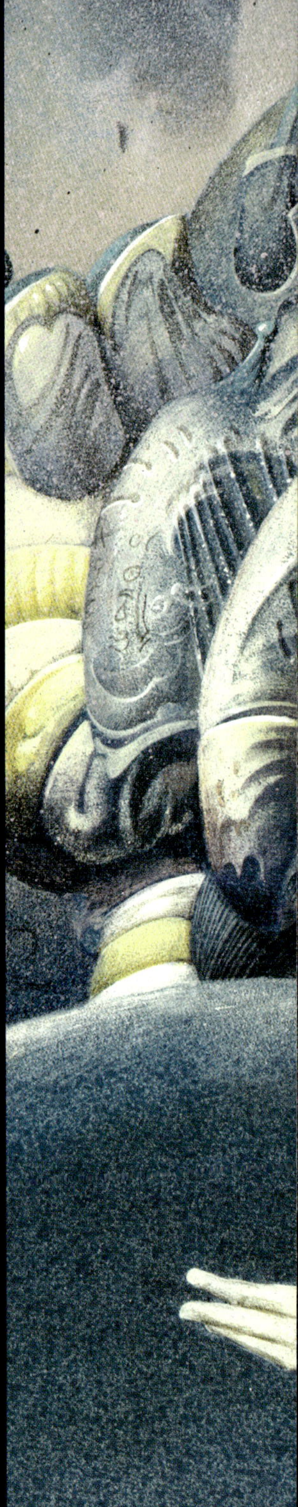

HERMES' DREAM - study ➤ ➤

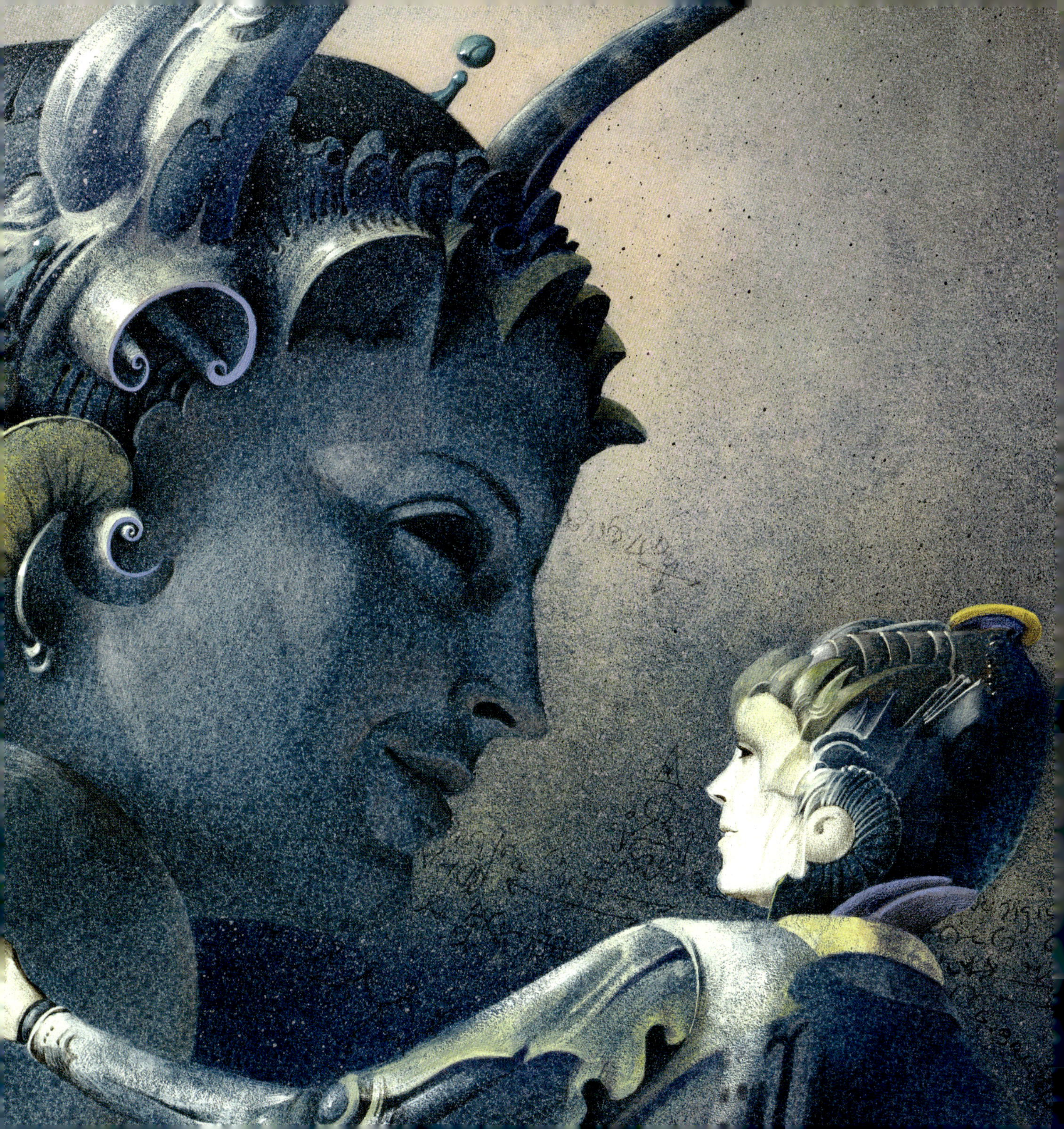

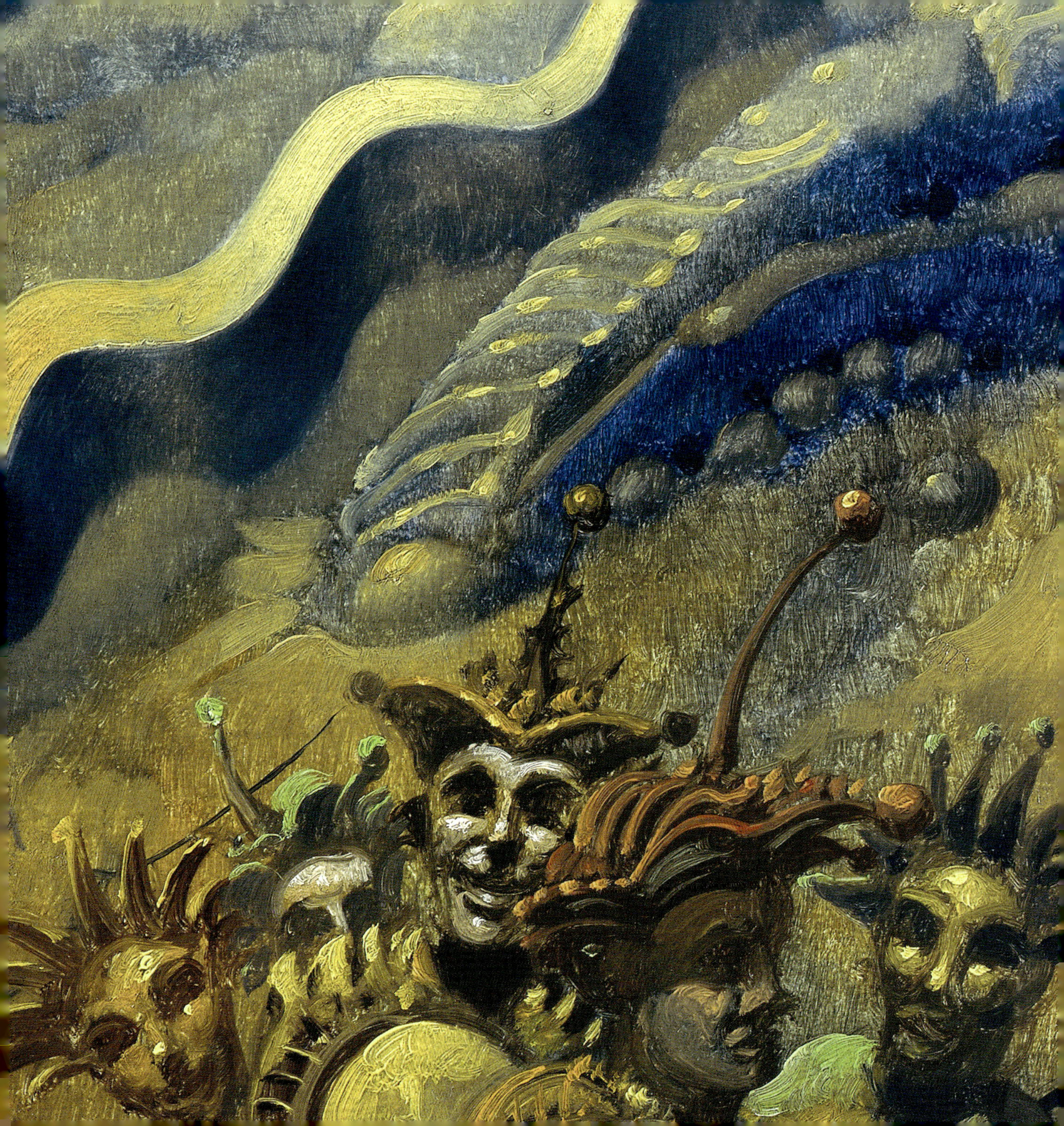

emerging /
emergence

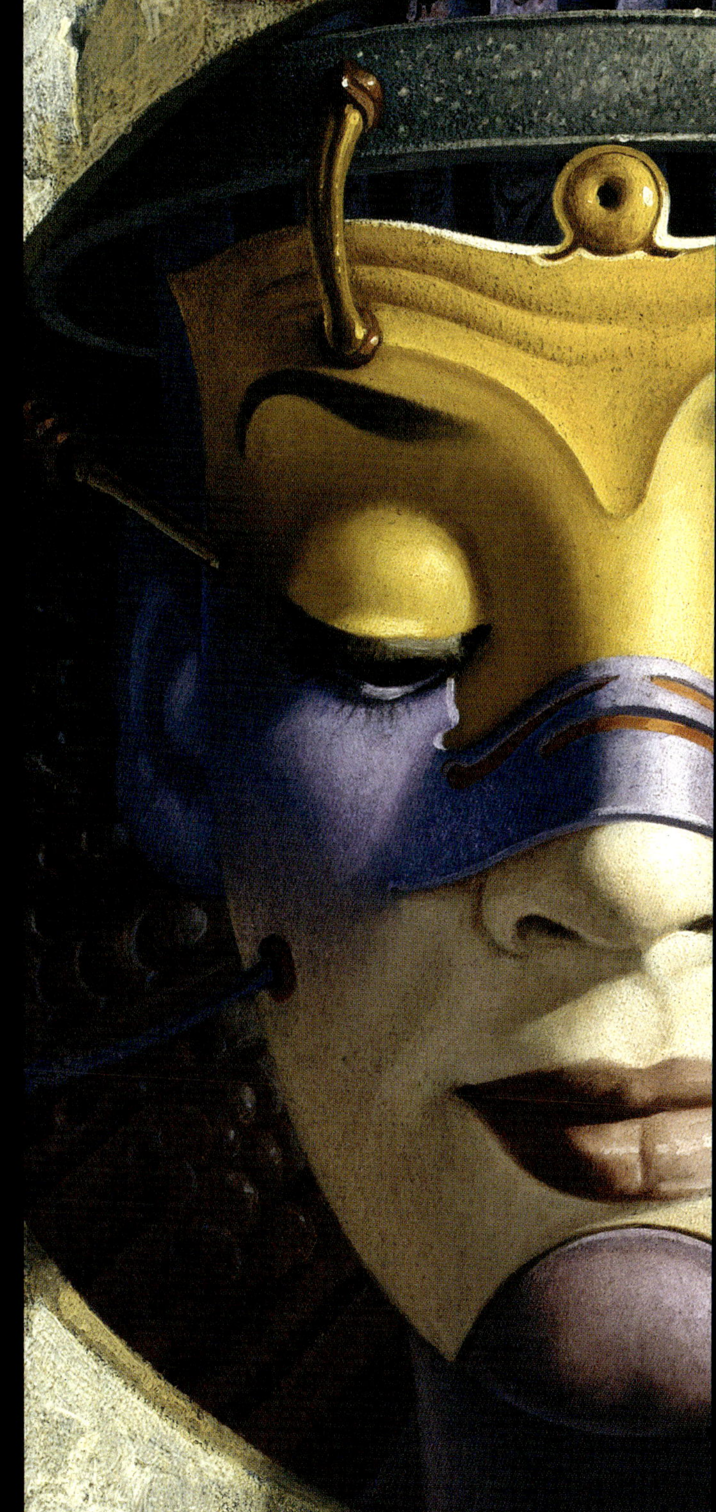

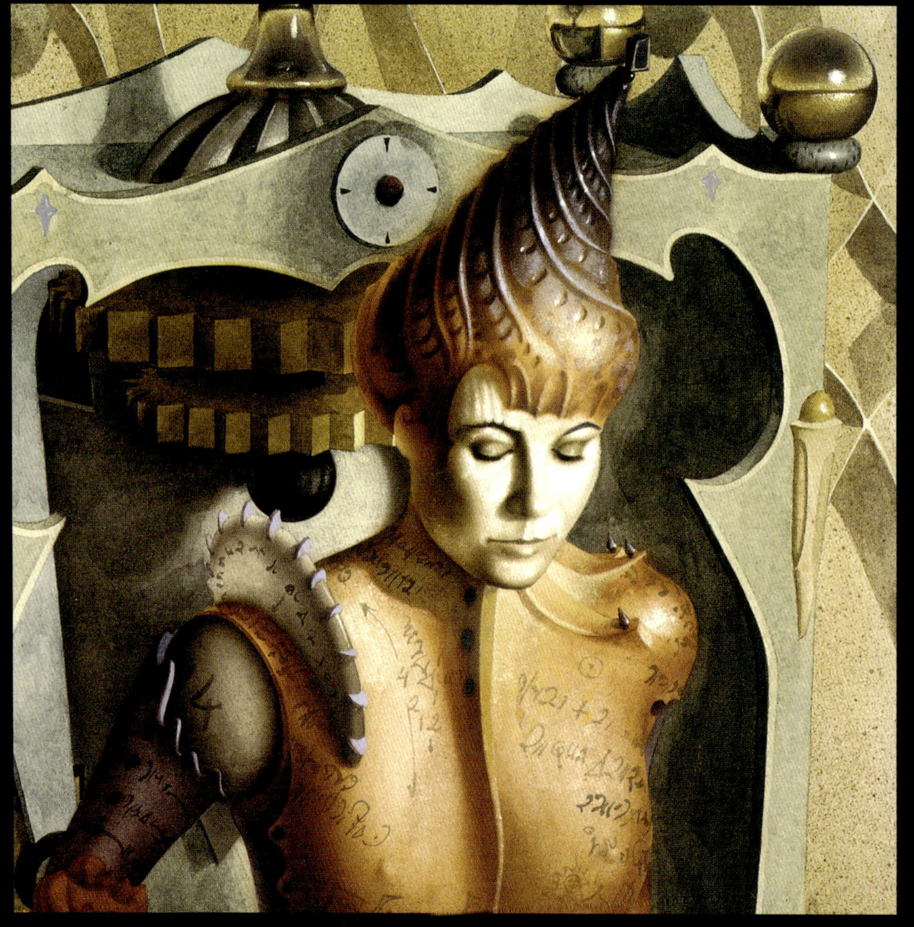

▲ TIME WATCHER

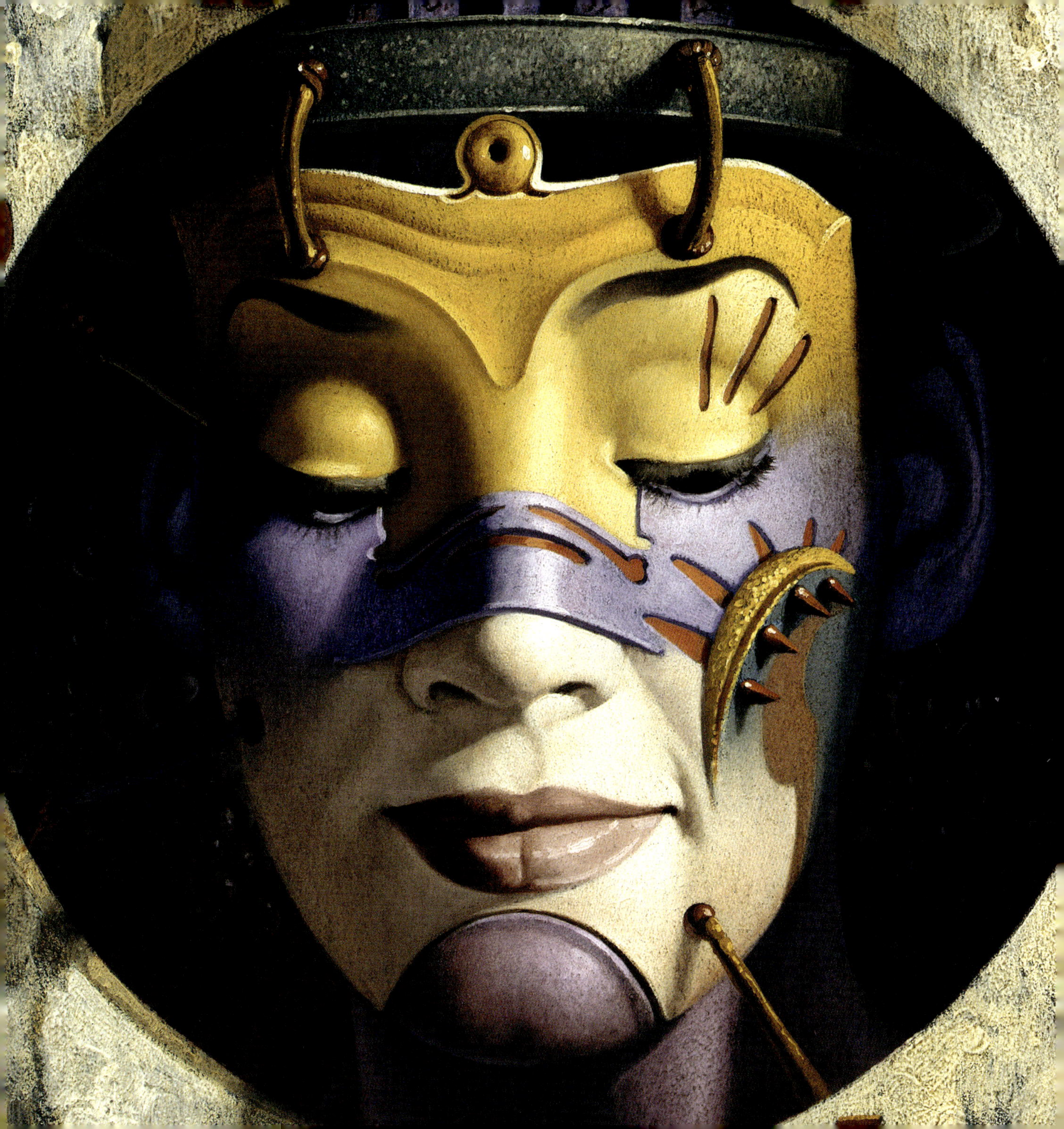

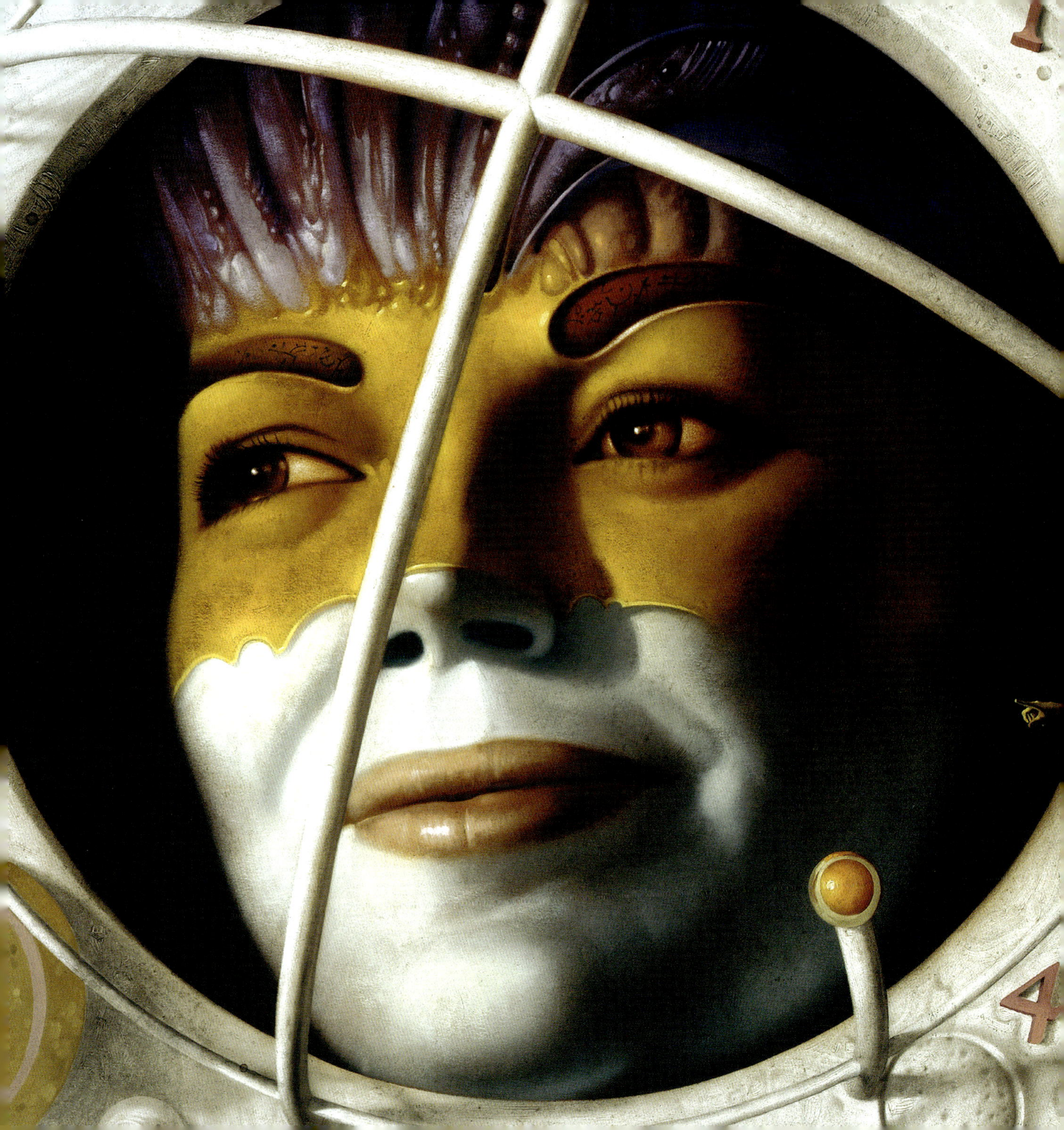

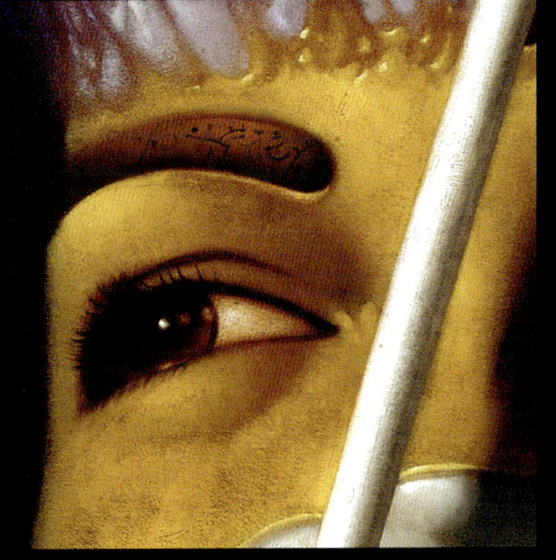

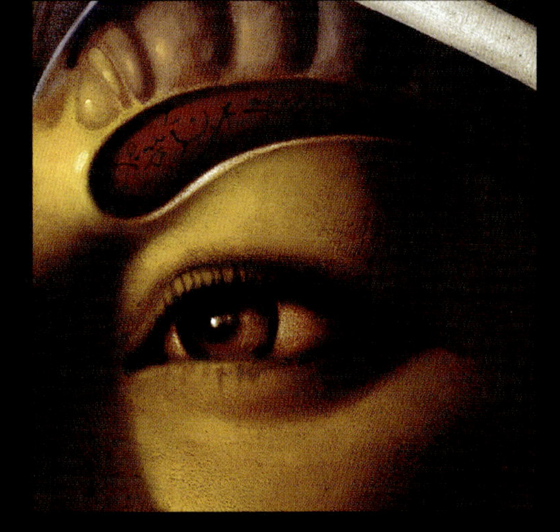

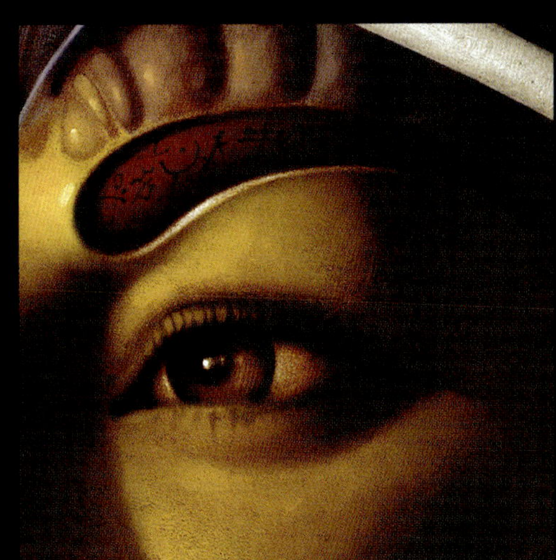

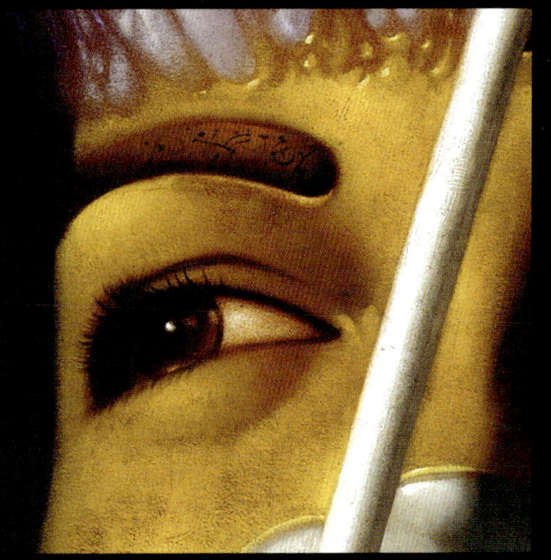

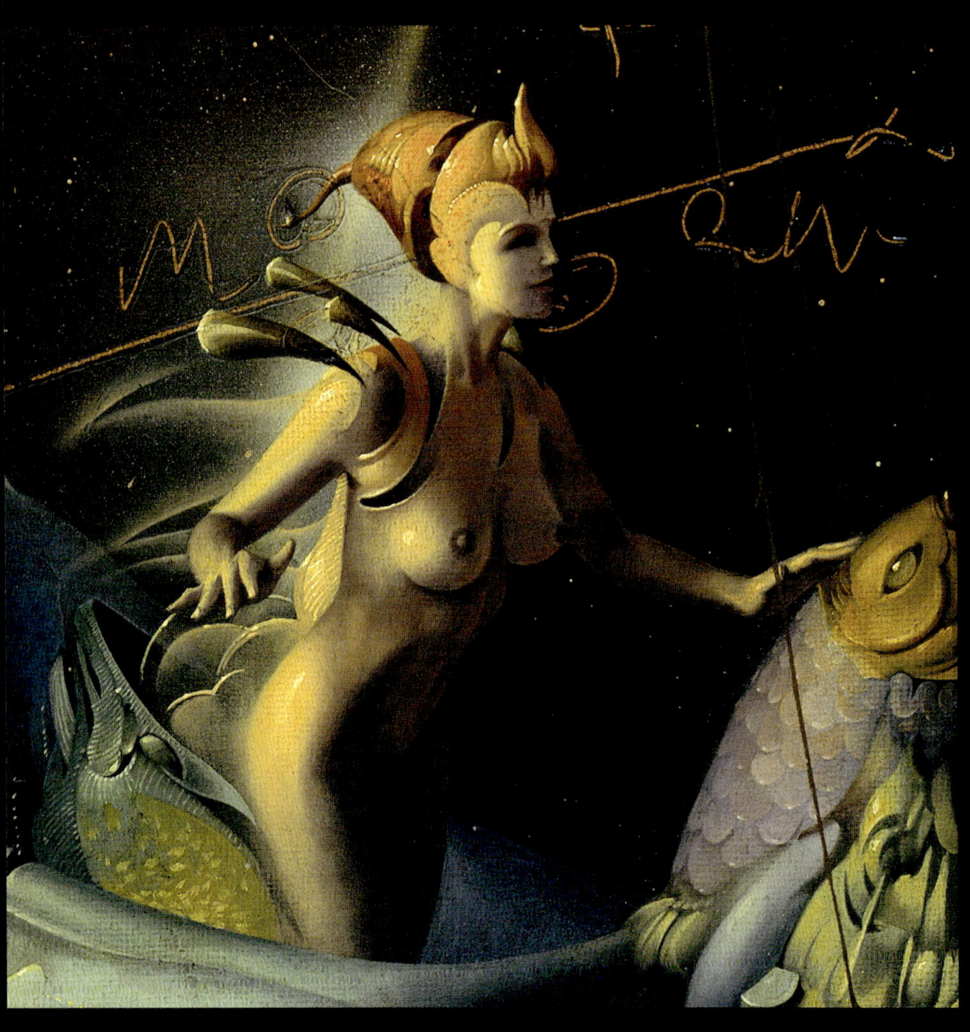

VOYAGE ON THE WATER

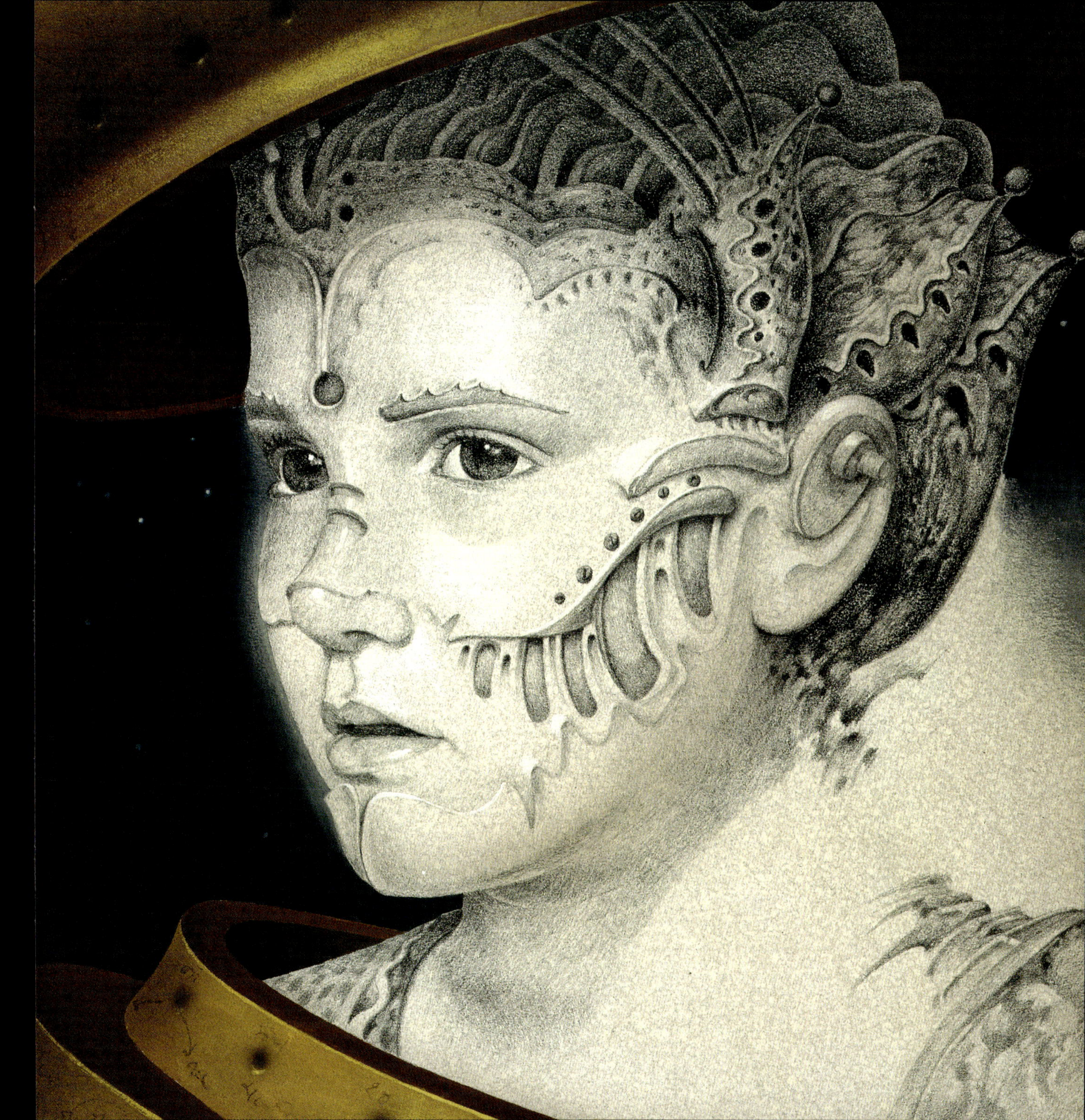

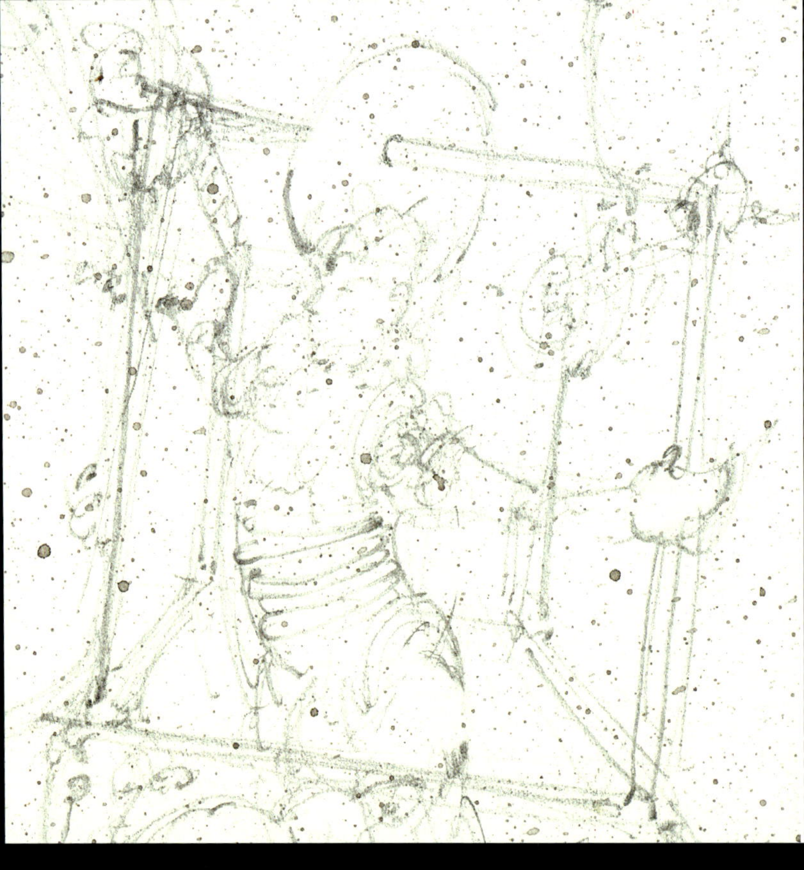

JUMP - study

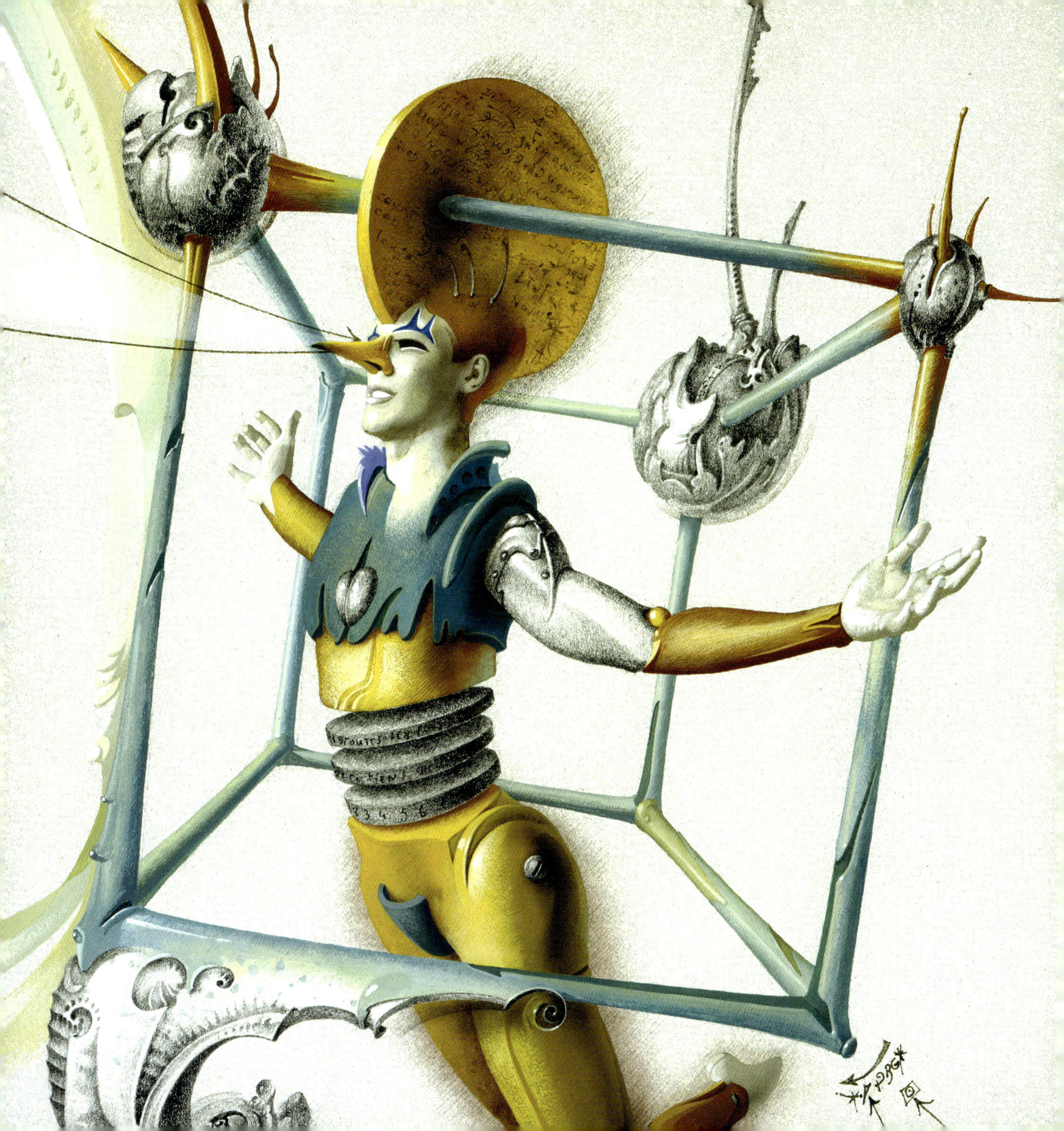

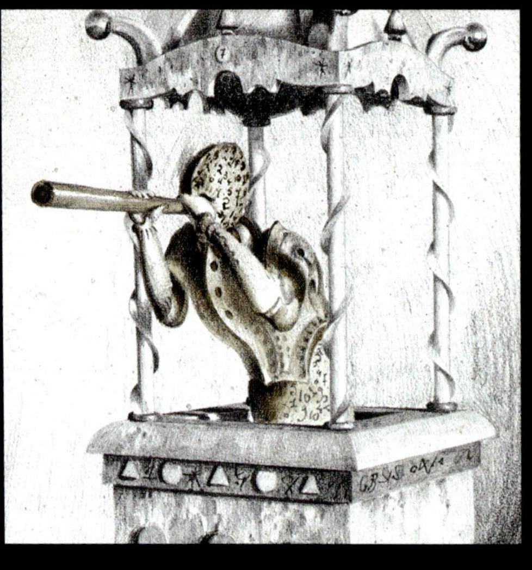

IT'S A MATTER ➤
OF TIME

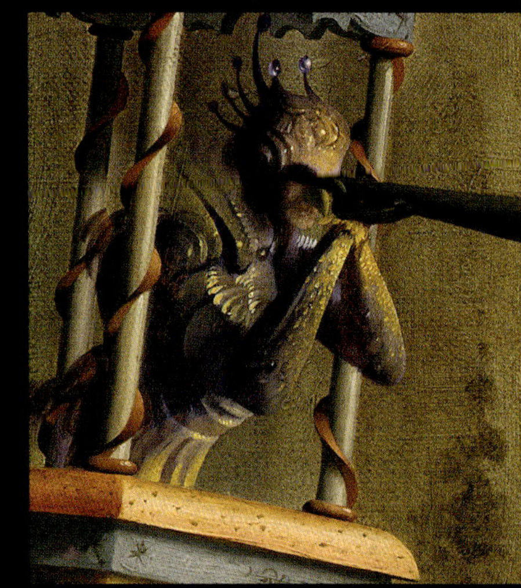

▲
THE FUTURE - study

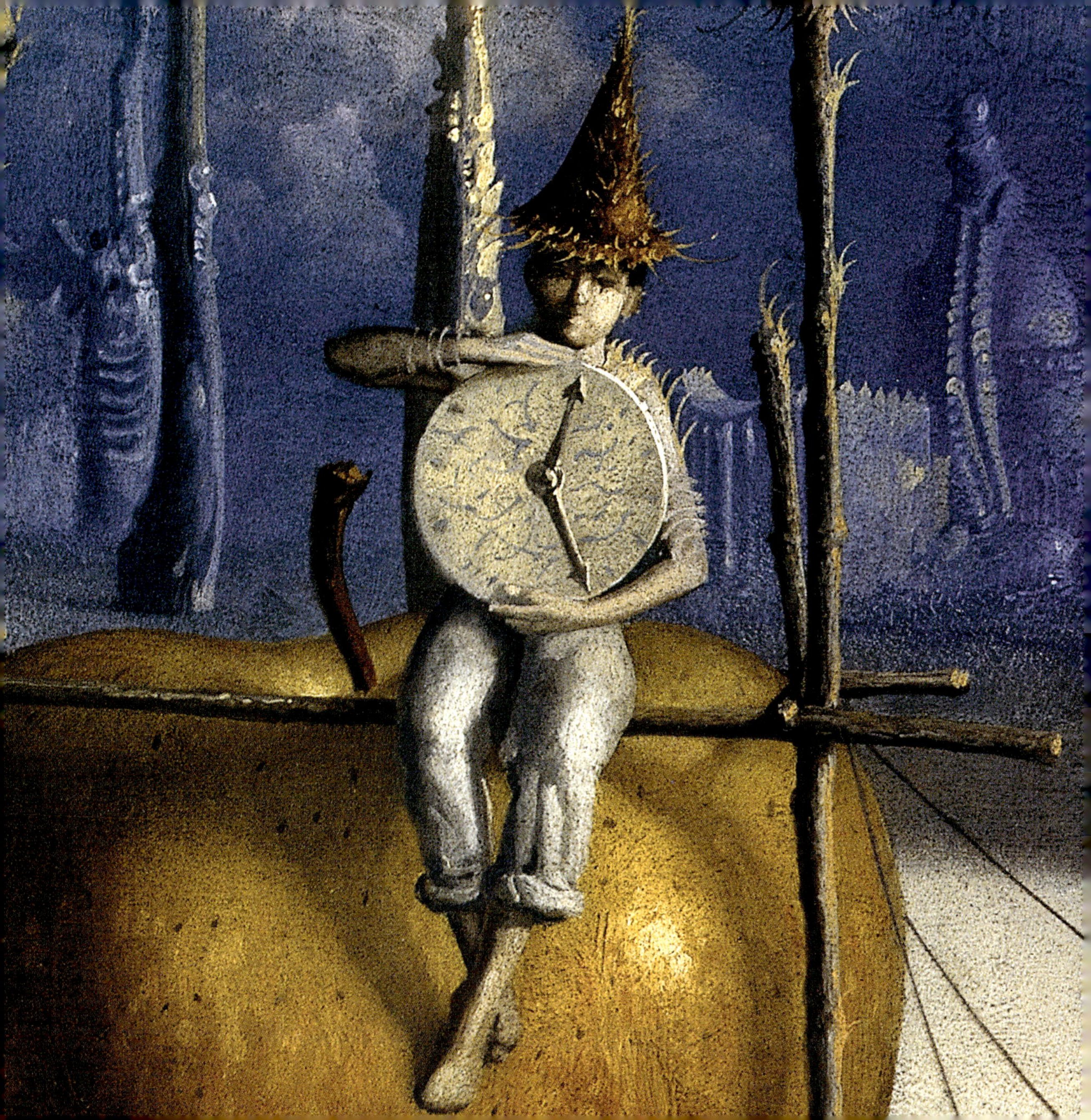

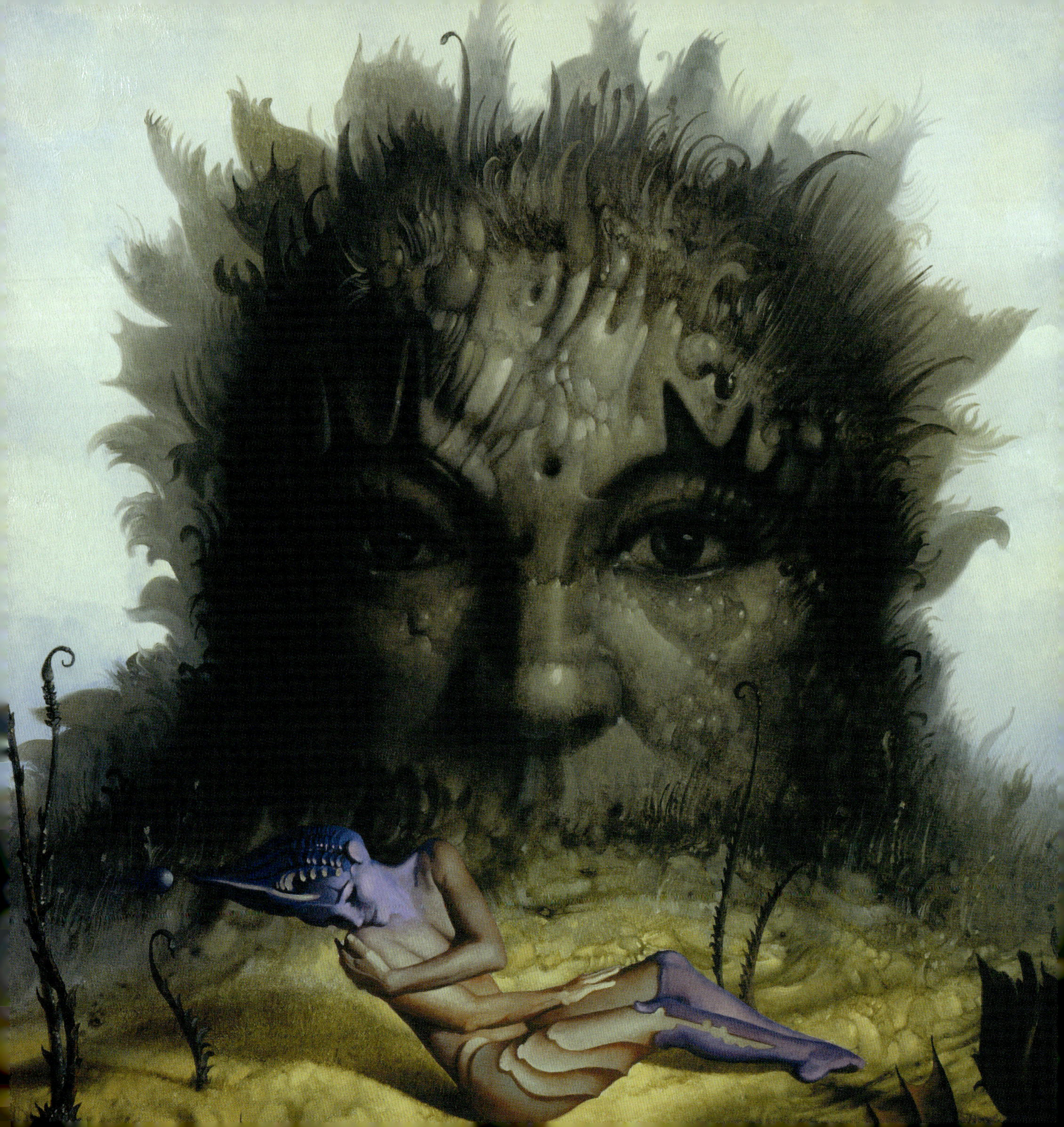

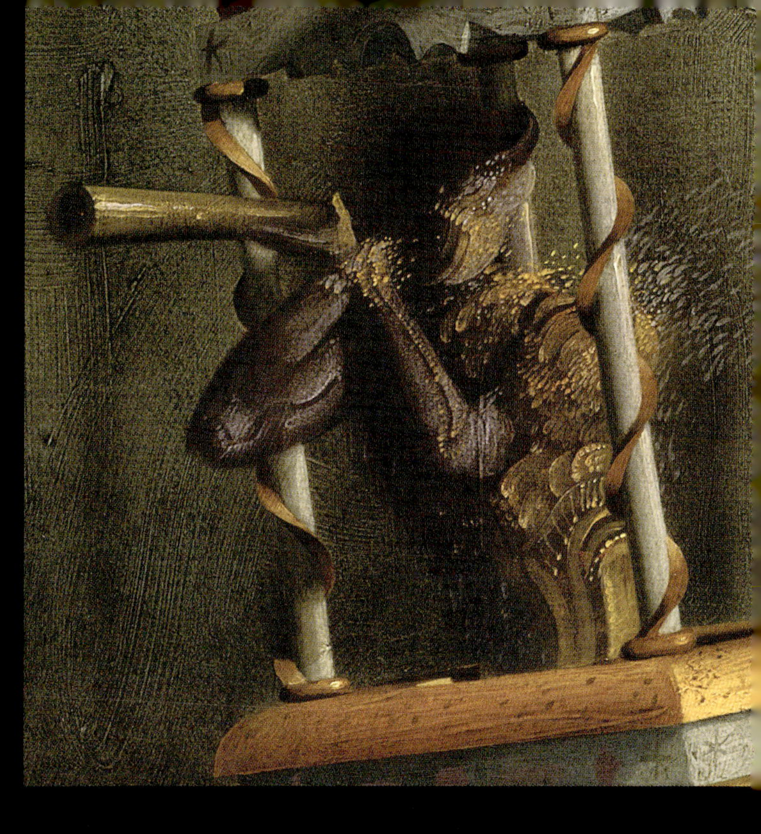

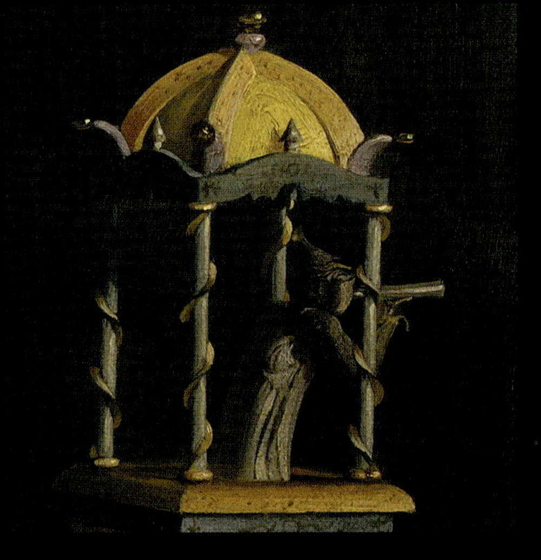

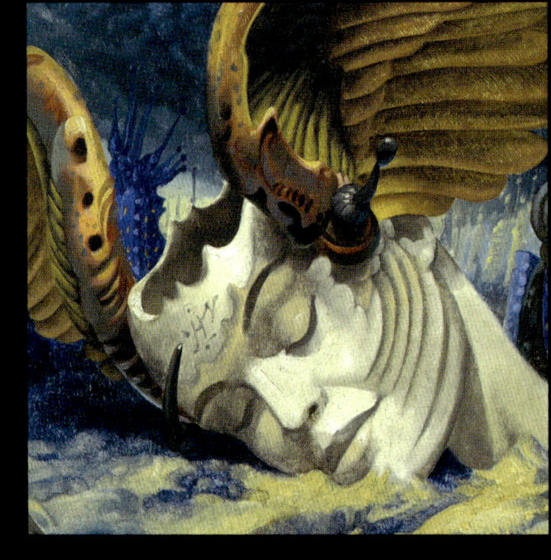

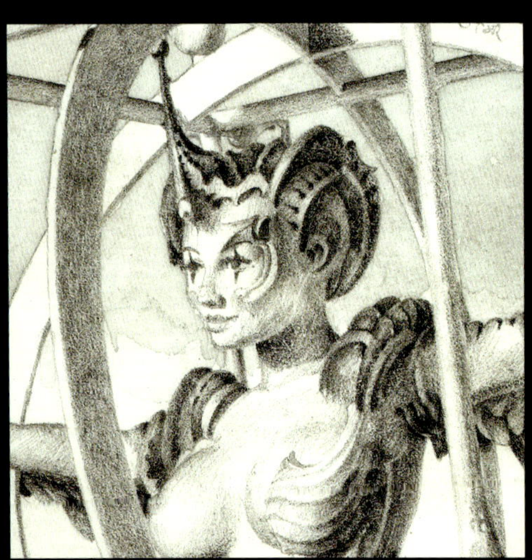

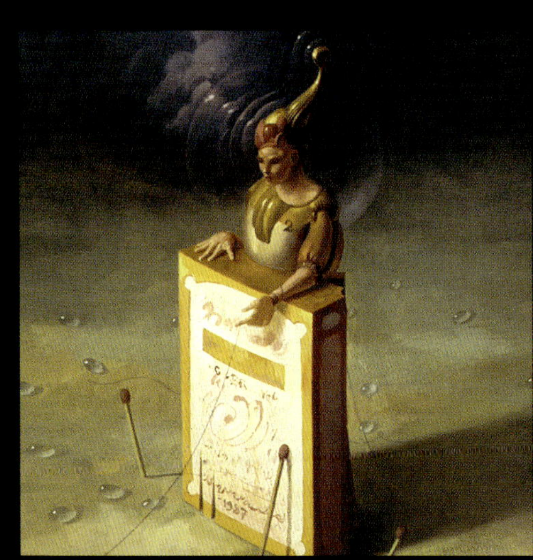

THE SEARCH - study

THE DRUNKEN MAN

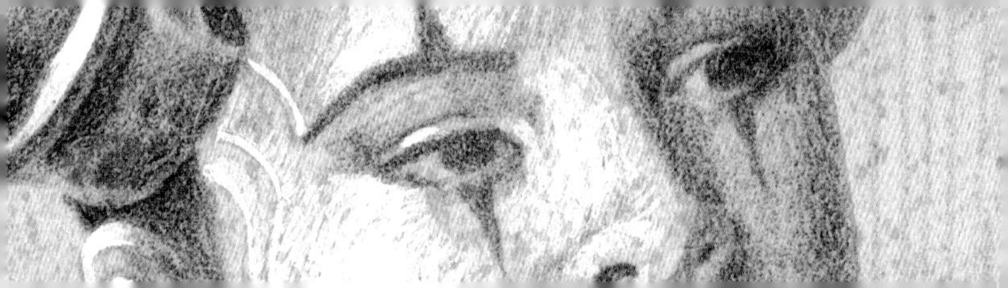

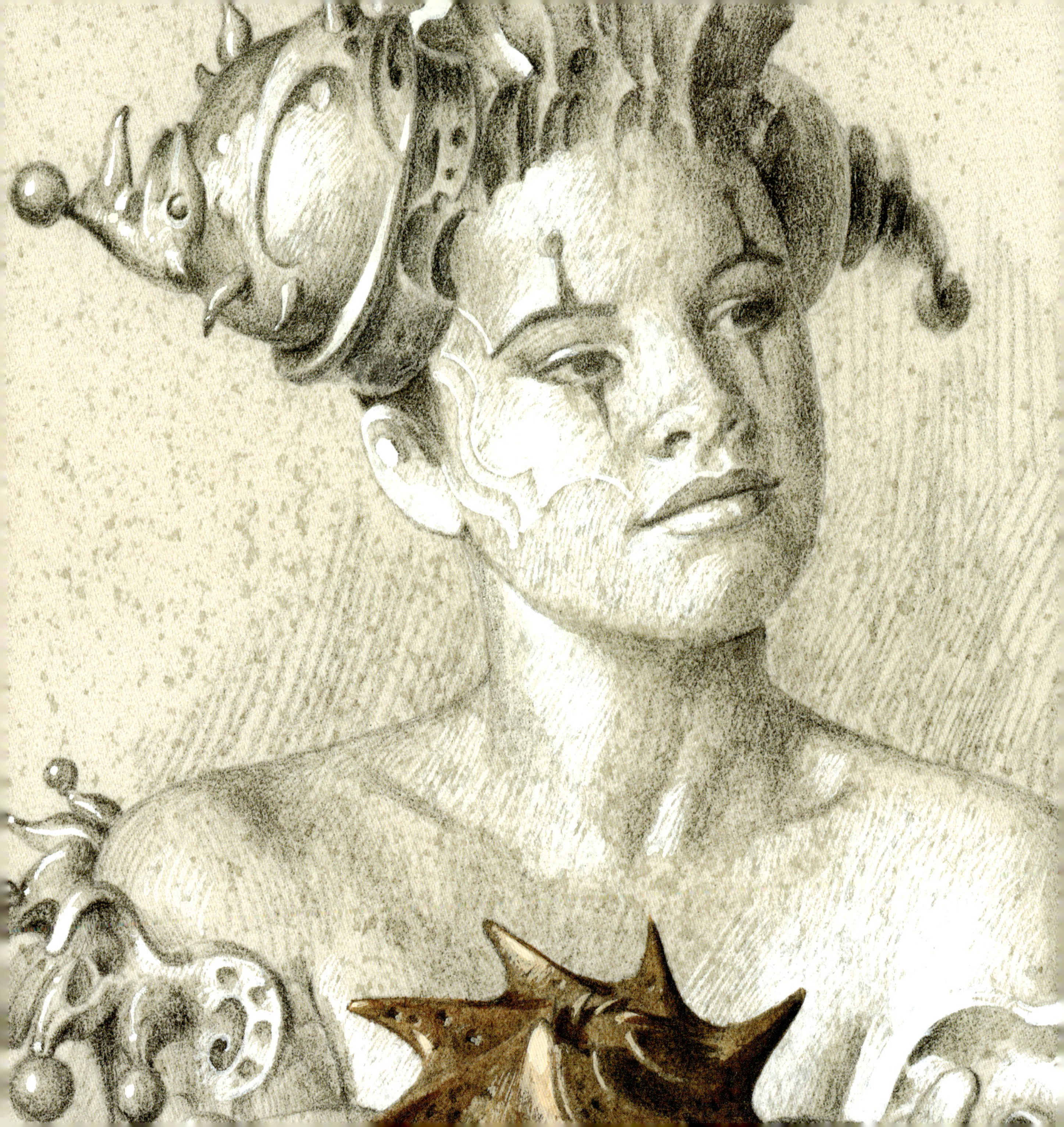

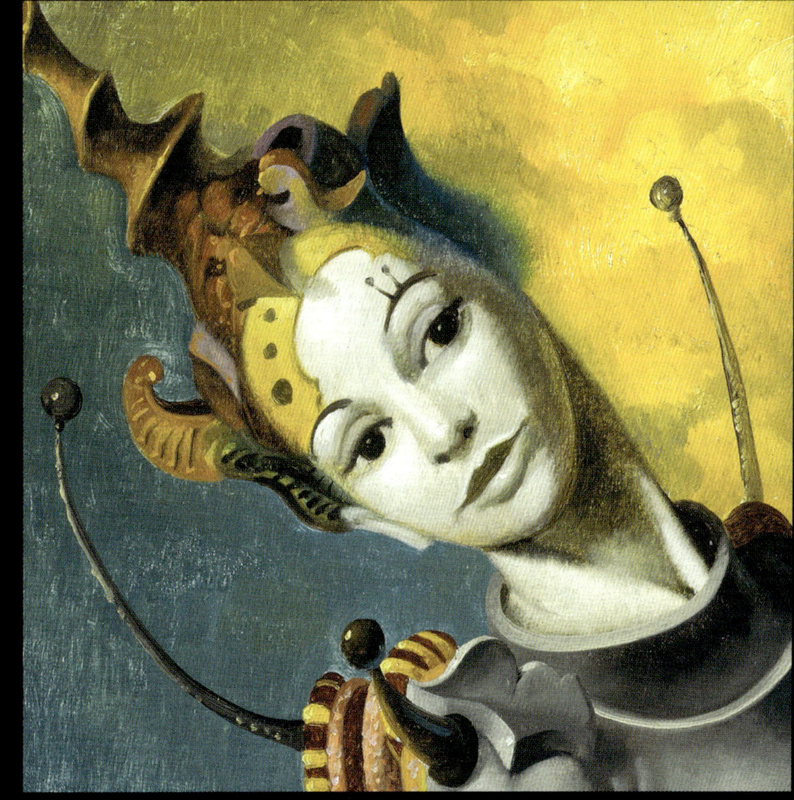

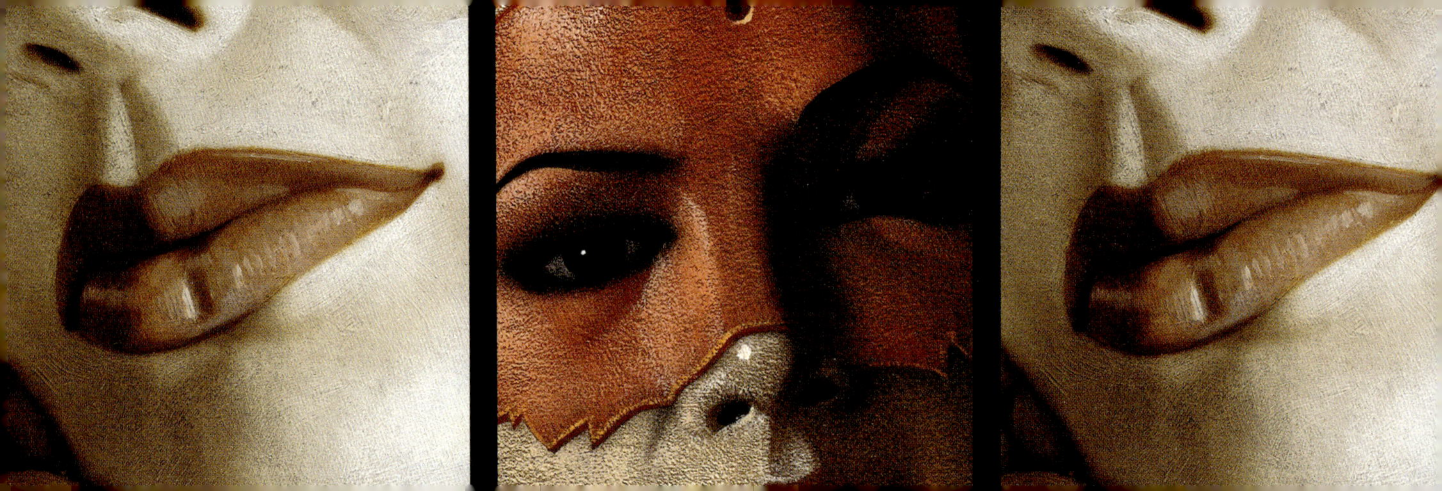

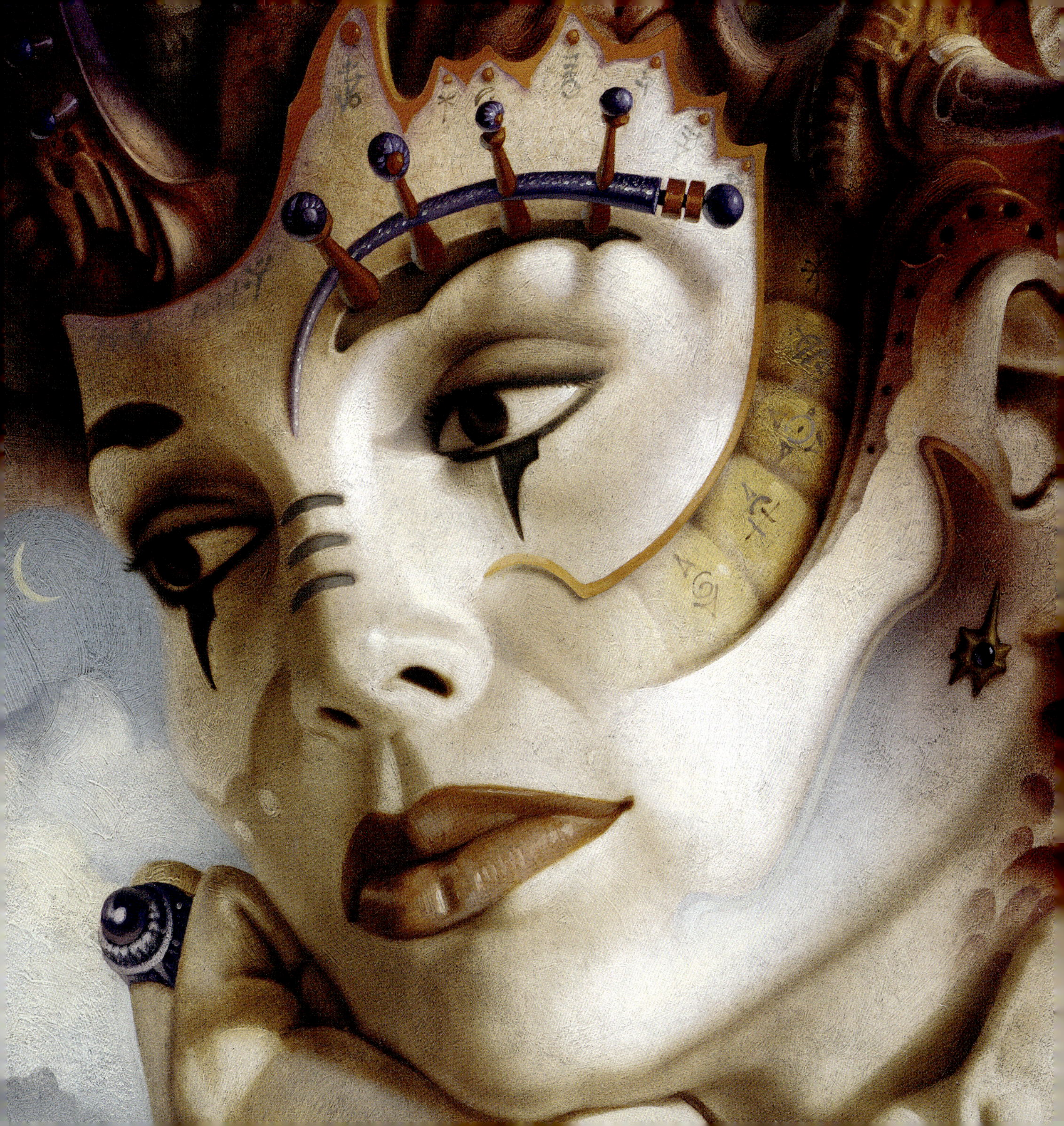

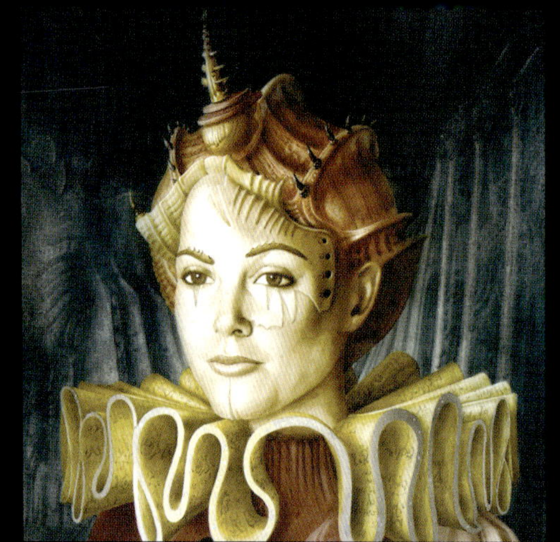

THE RETURN ➤

THE WIND ➤

THE GIFT ➤

▲
THE MAGICIAN

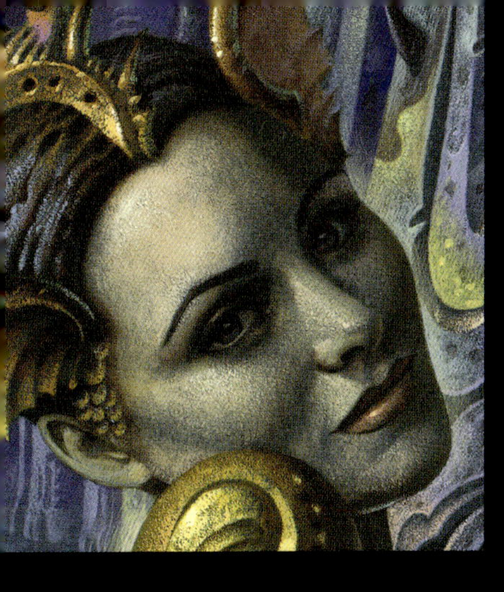
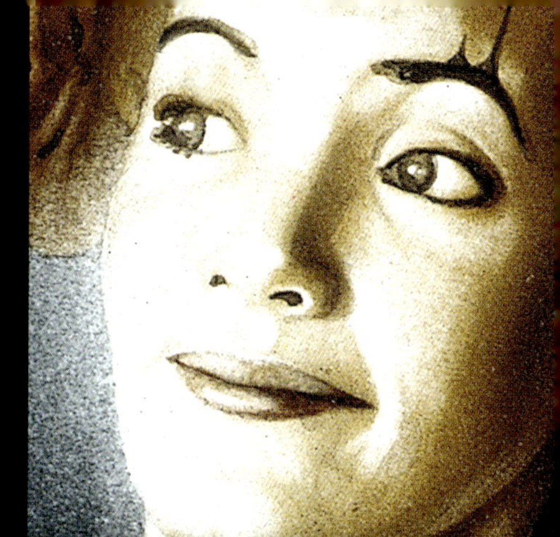
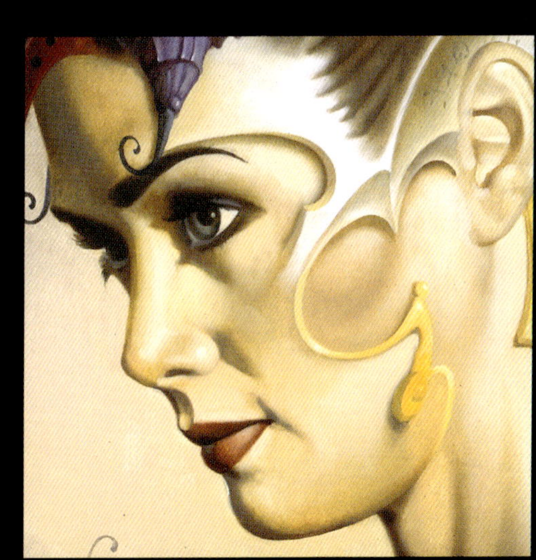
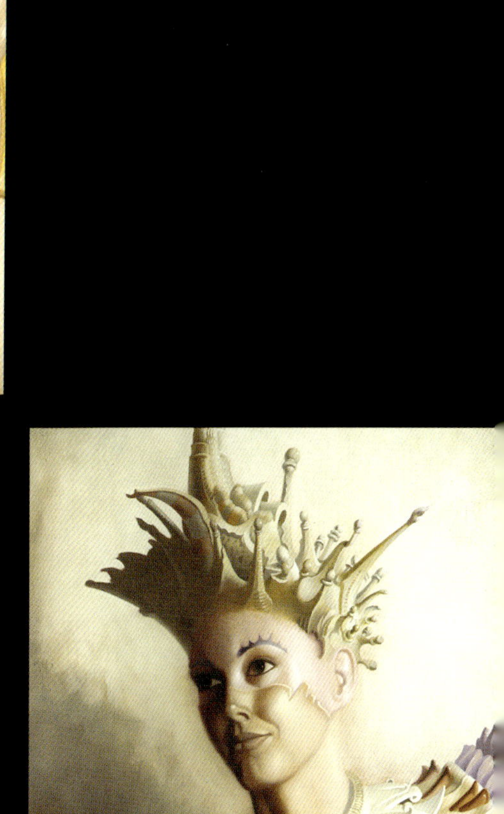
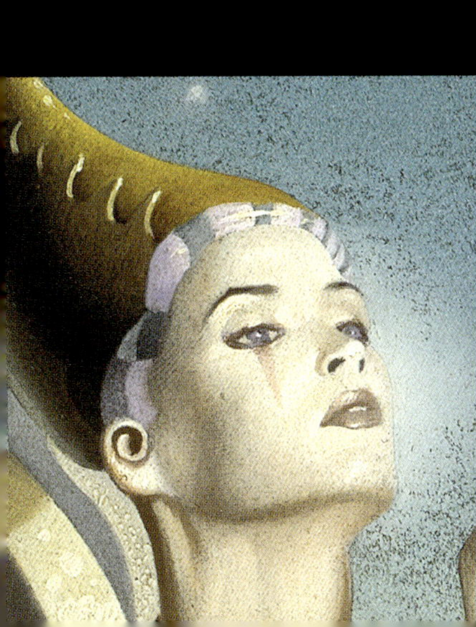

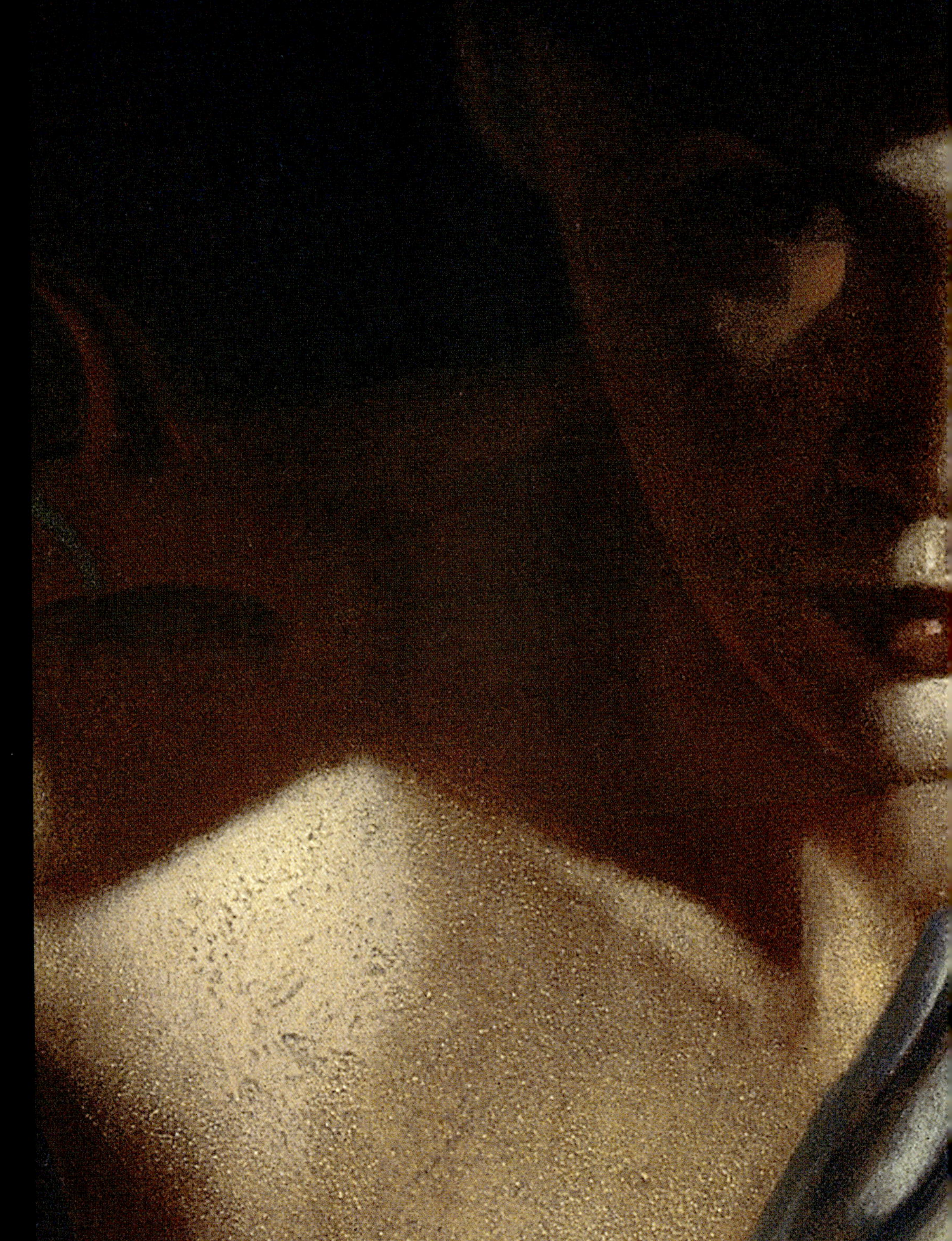

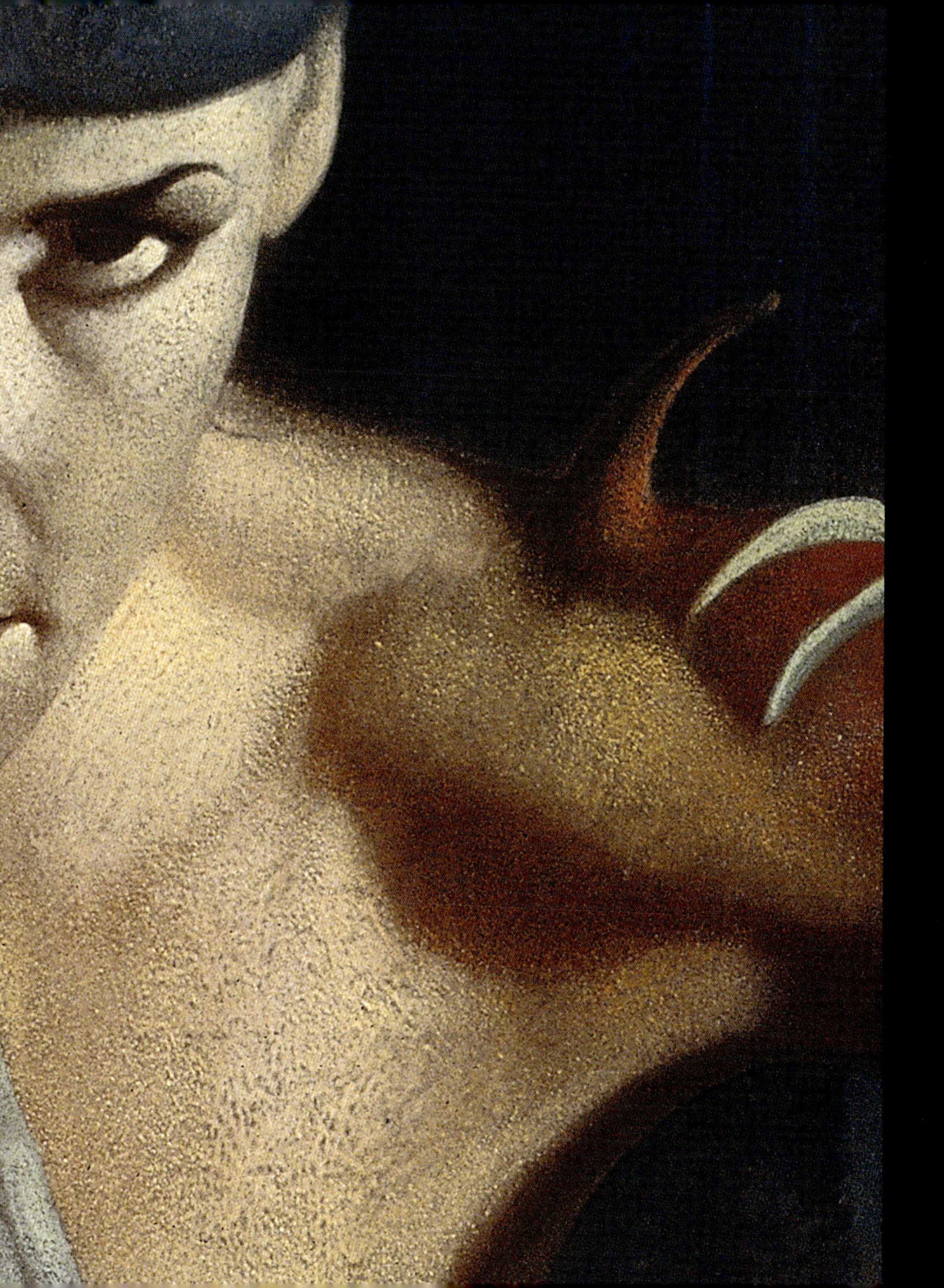

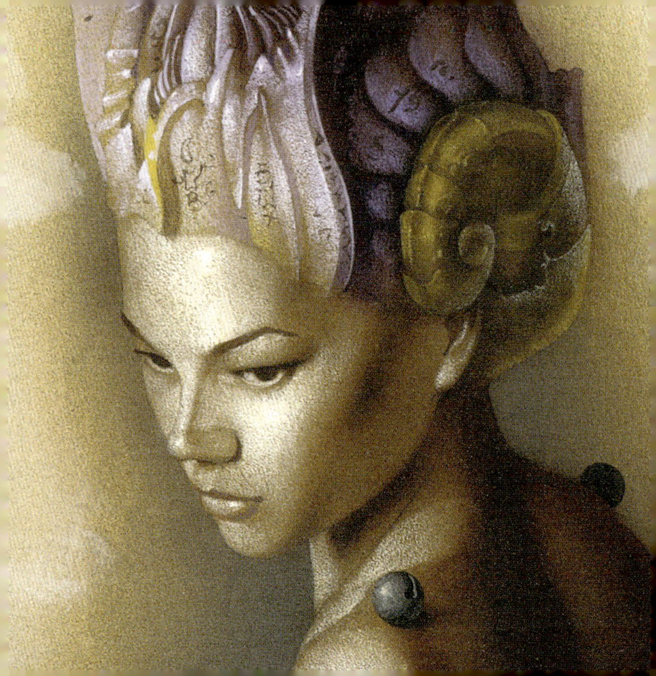

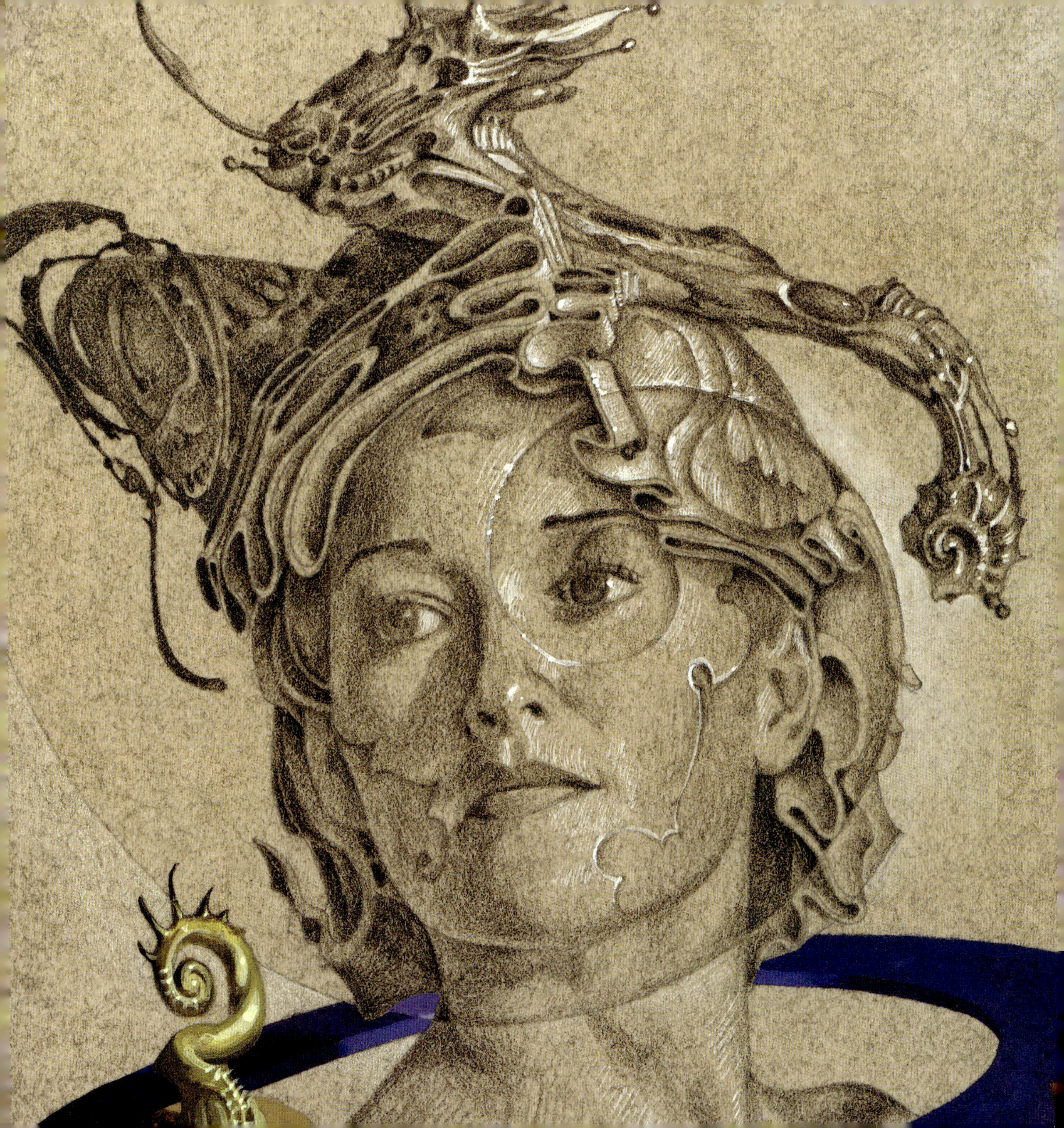

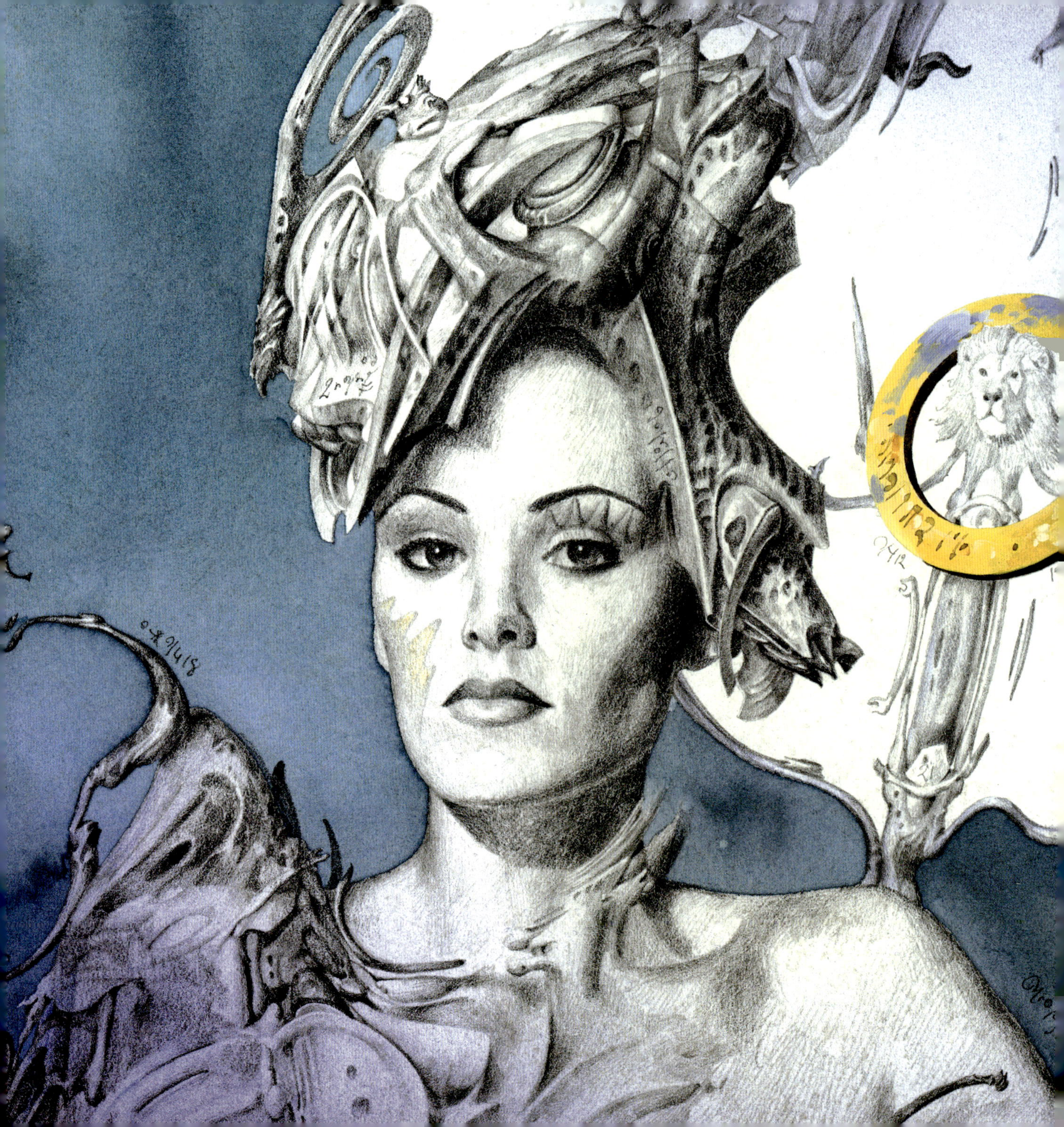

MORNING FROLIC - study

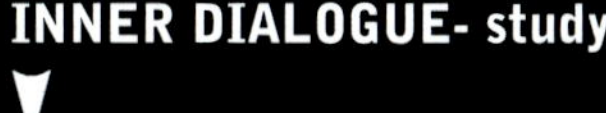

INNER DIALOGUE- study

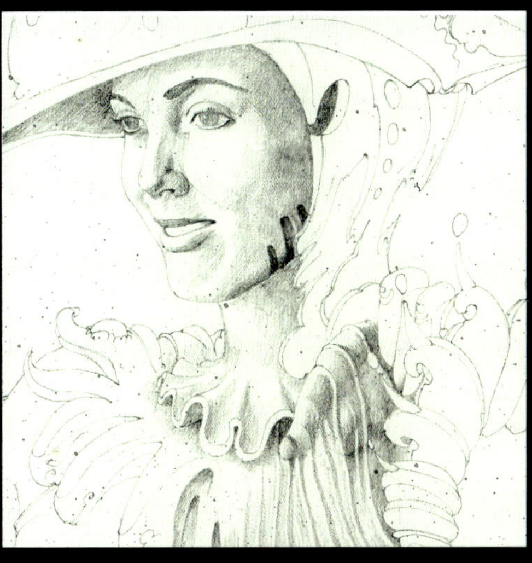

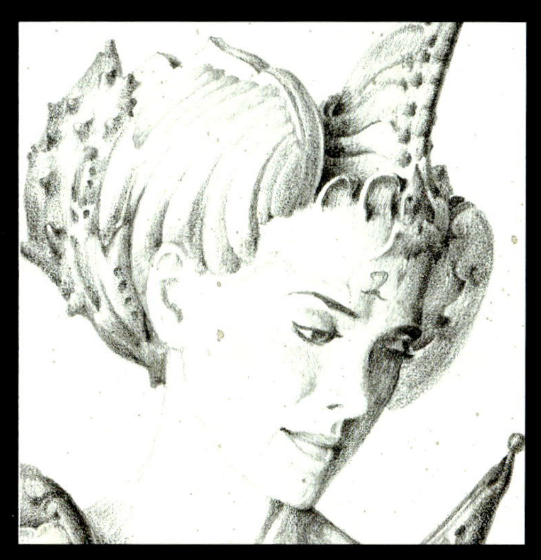

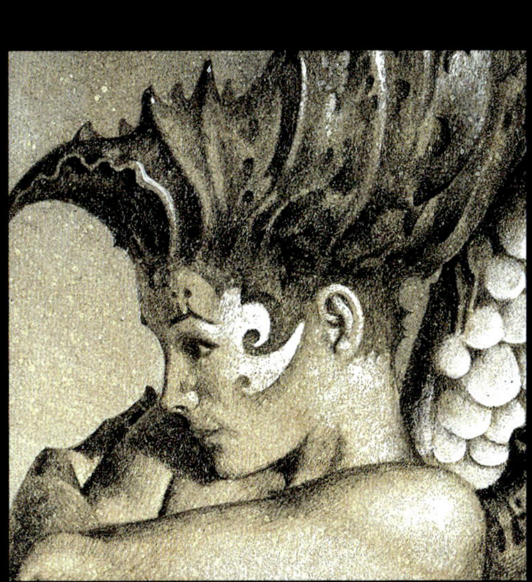

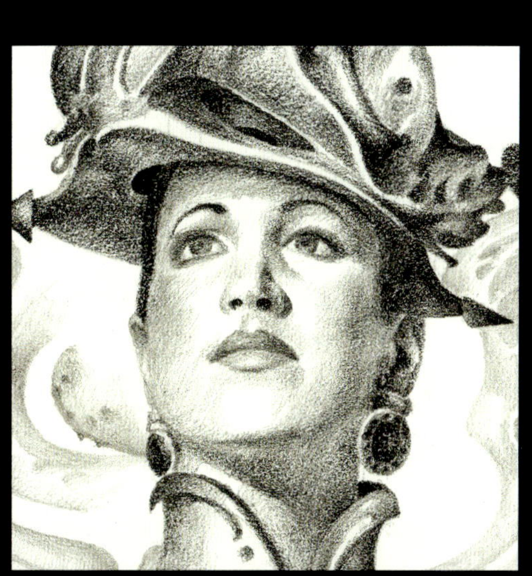

◄ FORTITUDE - study

EARTH ANGEL - study

ARIANNE - study

HOPE ➤

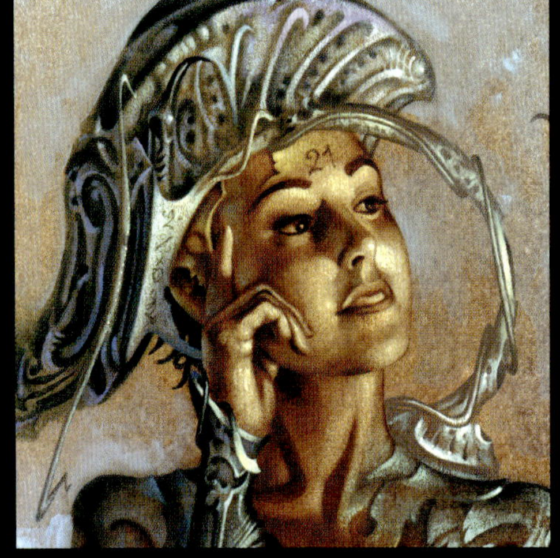

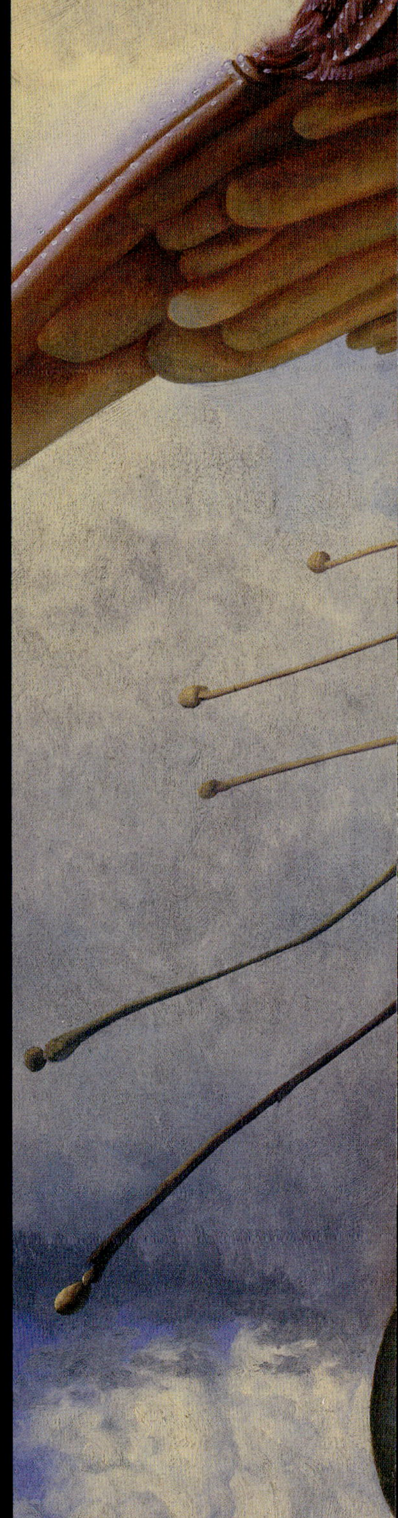

▲
FREEDOM - study

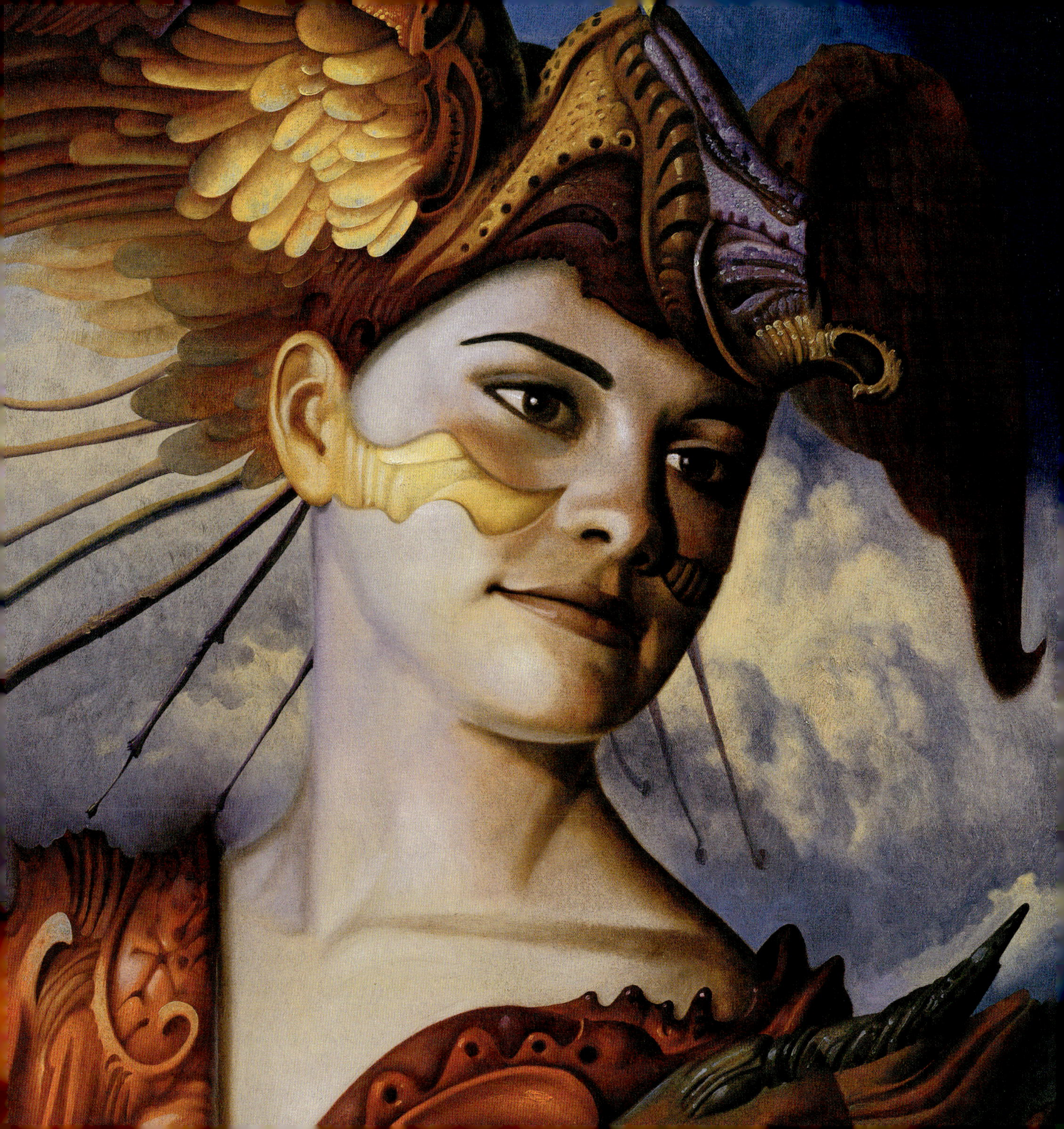

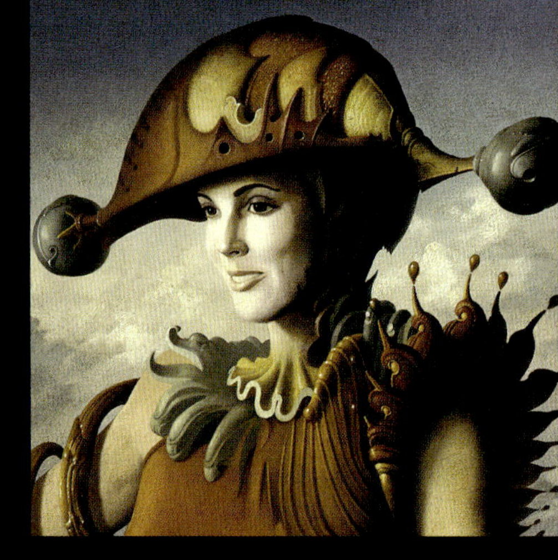

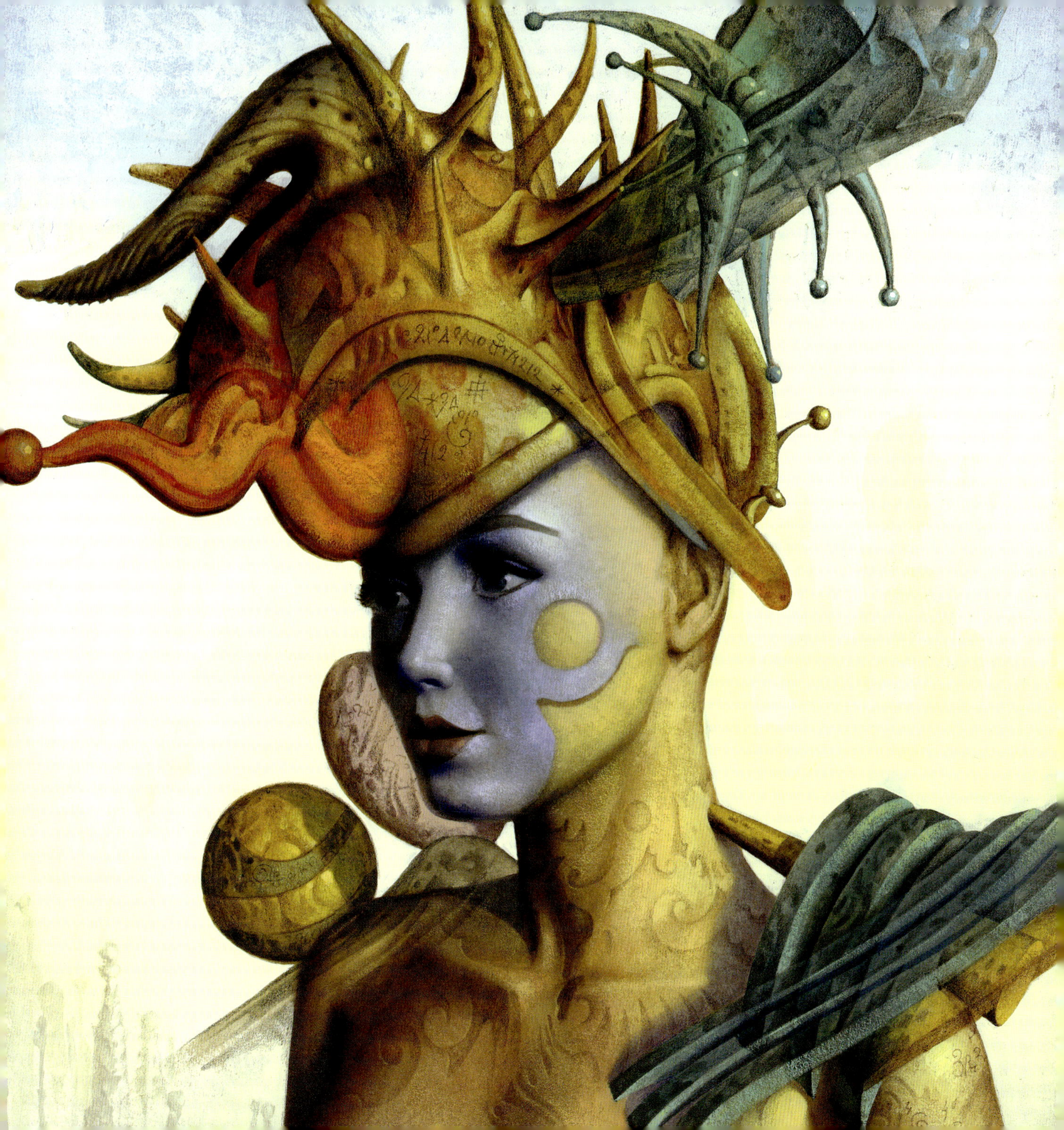

◄ THE GIFT - study

MUSE ►

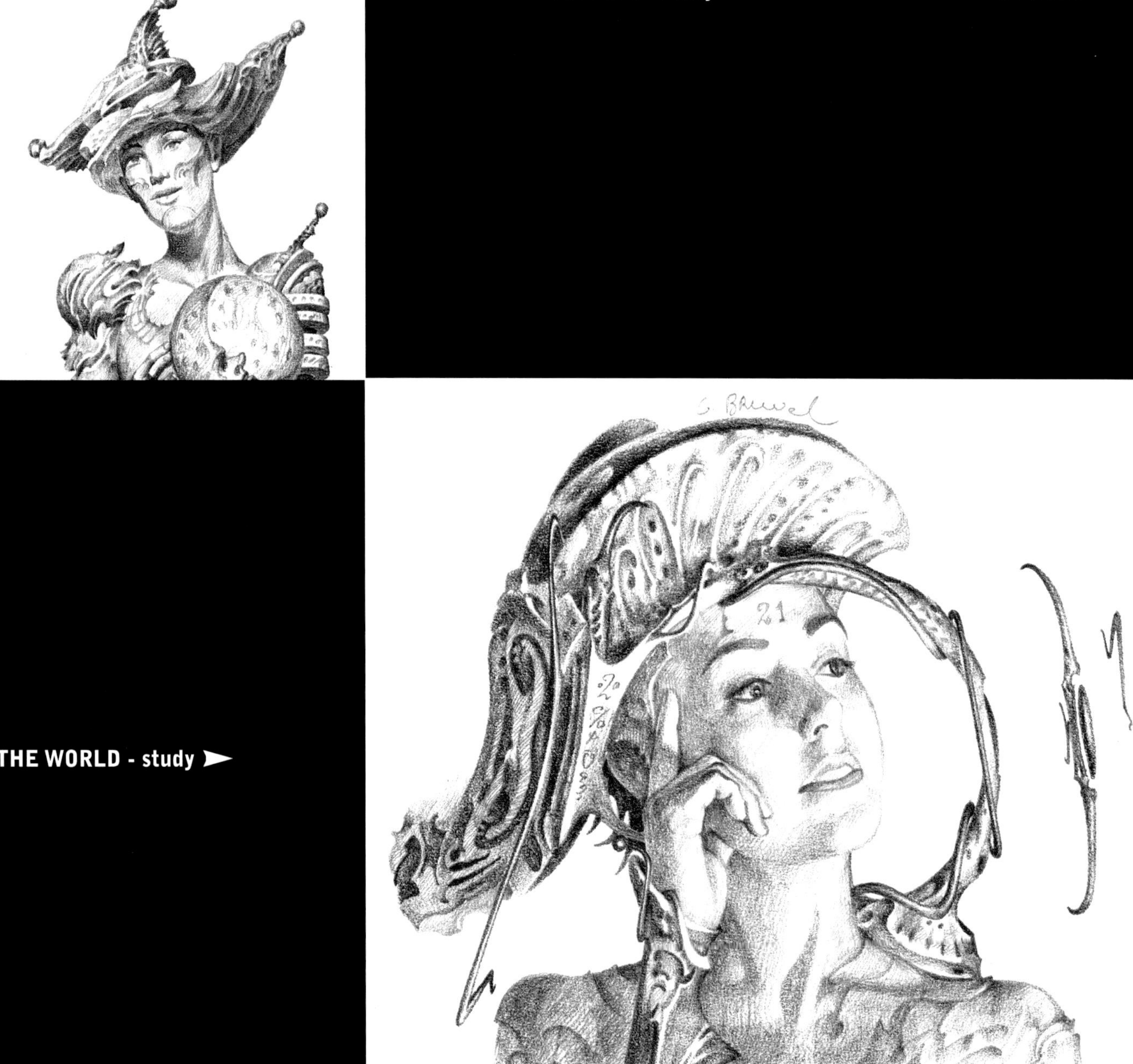

THE WORLD - study ►

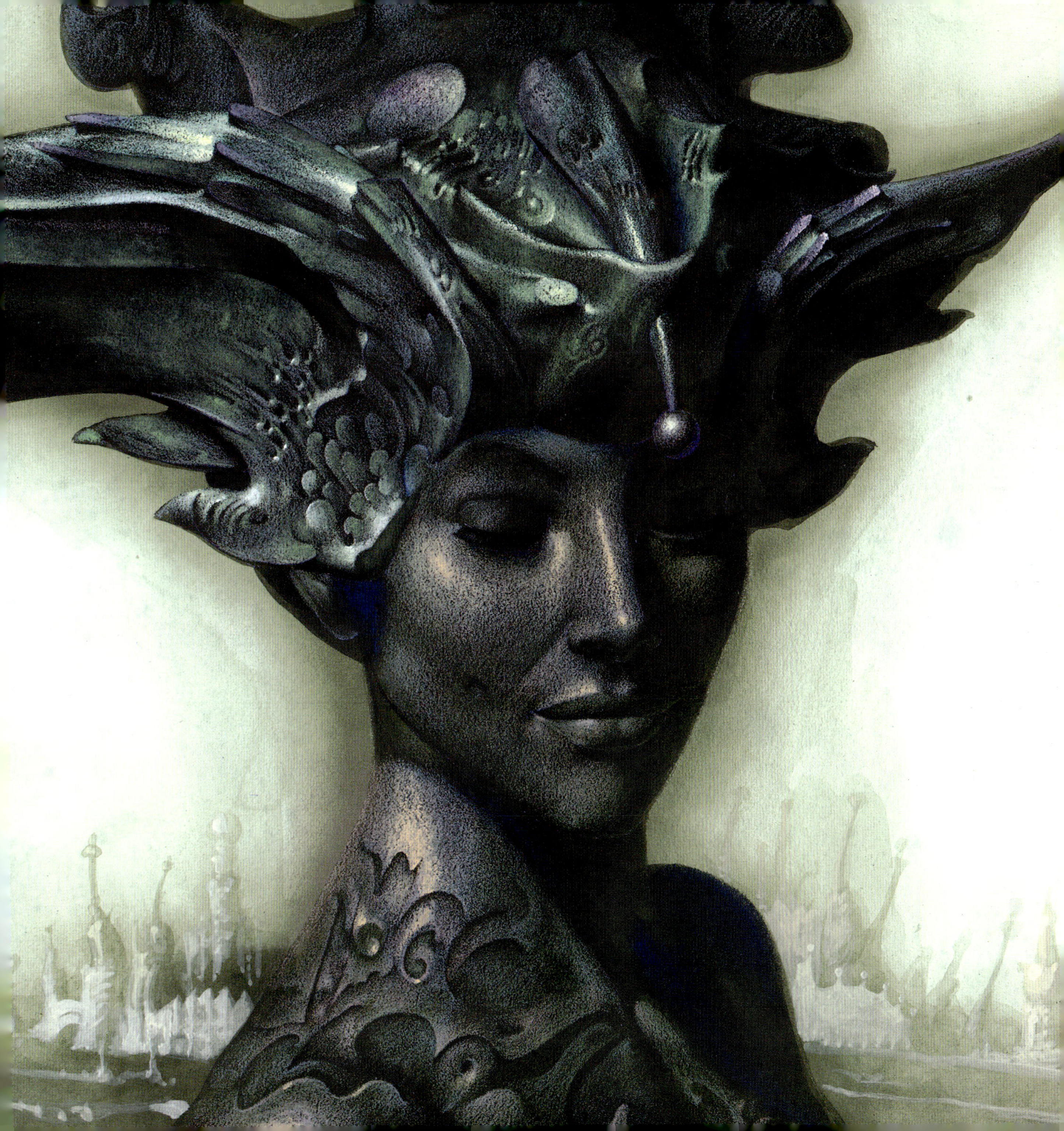

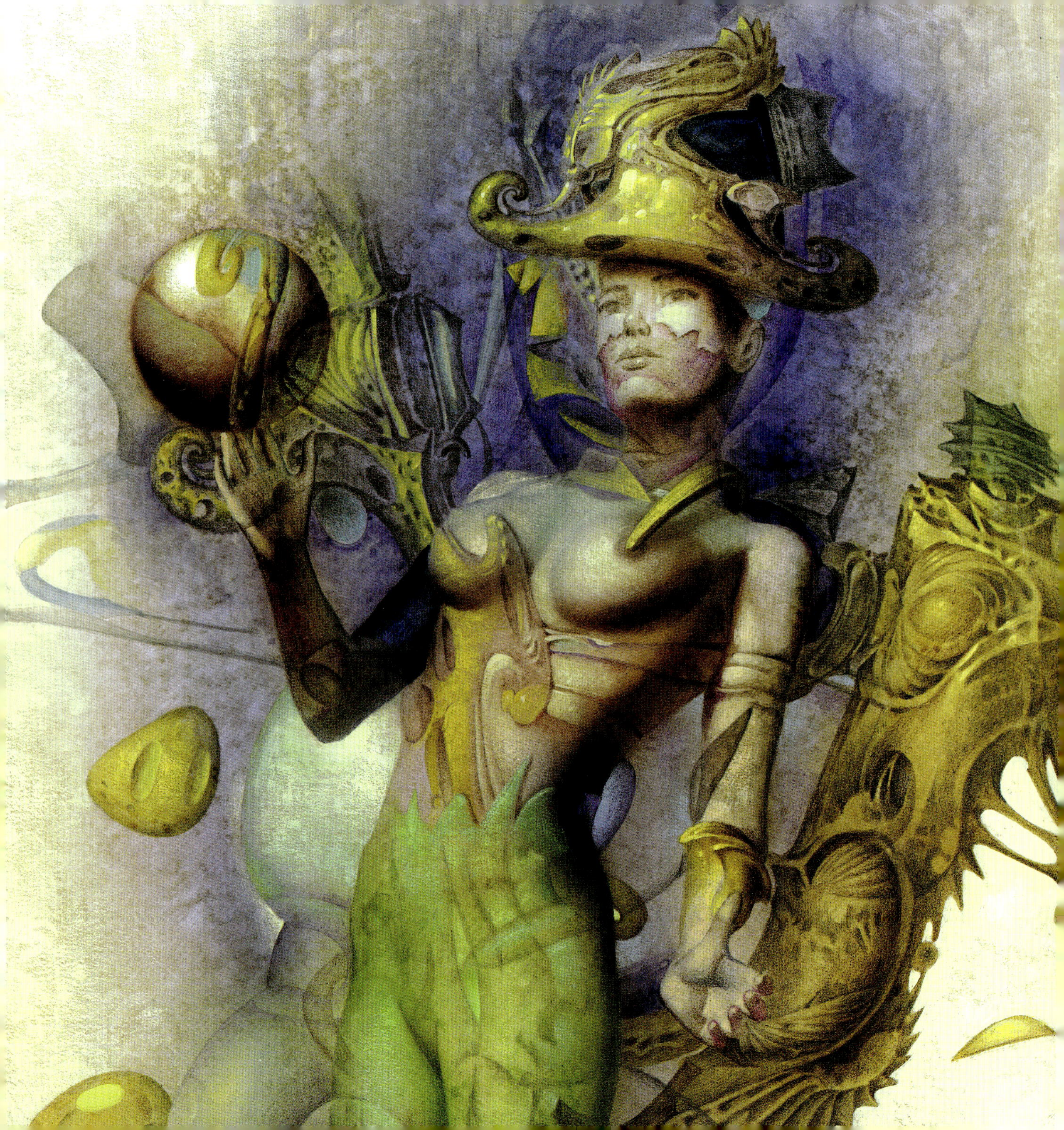

EMPERANCE - study

THE QUEST - study ➤

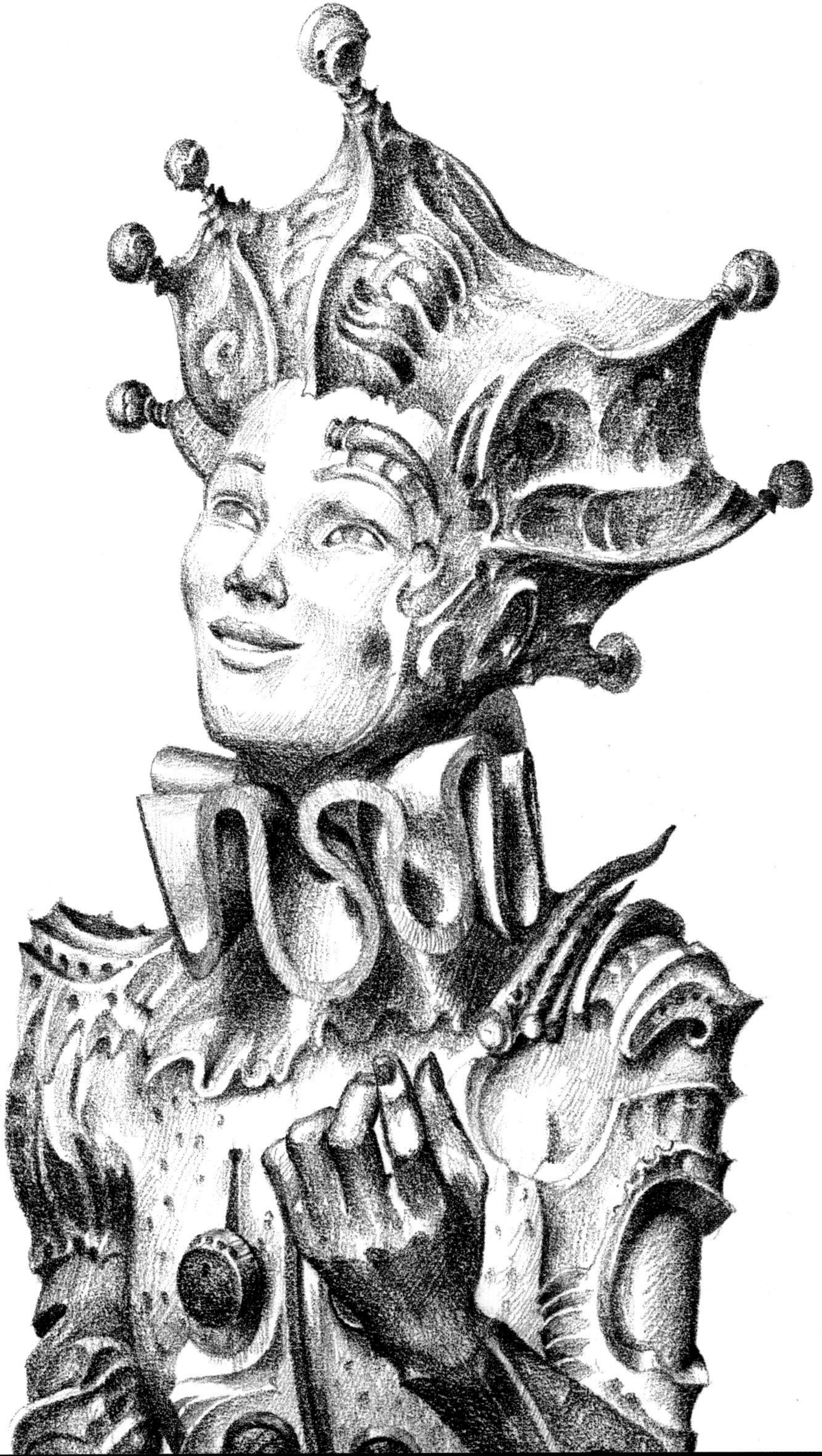

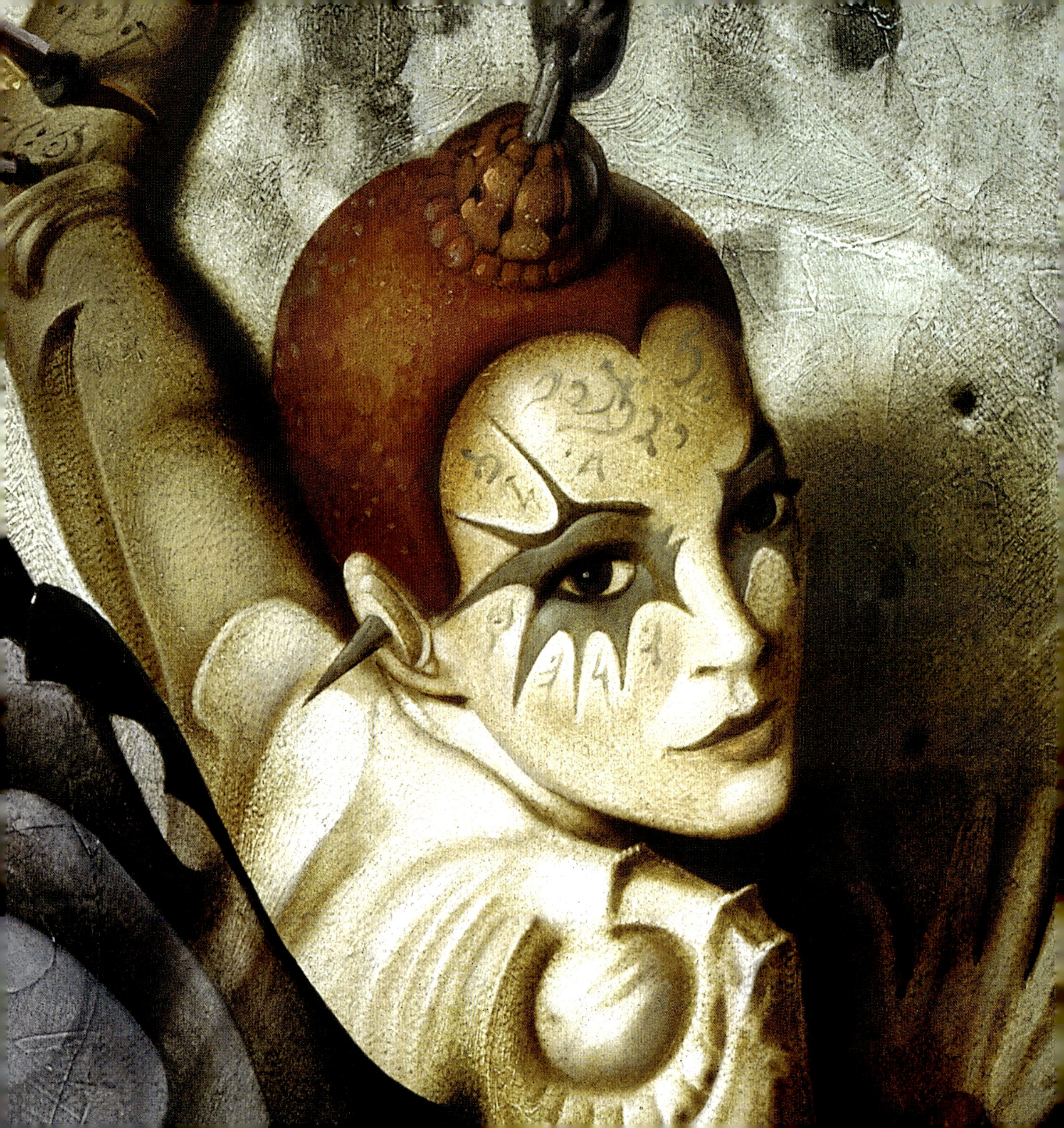

PERFUME OF GEOMETRY

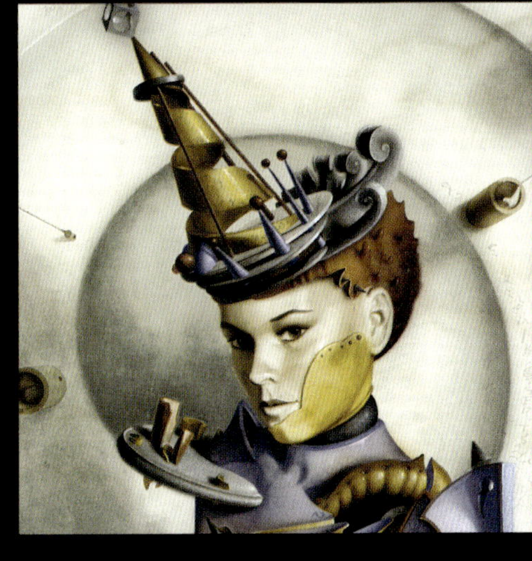

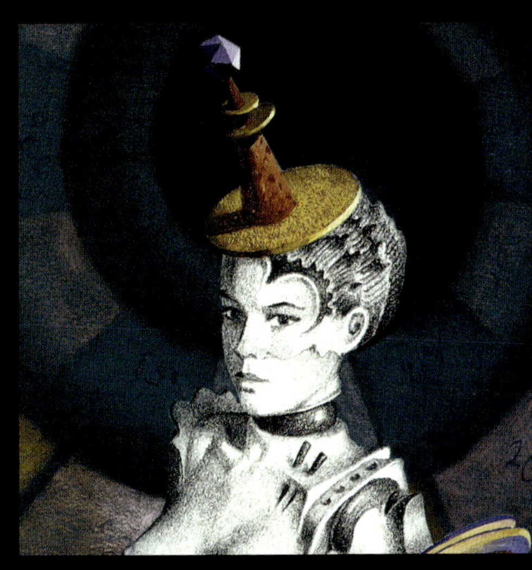

OTHER SIDE

PERFUME OF GEOMETRY - study

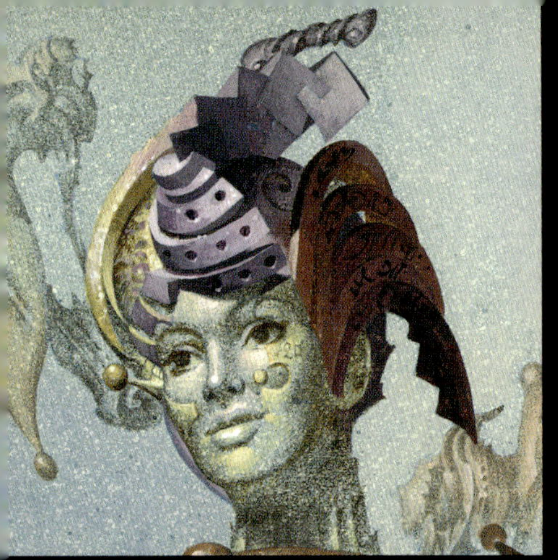

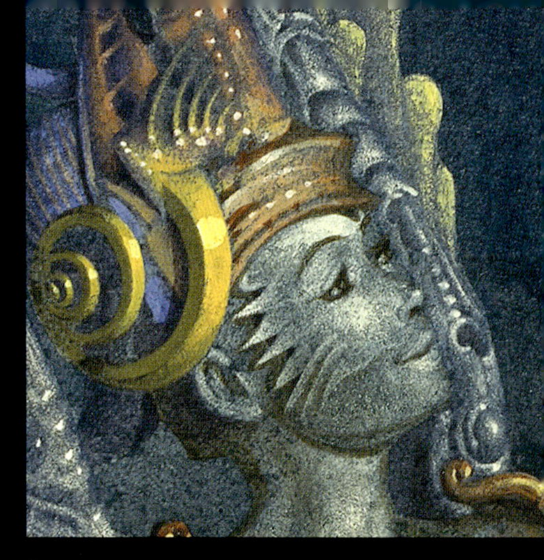

JUST A WALK

THE WORLD - study

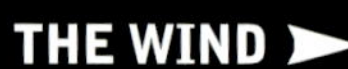

QUEEN

THE DESCENT

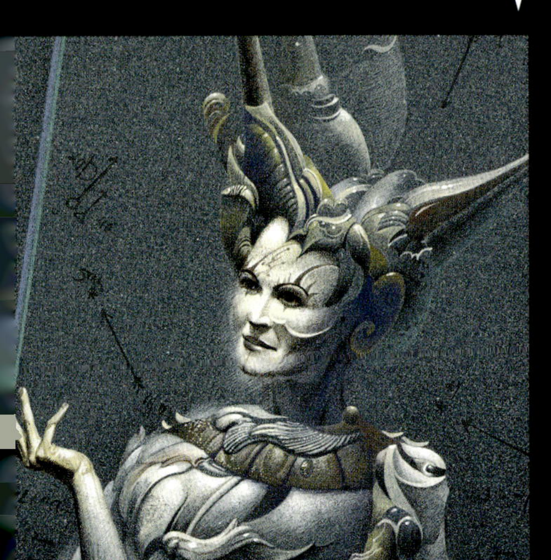

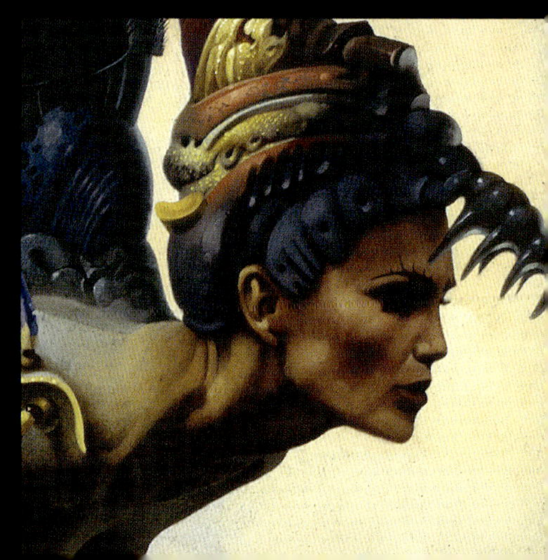

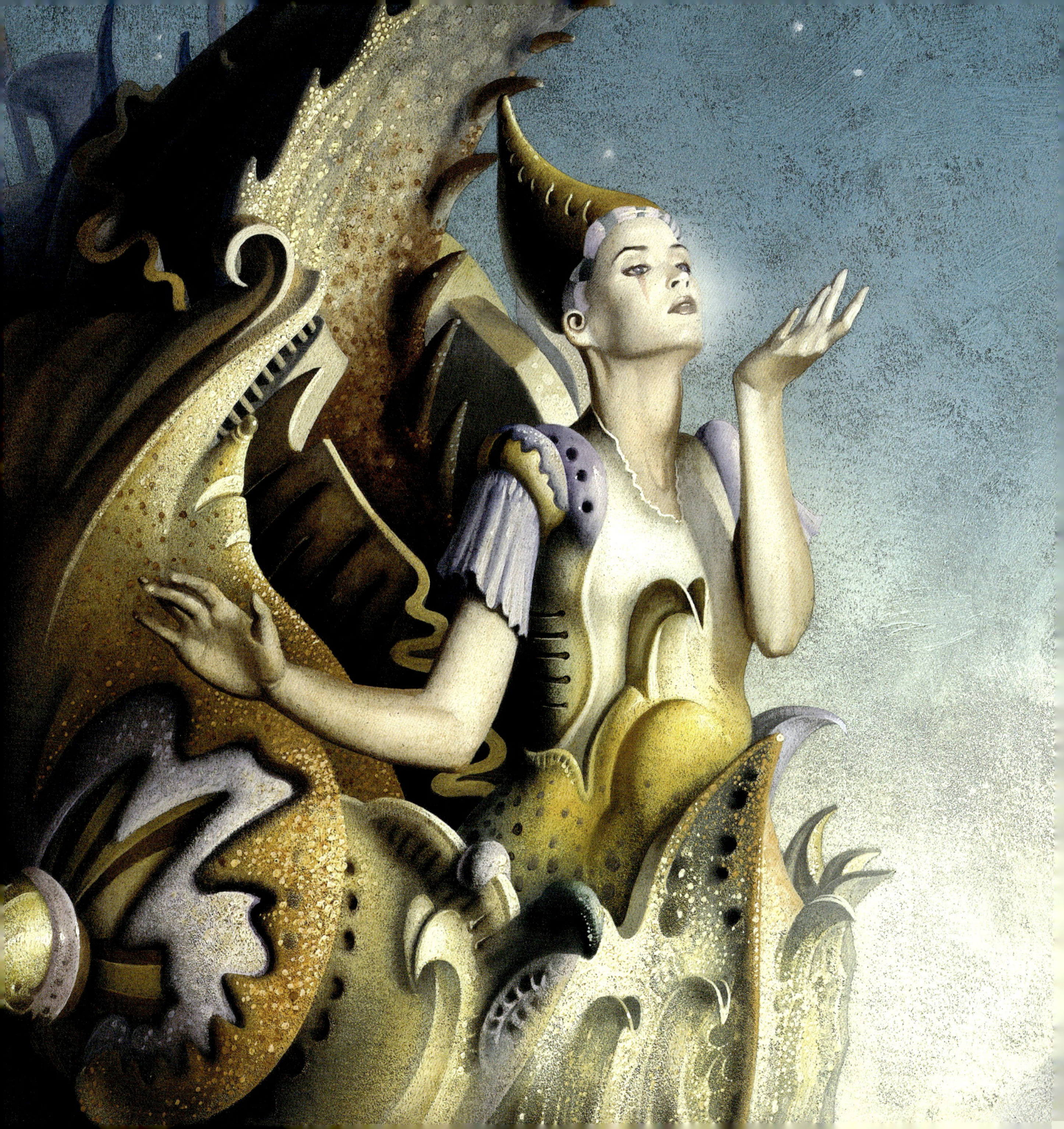

MARIANNE

SENSUOUS MACHINE

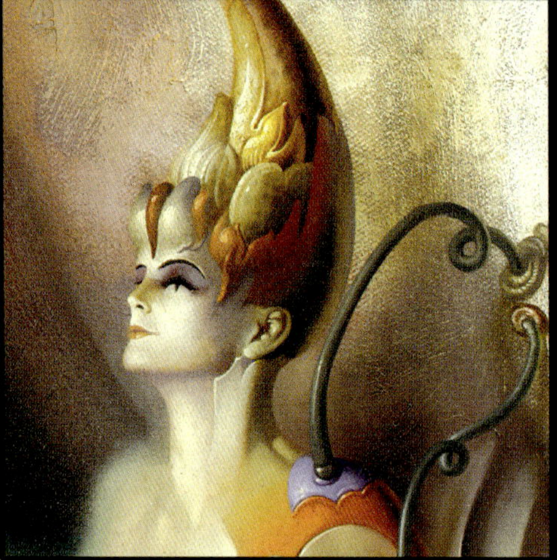

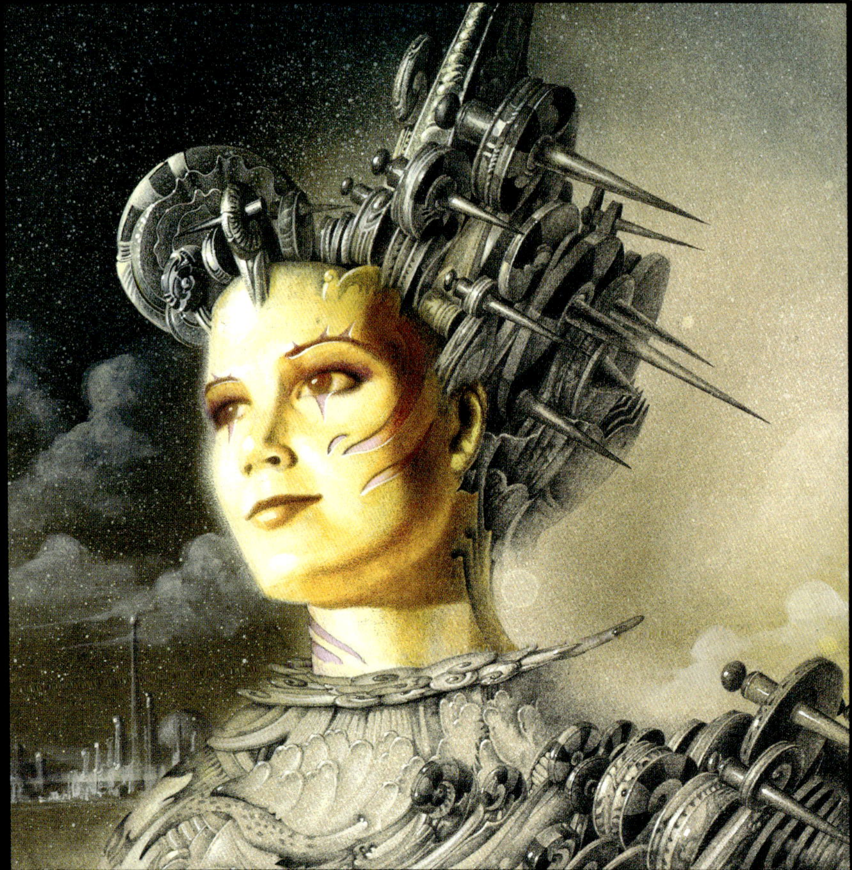

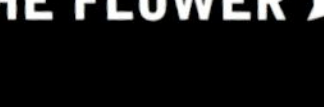

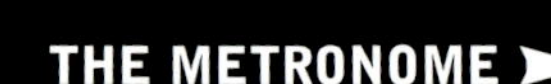

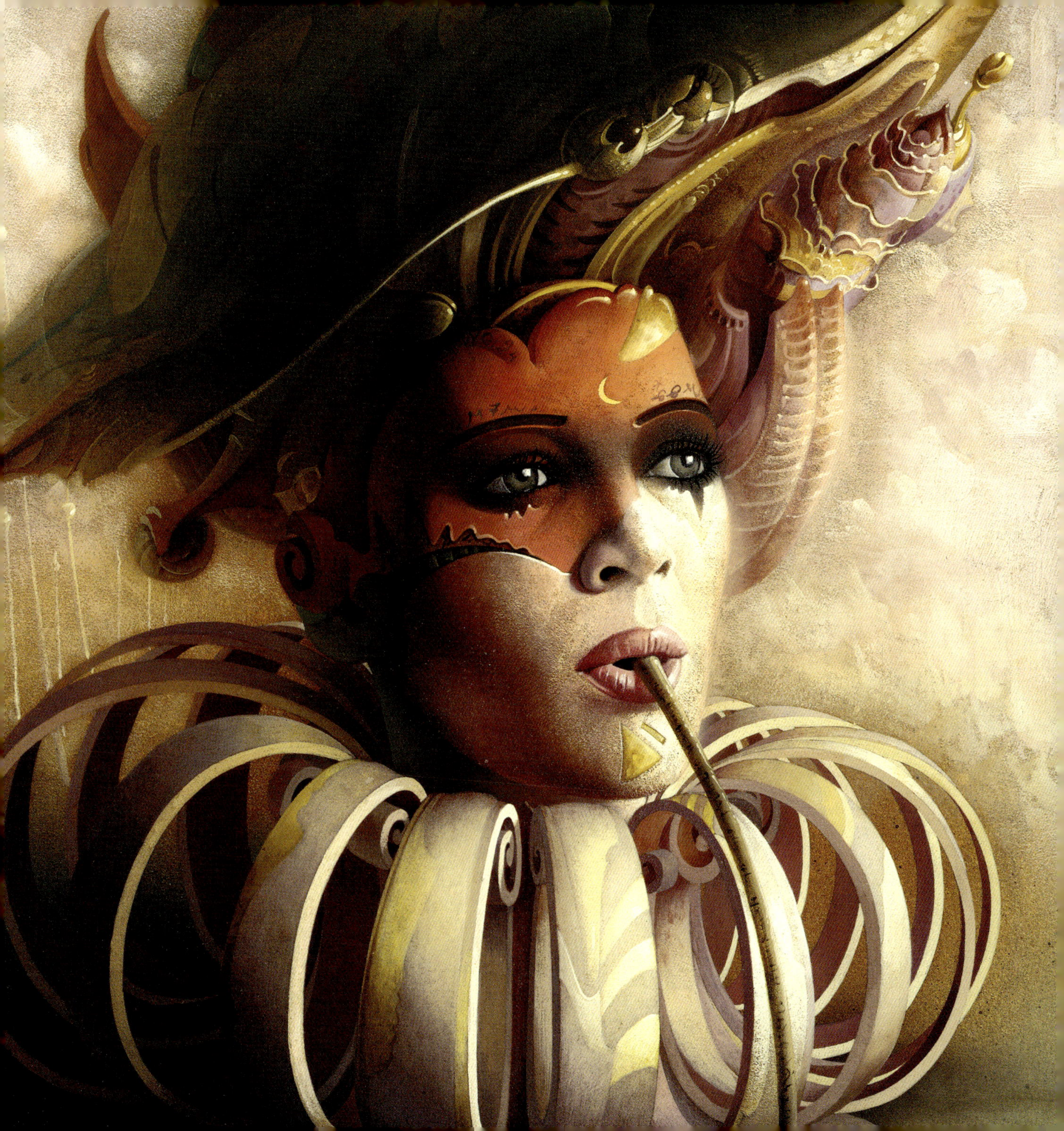

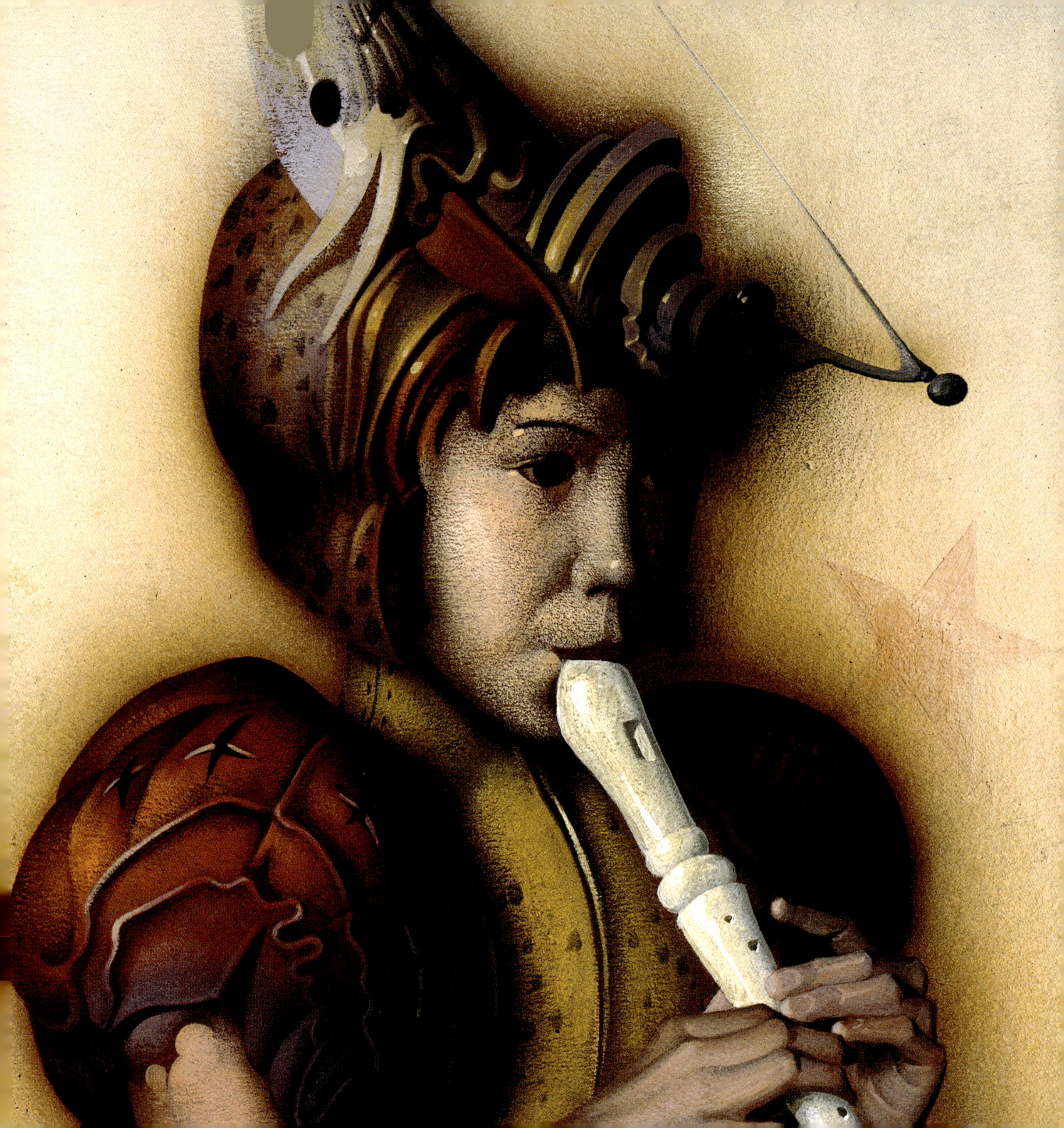

timeless travelers / les voyageurs intemporels

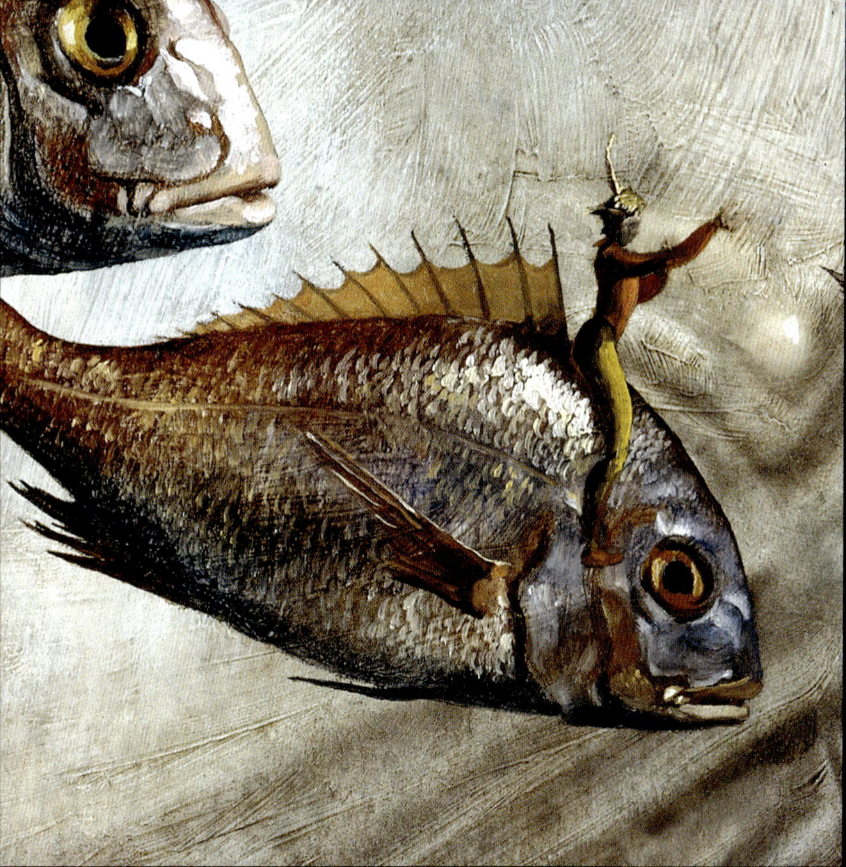

◀ **SILENT CITY**

HOW A FISH CAN MAKE A PORTRAIT ▶

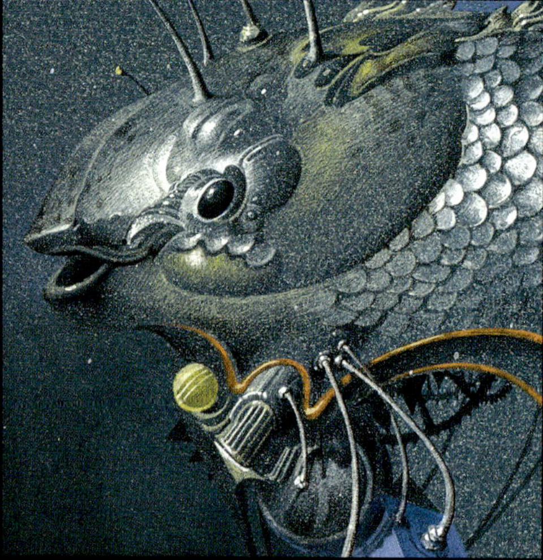

THE SLEEP GOES AWAY ▶

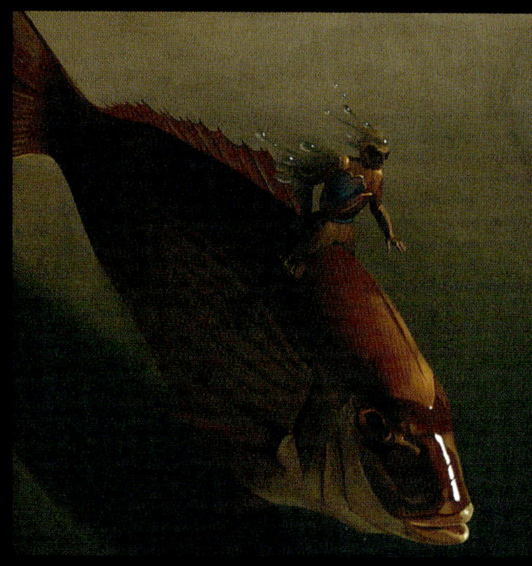

OCEAN MEMORY ▶

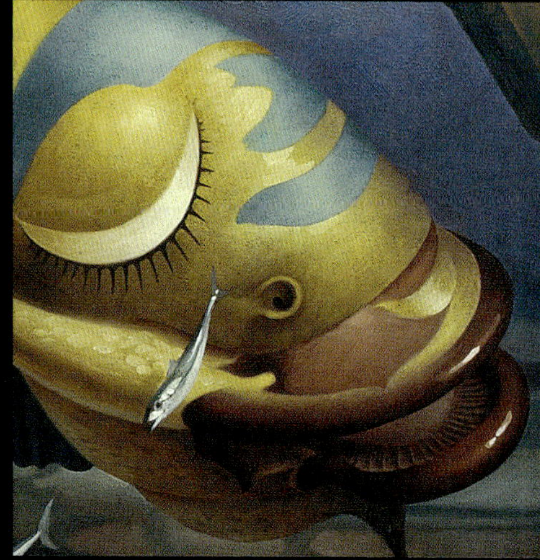

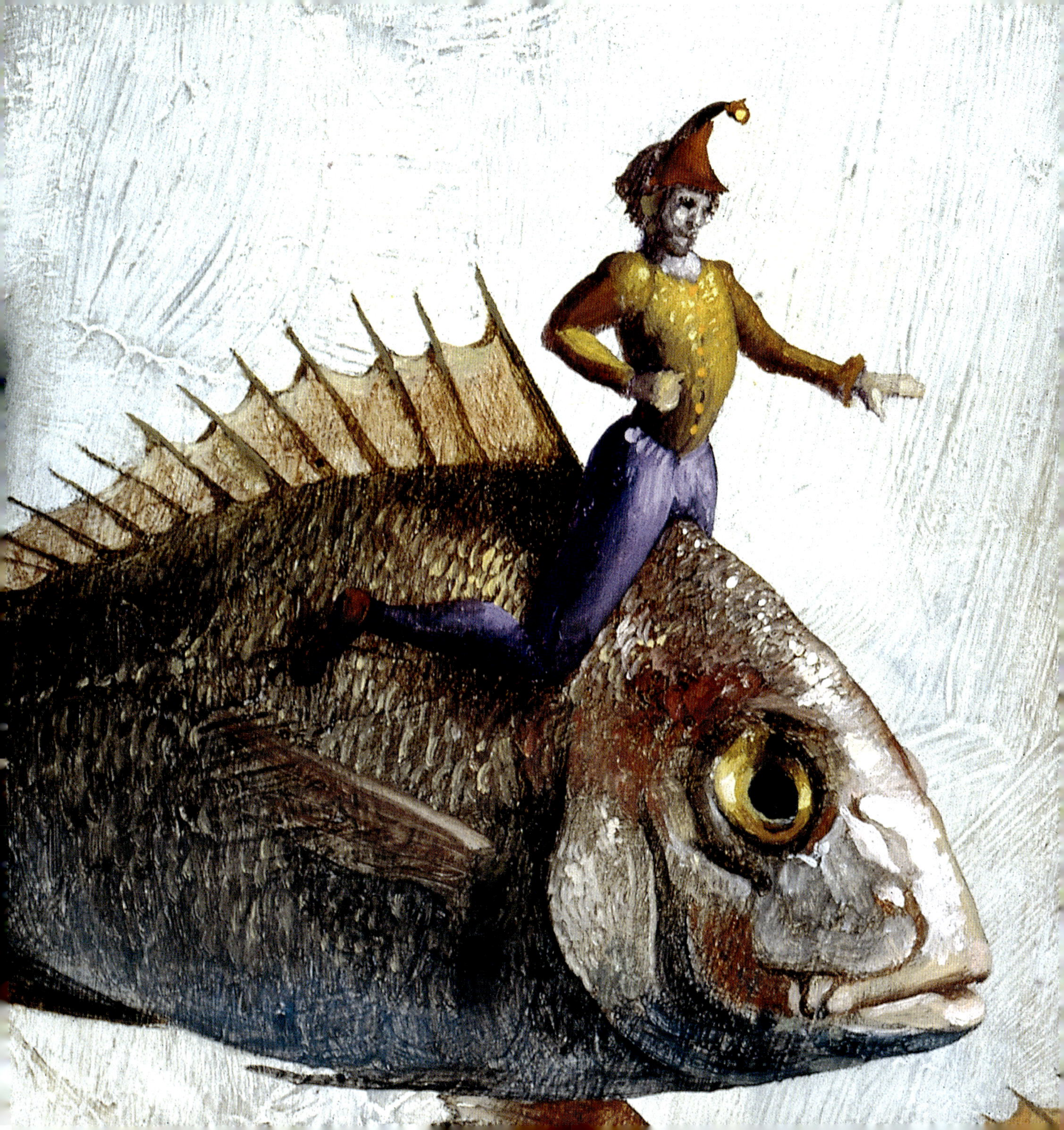

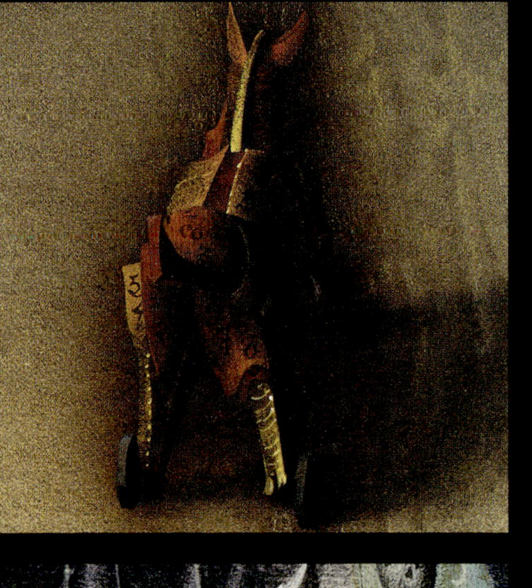

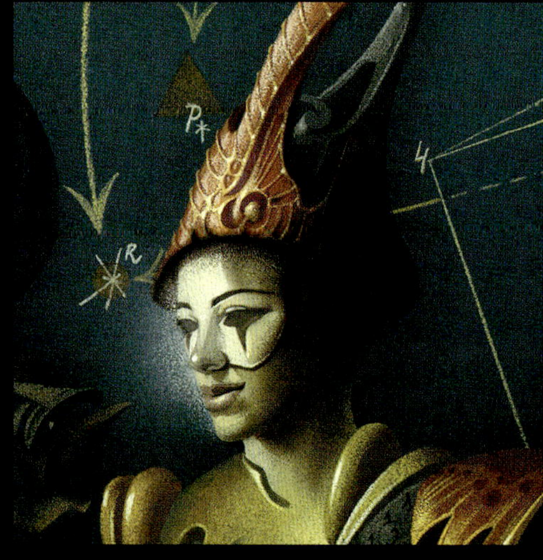

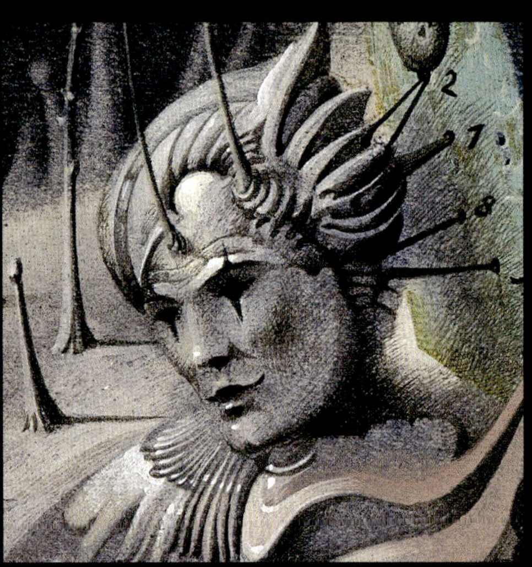

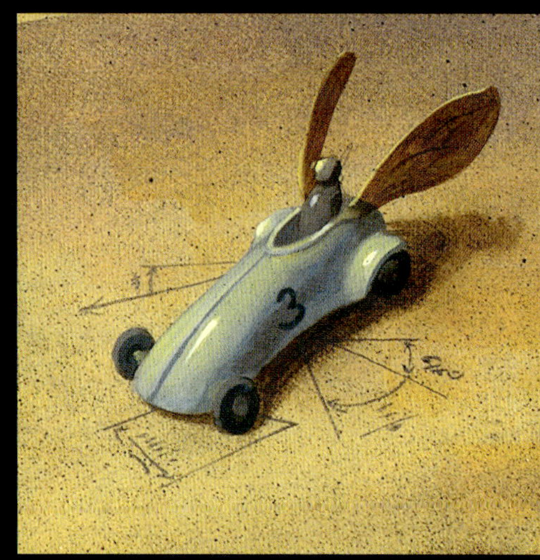

THE THOUGHT AMPLIFIER

THE INVISIBLE VOYAGE

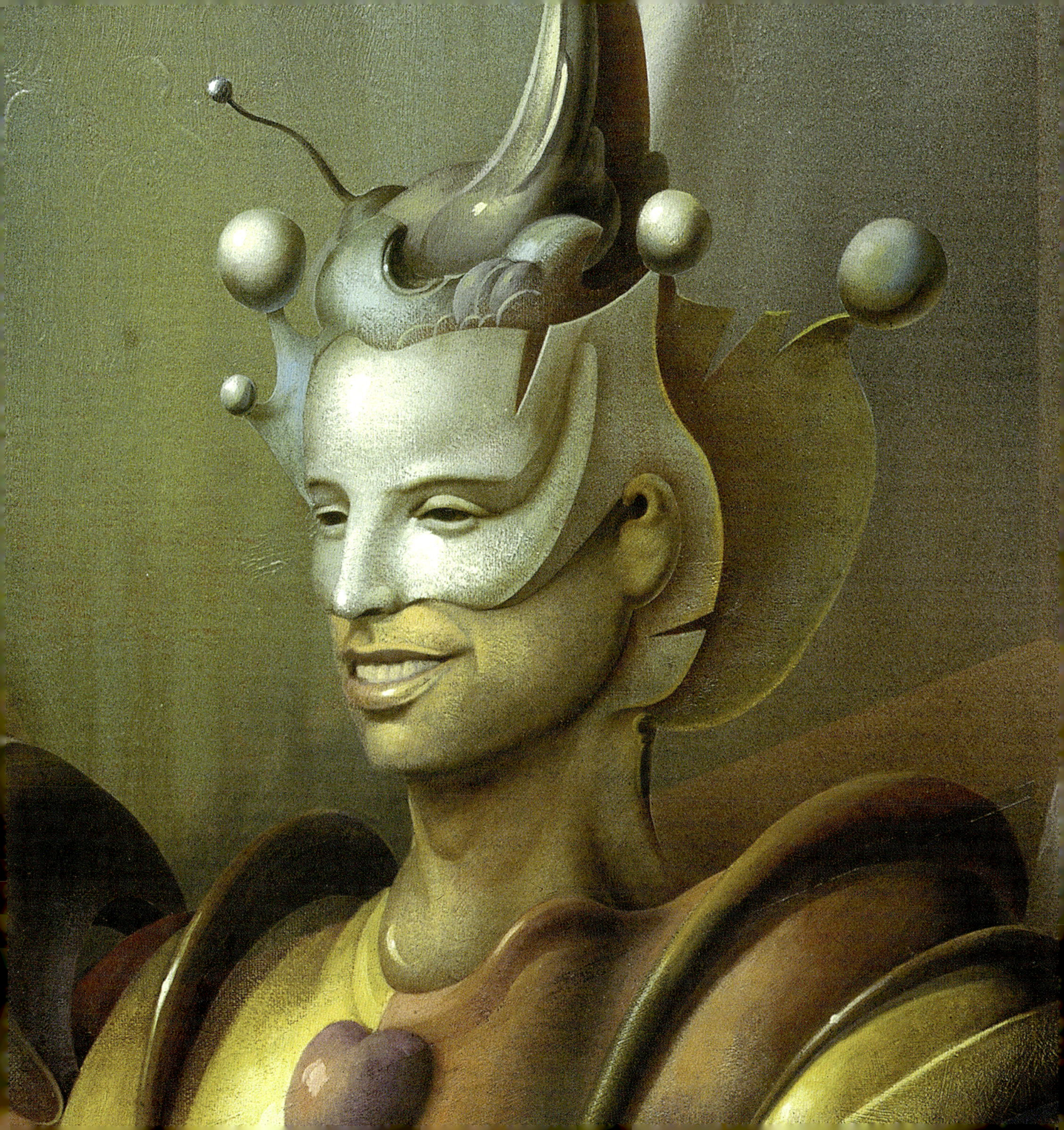

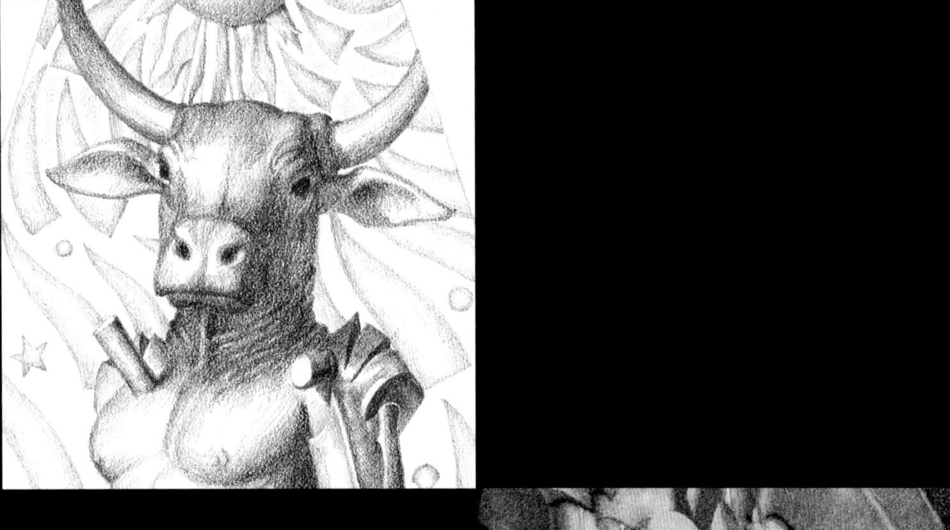

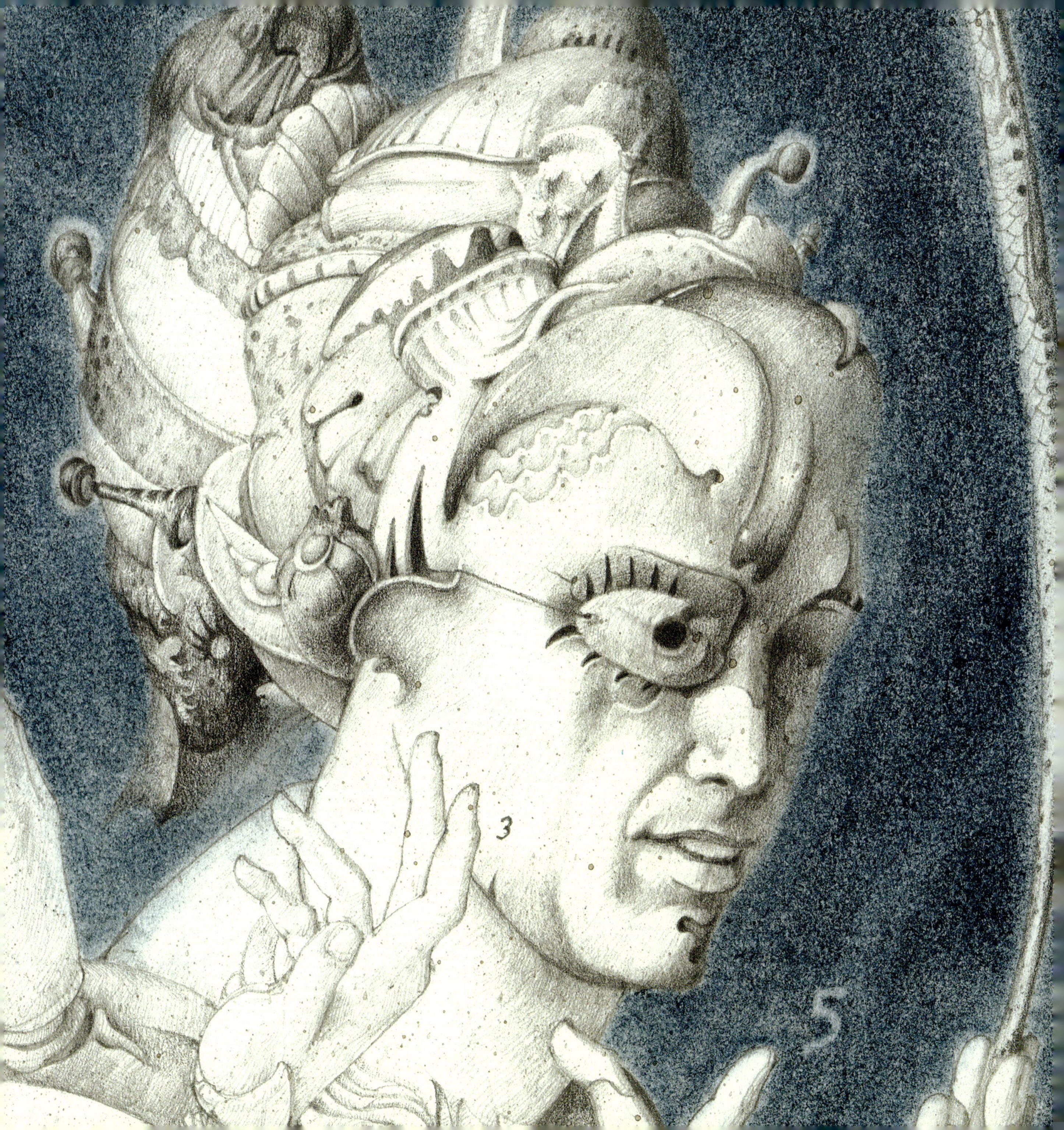
3
5

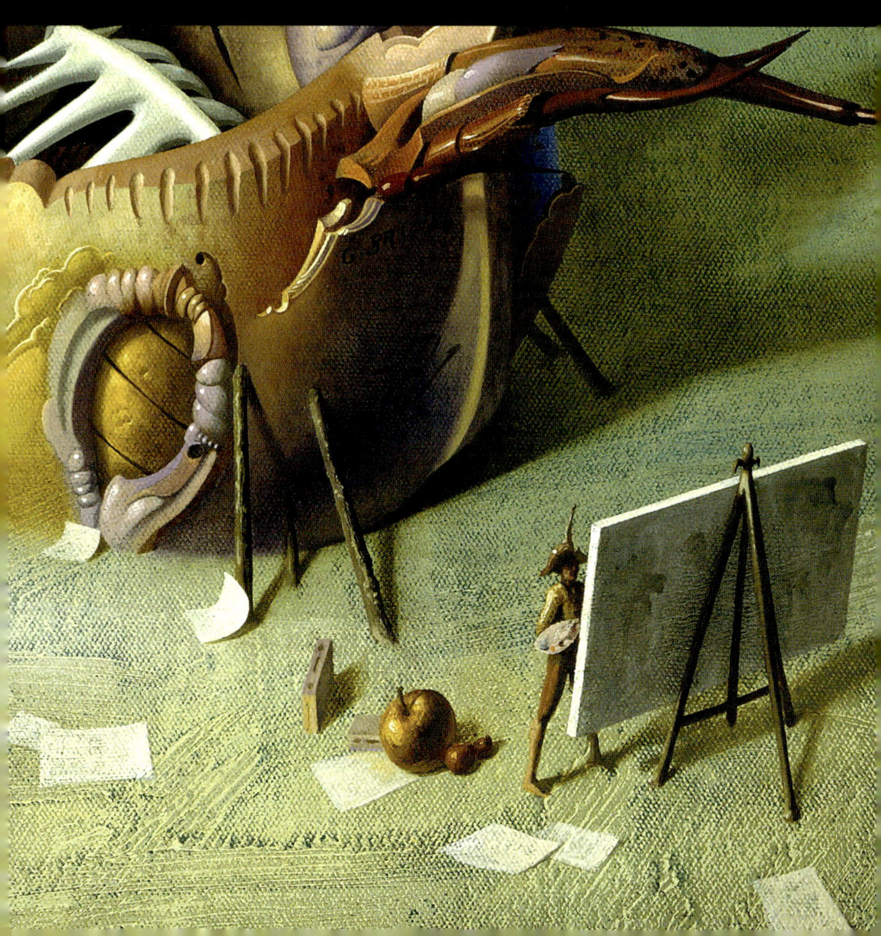

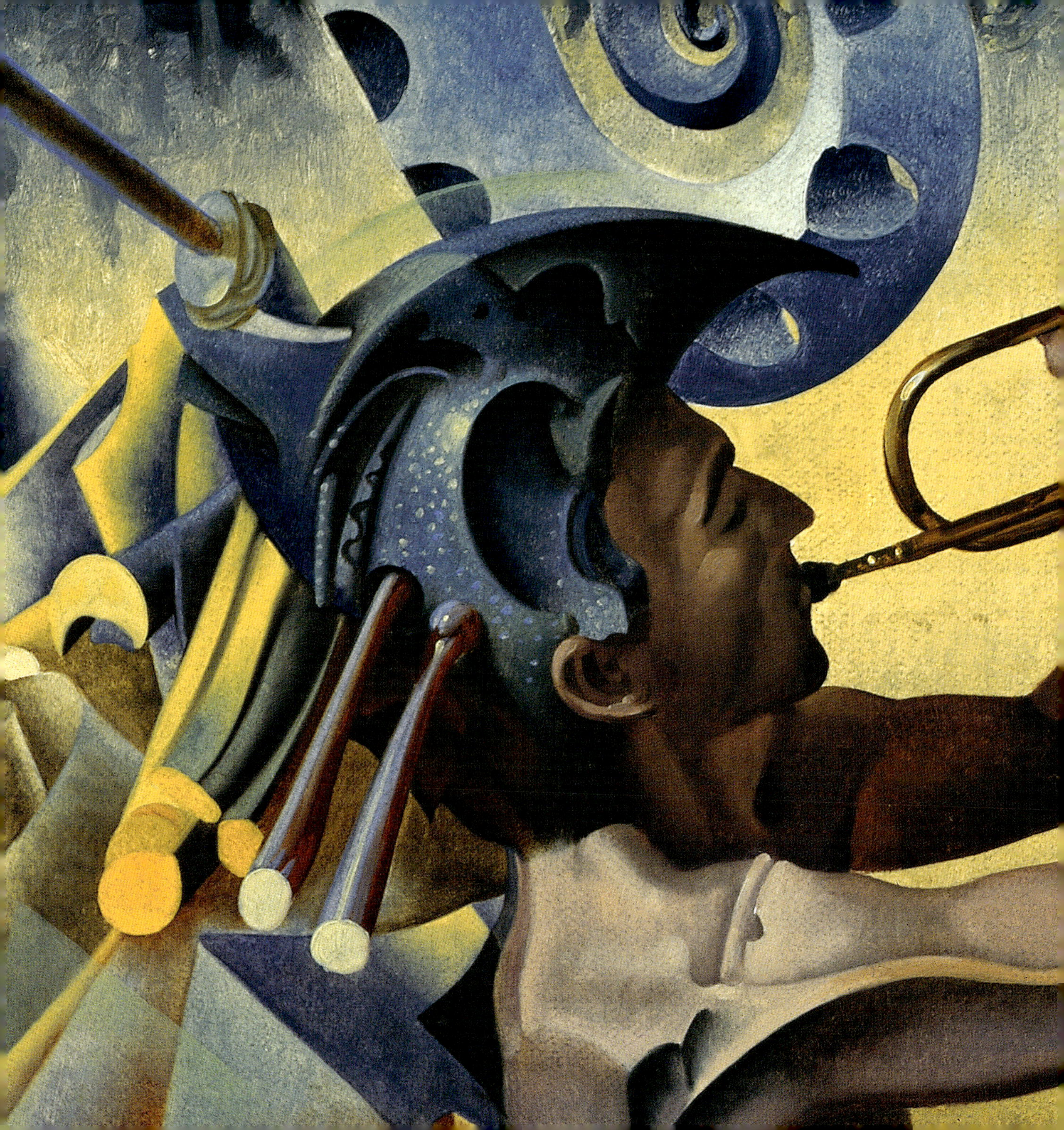

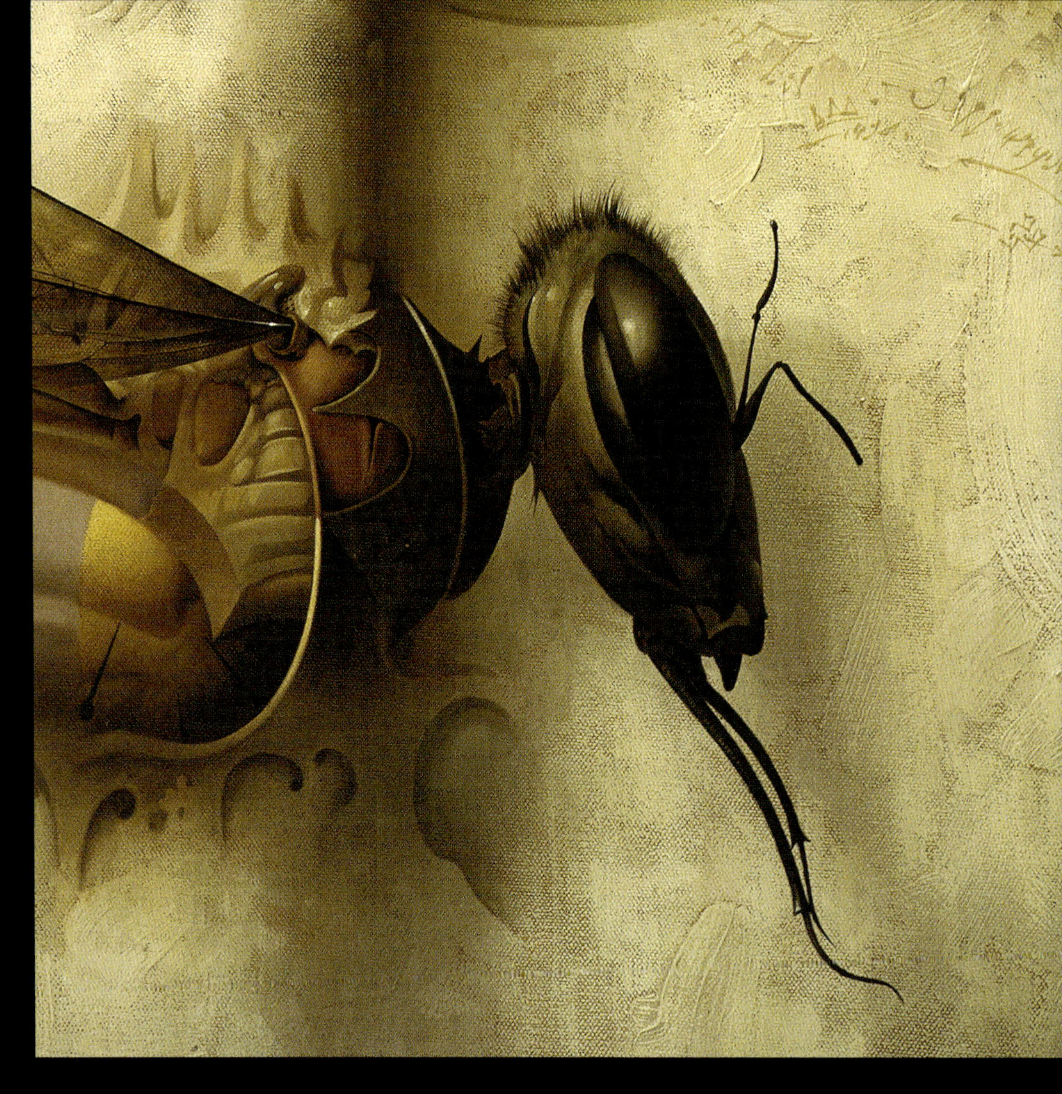

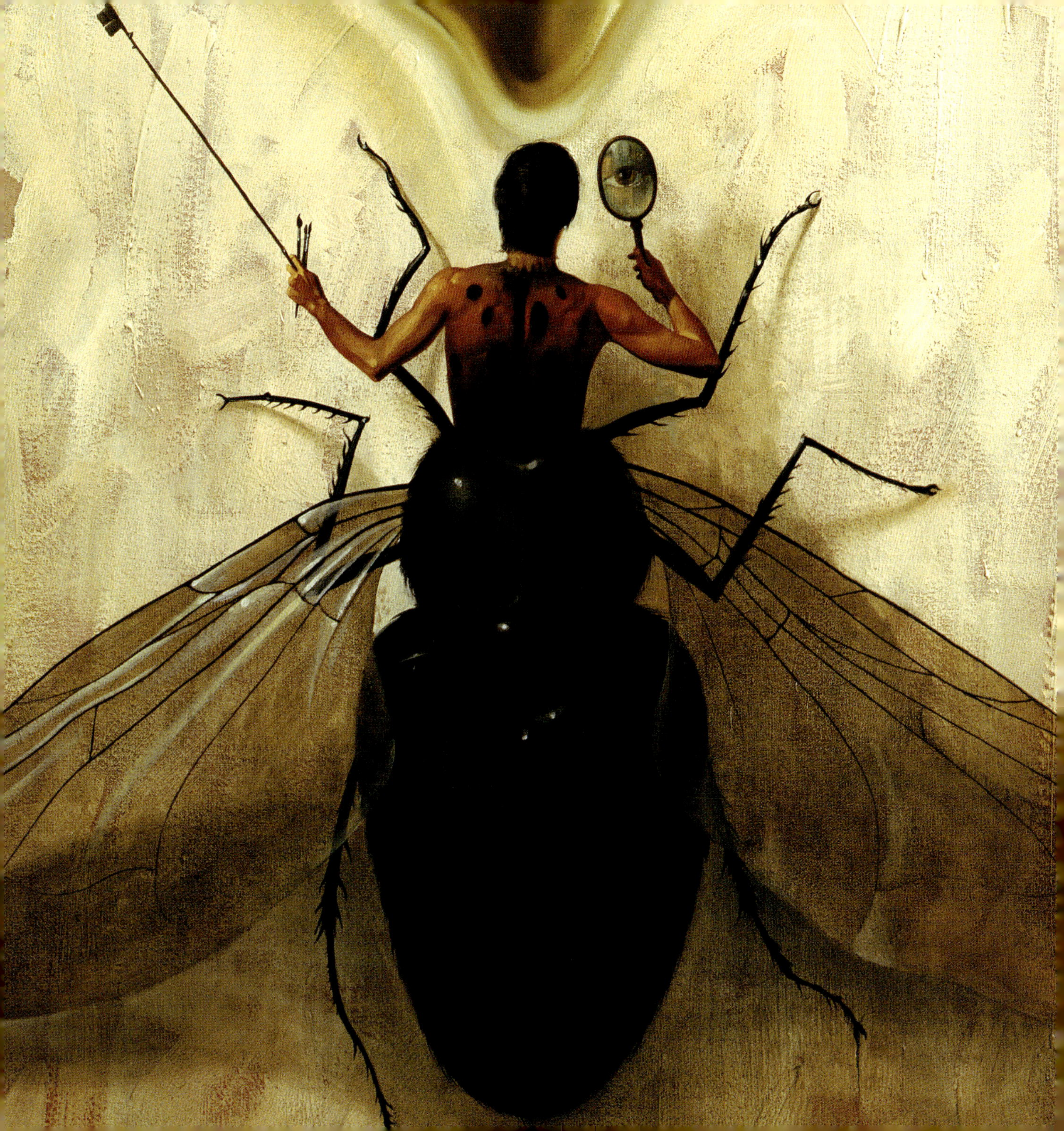

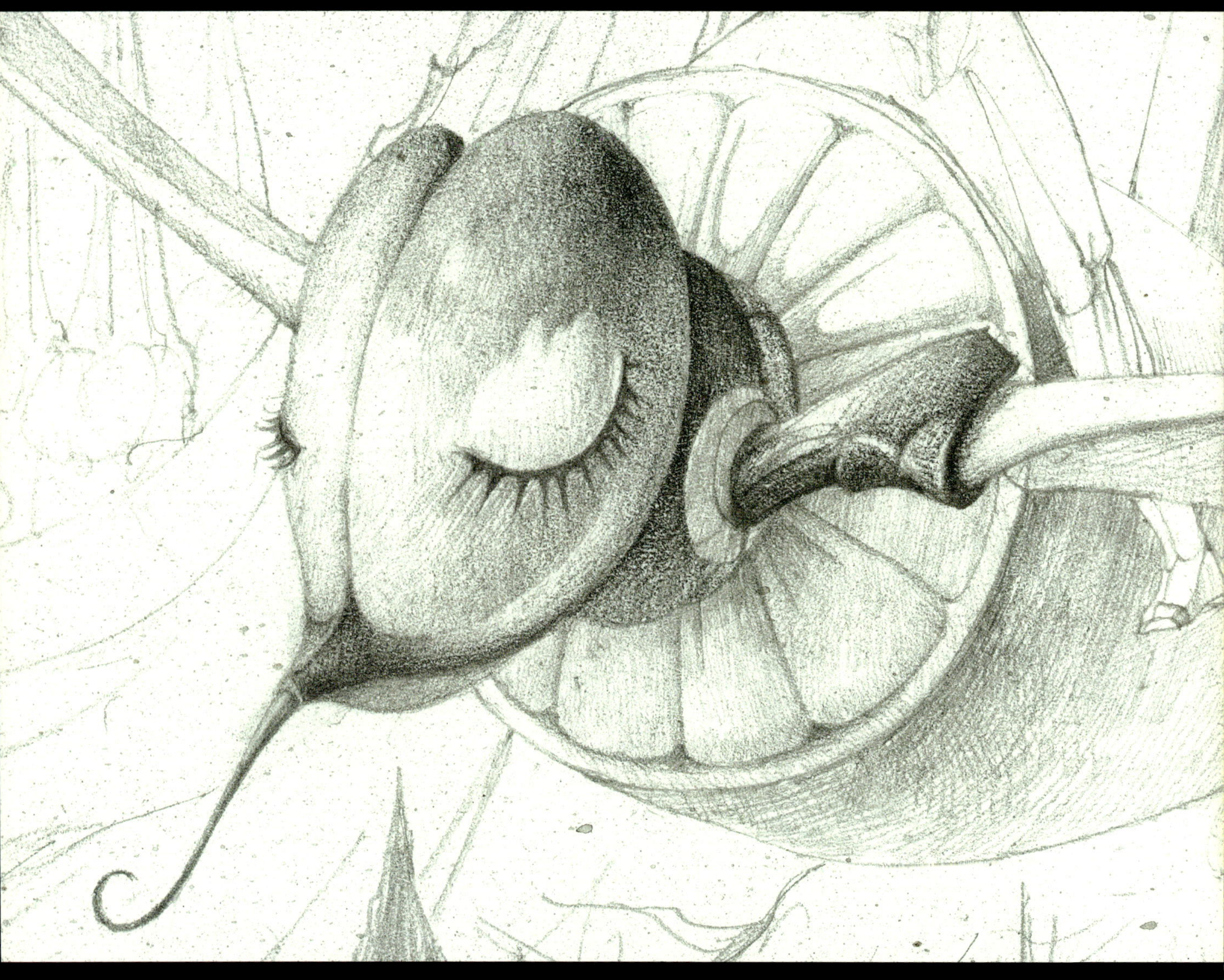

TAKE OFF - study

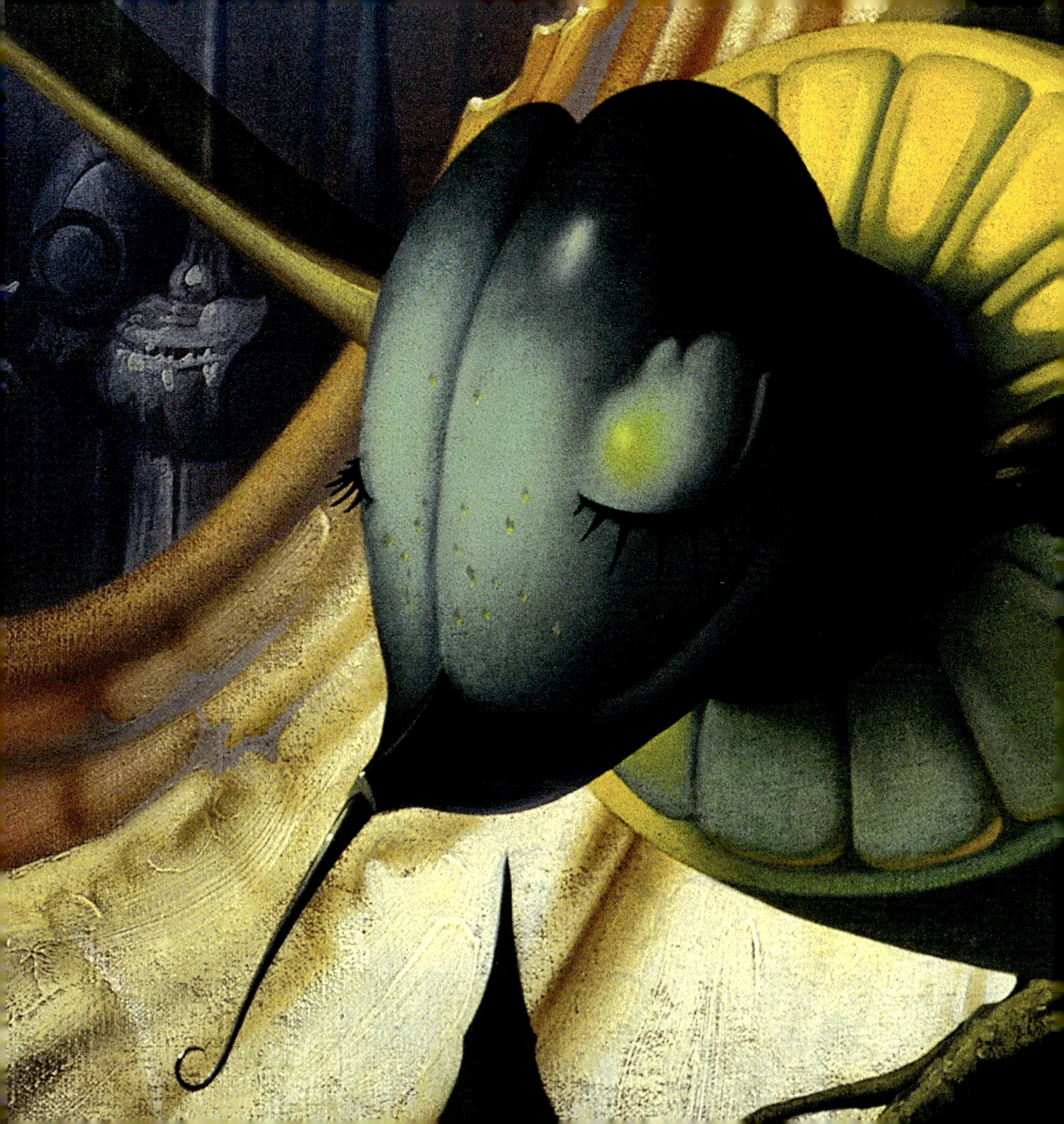

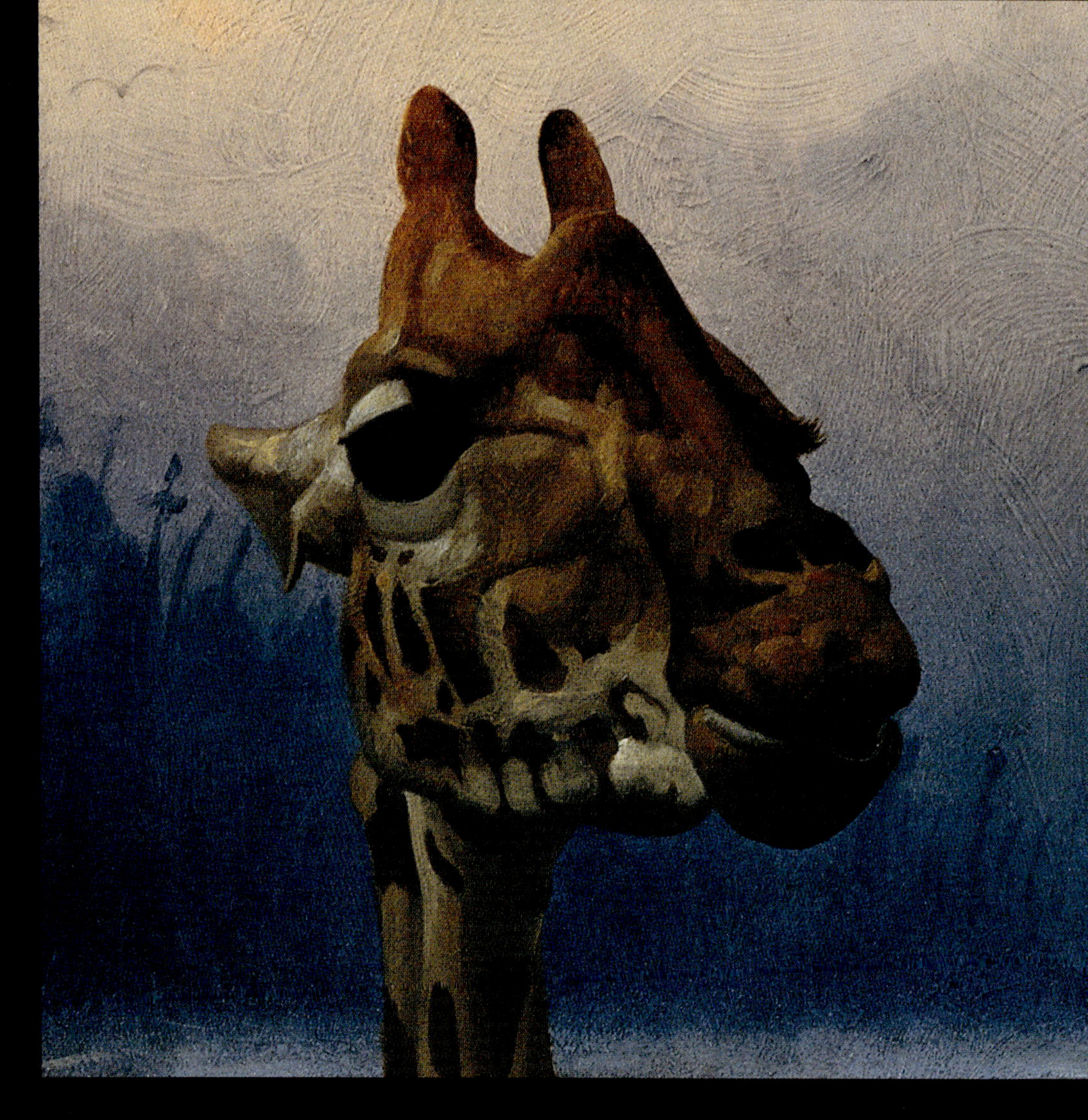

gazed upon /
le regard rêveur

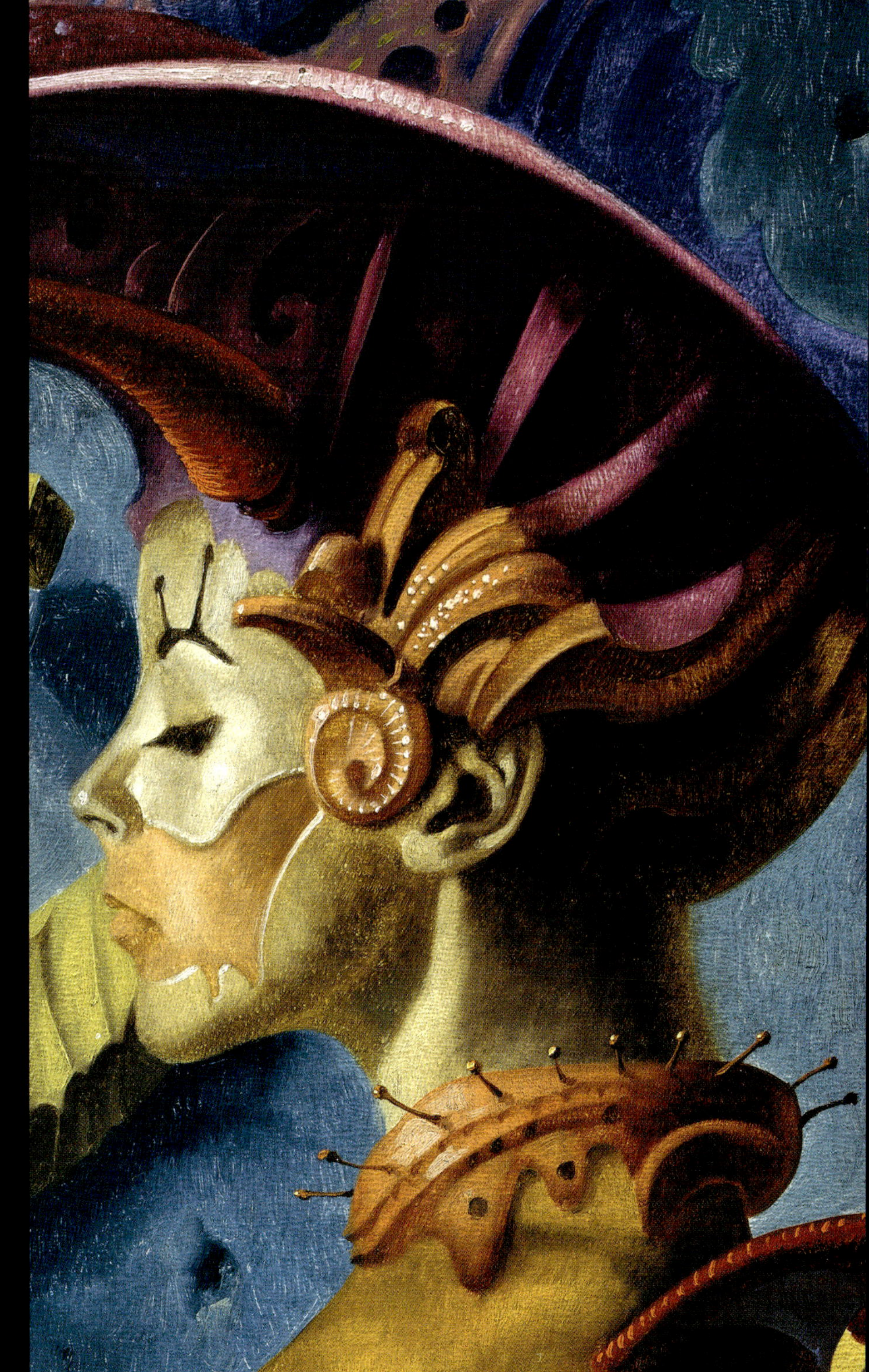

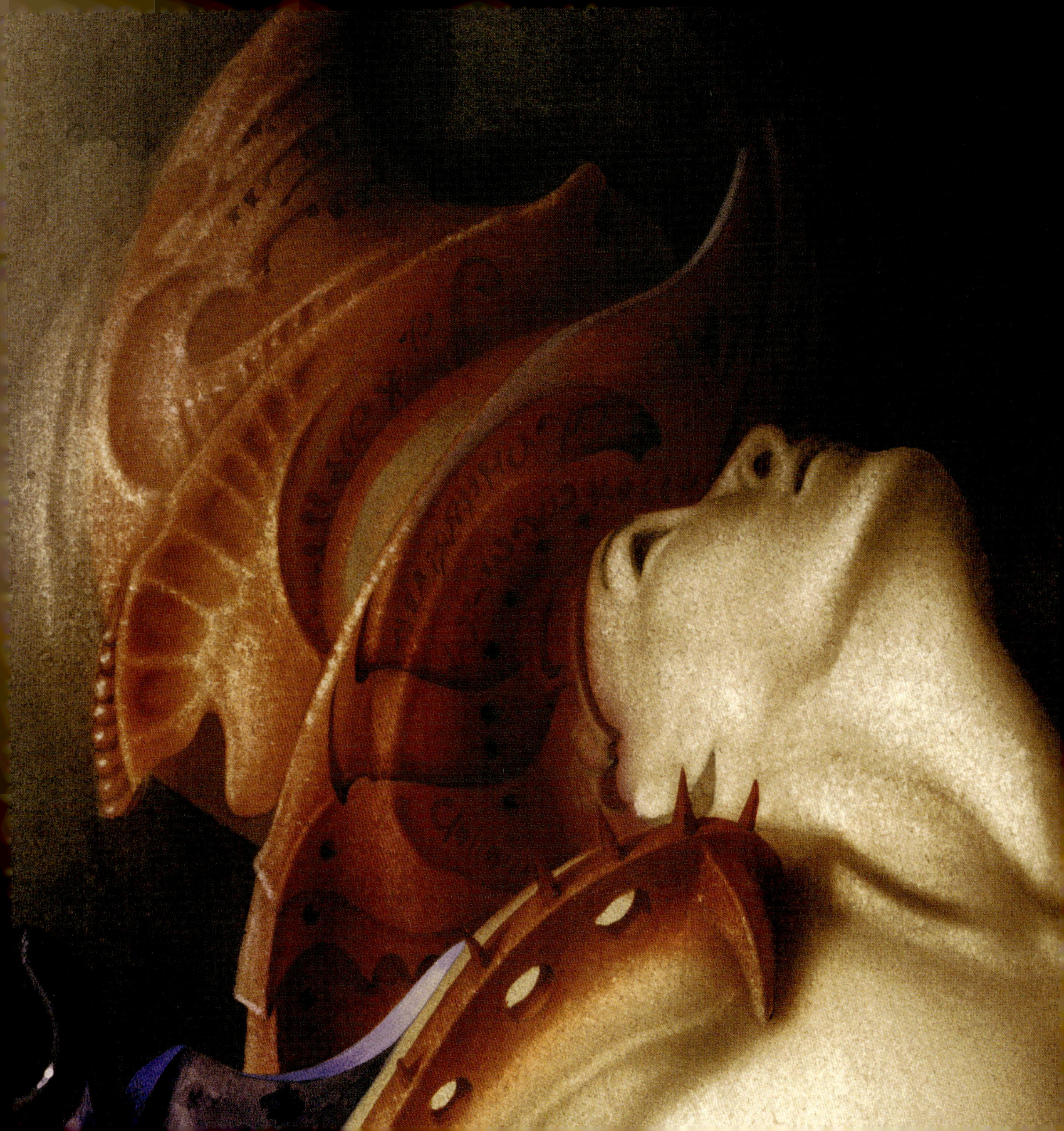

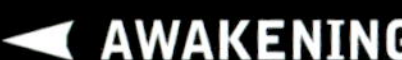

AWAKENING

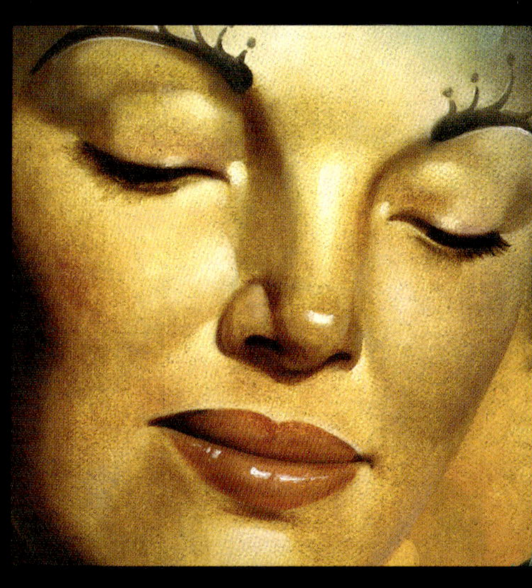

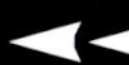

PANDORA - study

AS TIME GOES BY

TIME WATCHER ➤

THE ARCHITECT - study ➤

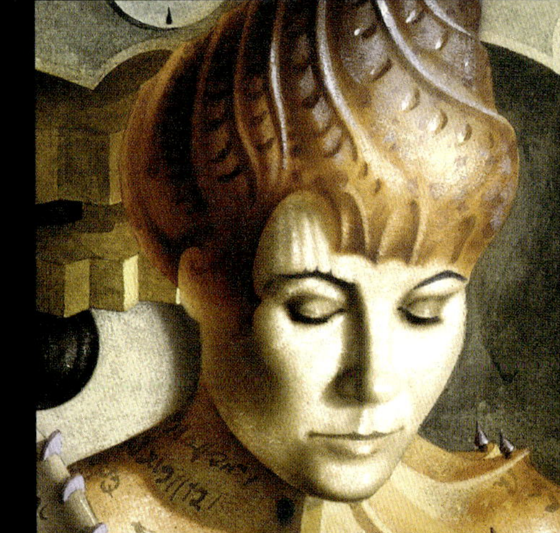

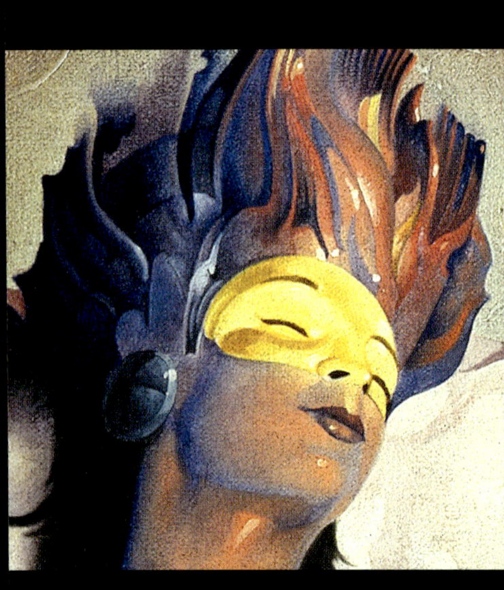

▲ THE NIGHT

▲ THE MERMAID

◄ WHAT TIME IS IT?

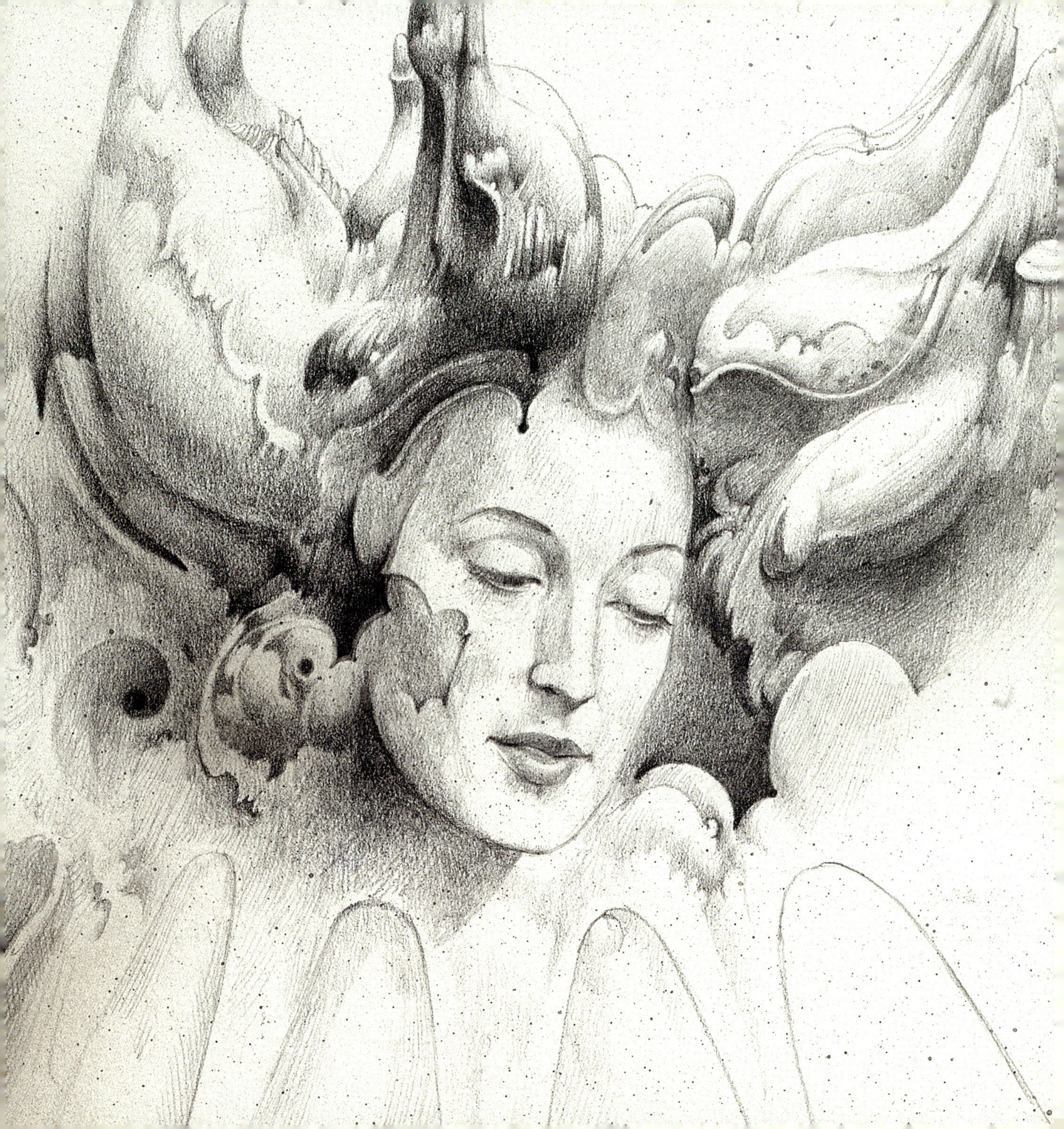

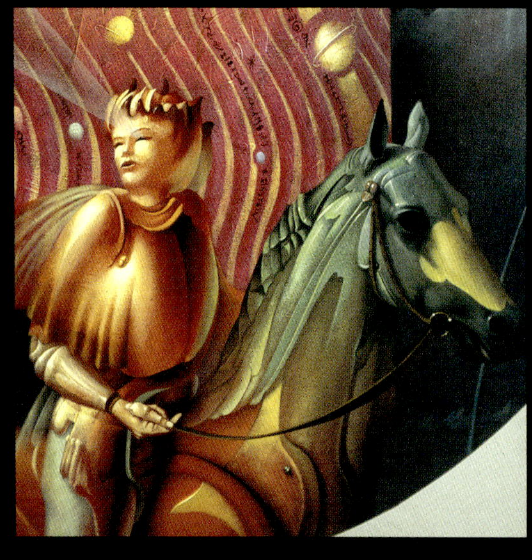

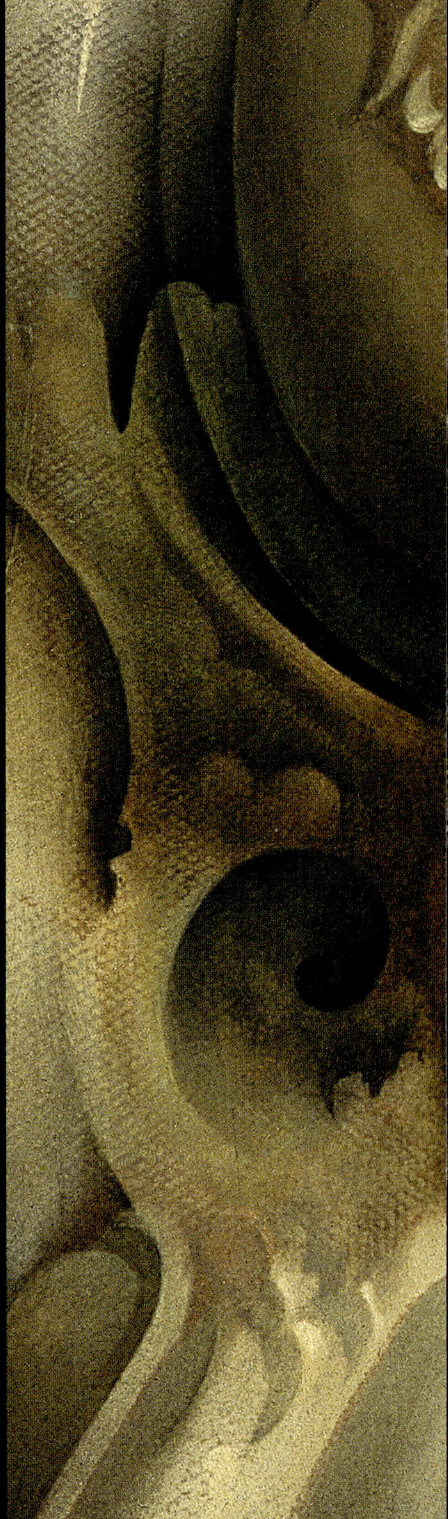

INFINITY

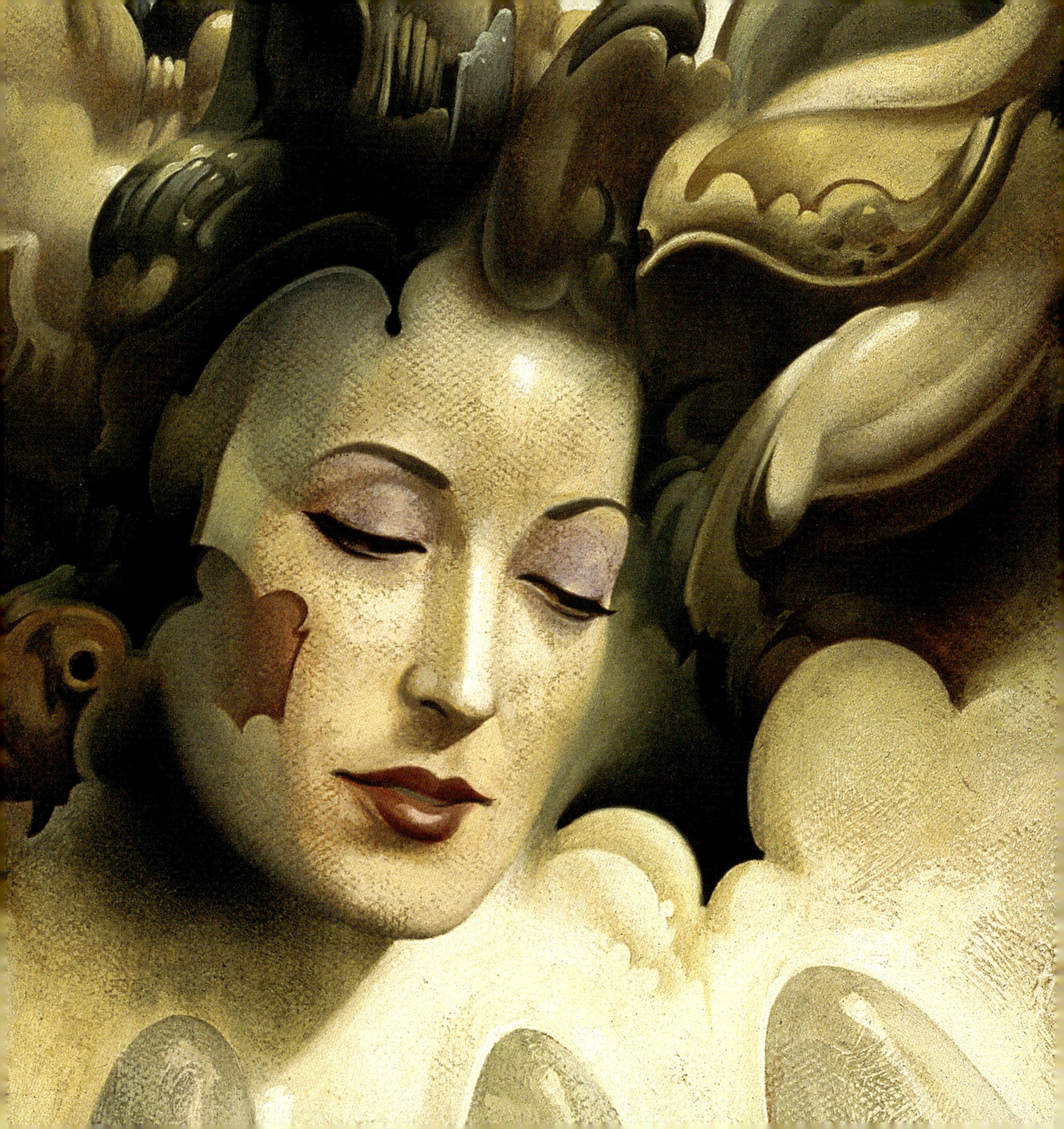

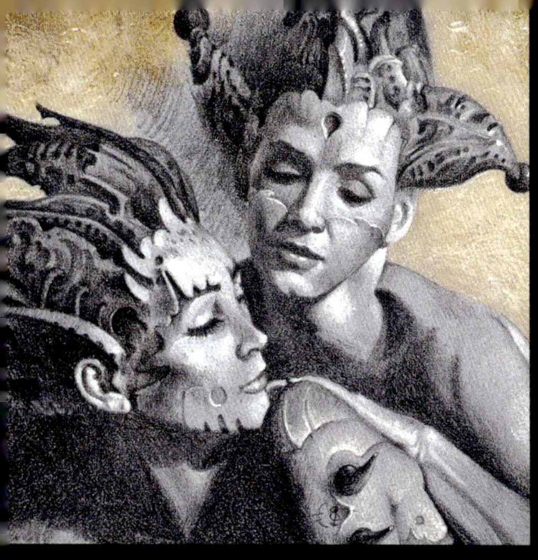

THE MESSENGER

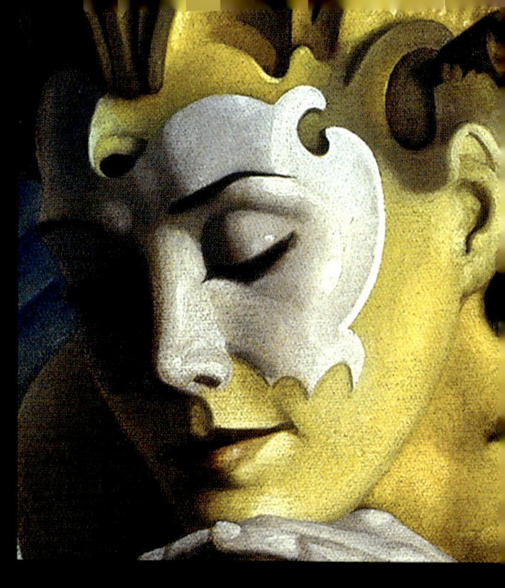

SECRETS - study

THE MESSENGER - study

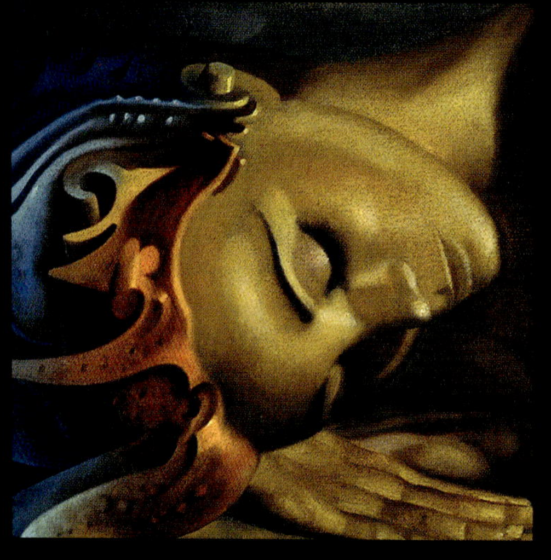

CUBIC WALK - study

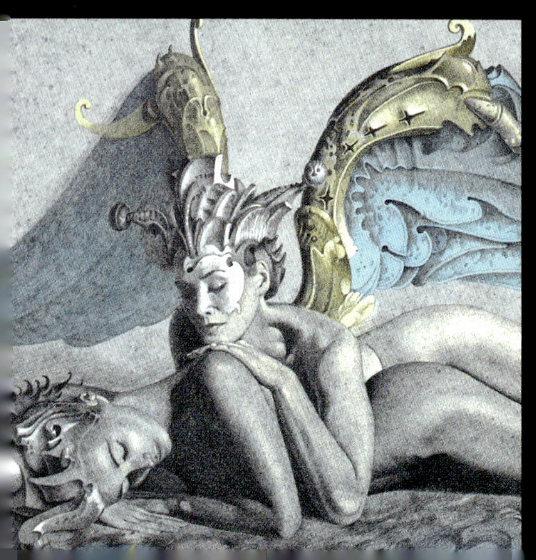

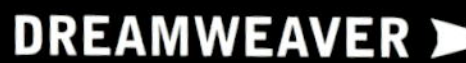

DREAMWEAVER

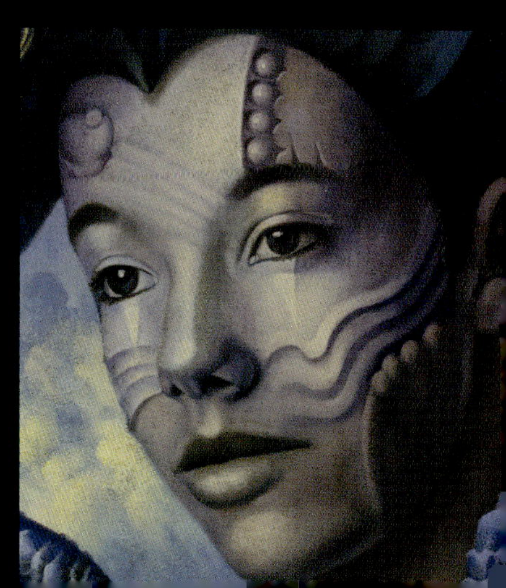

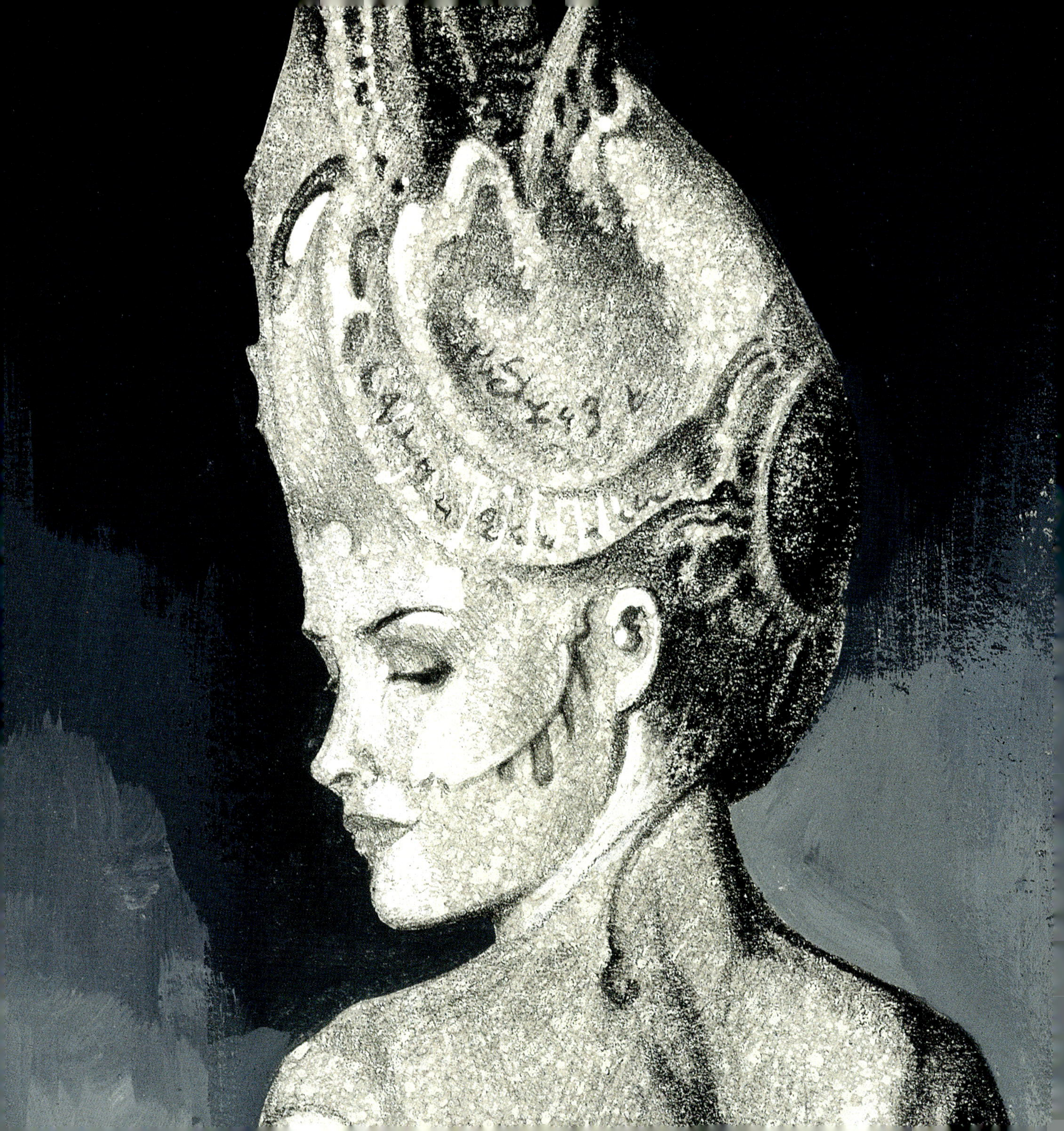

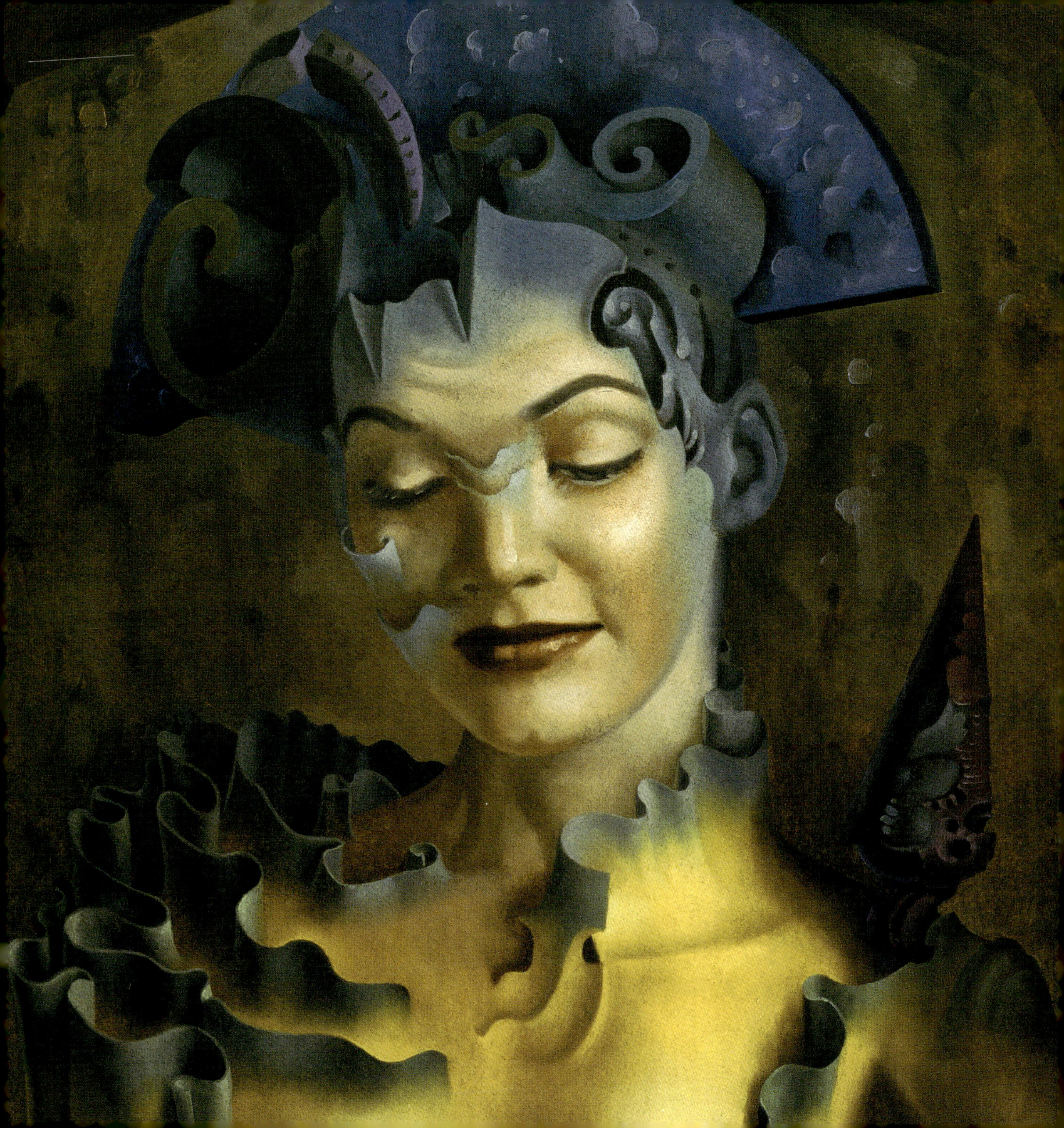

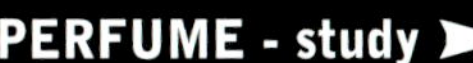
PERFUME - study

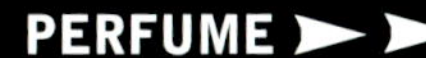
PERFUME

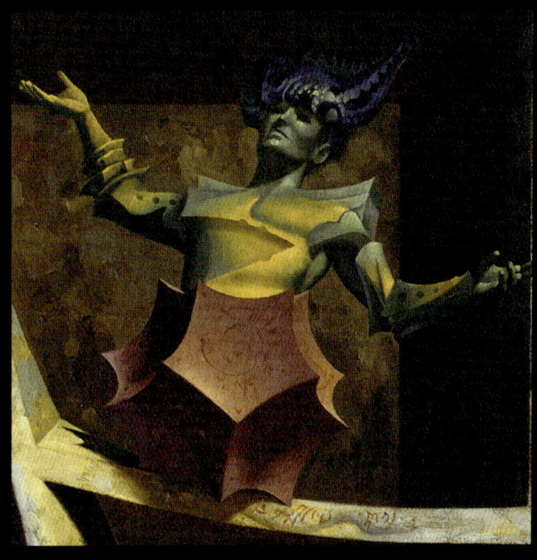

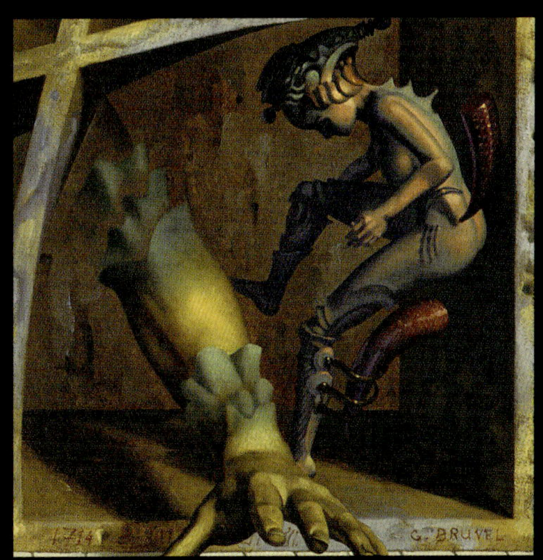
G. BRUVEL

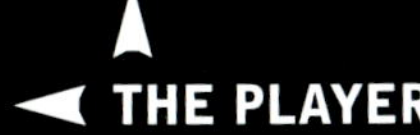
THE PLAYER

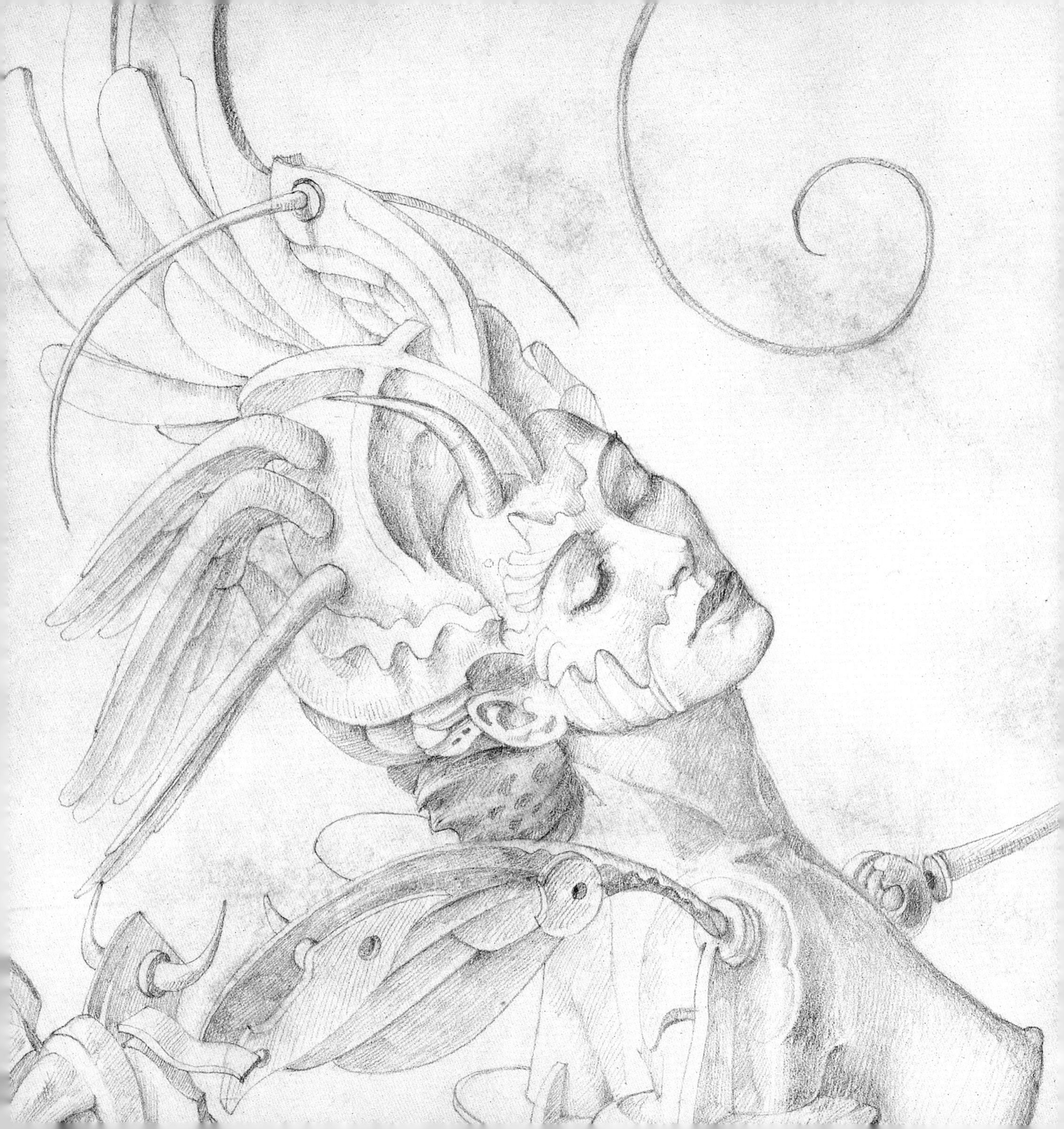

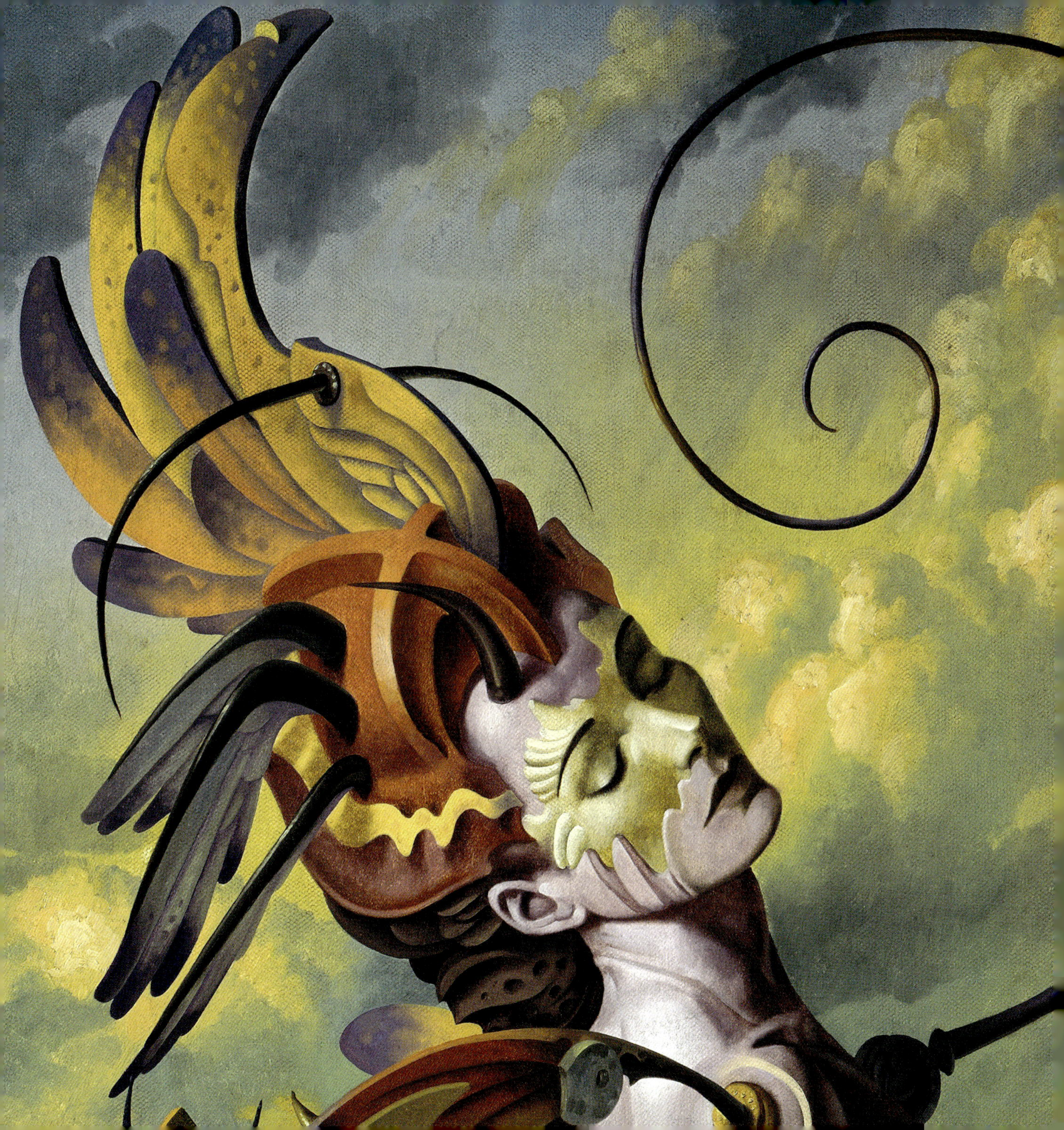

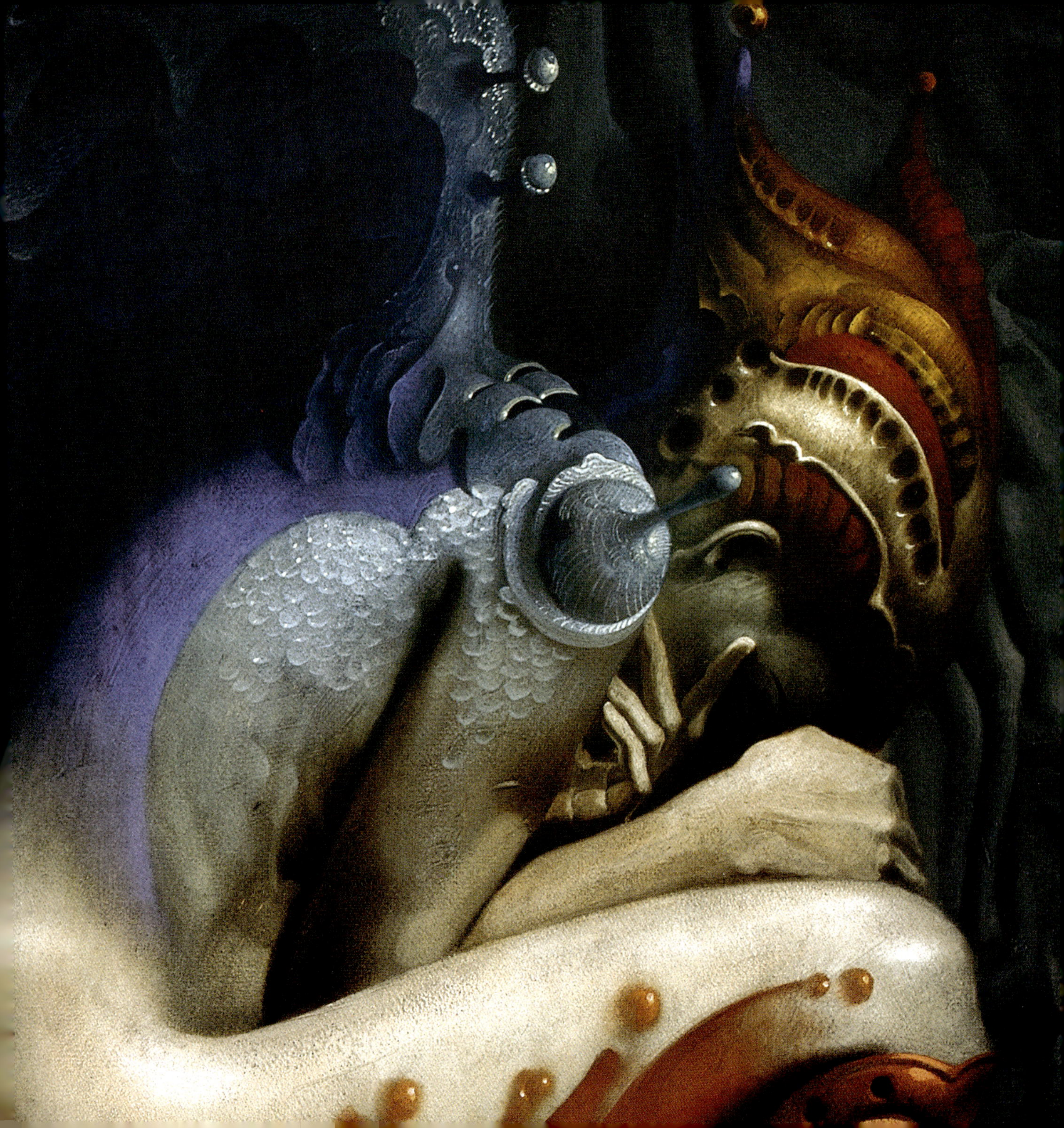

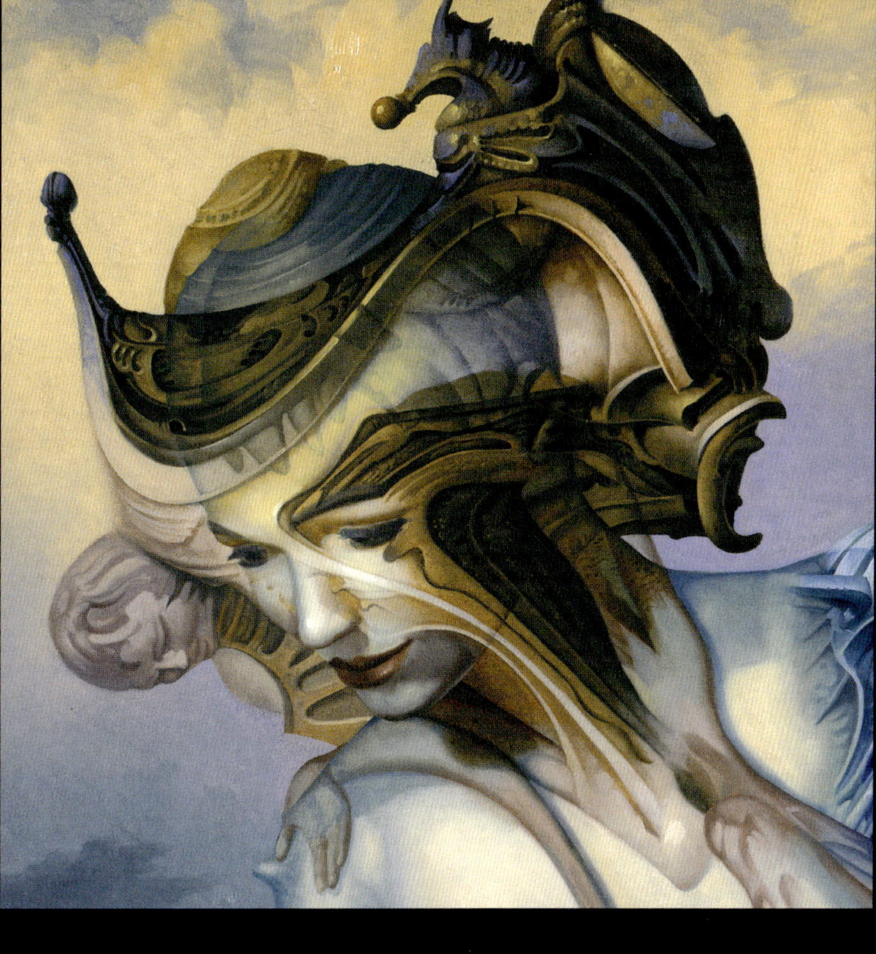

TIME TRANSFERS

REST UPON THE DREAM

TRANSFERENCE

THE JOURNEY

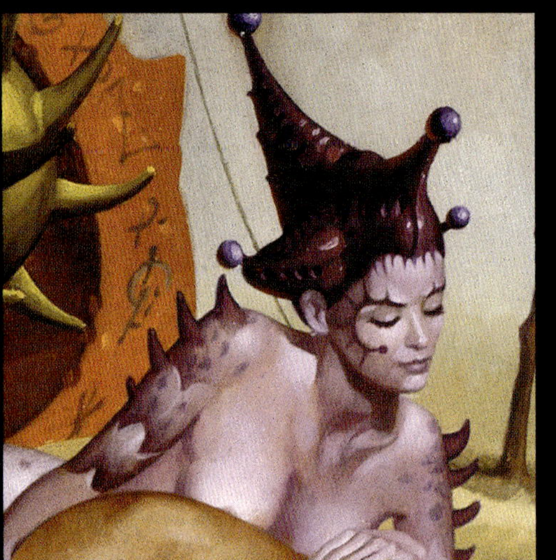

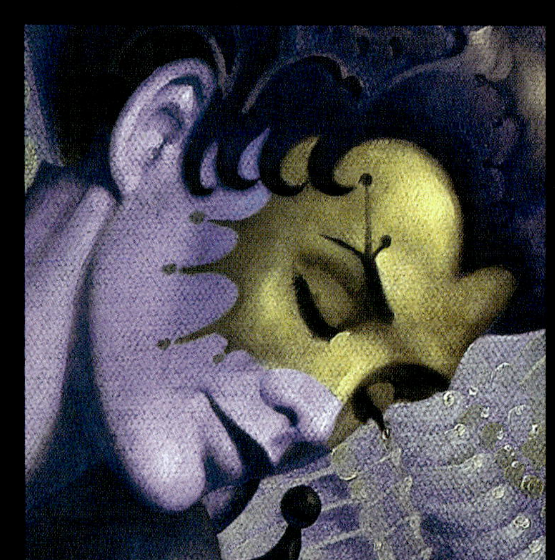

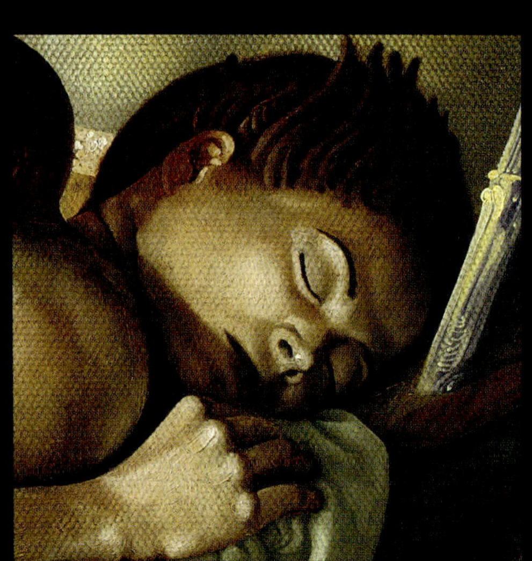

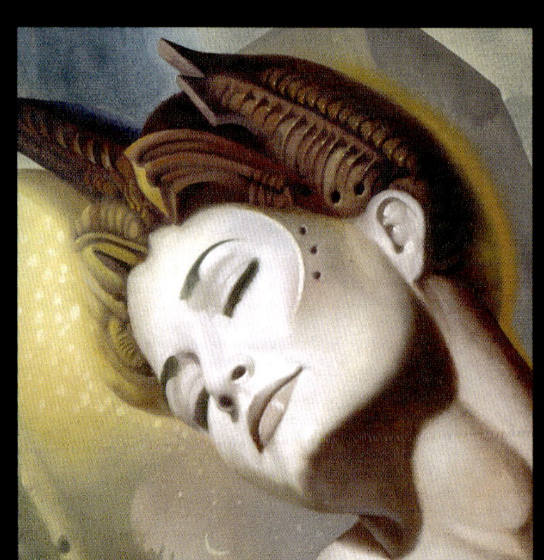

AT THE GATE

THE FLIGHT INSIDE

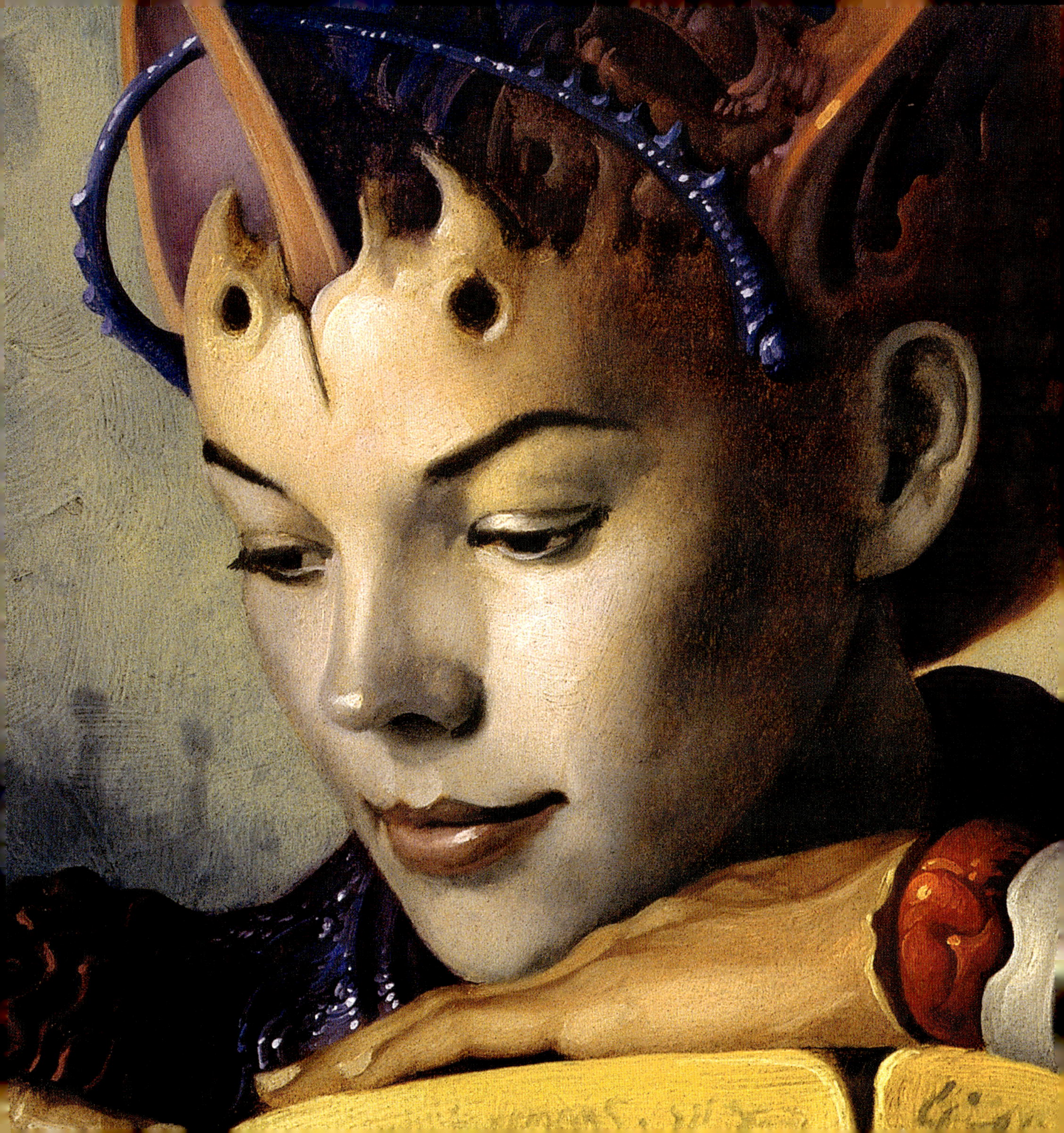

THE NIGHT - study

THE WORLD - study

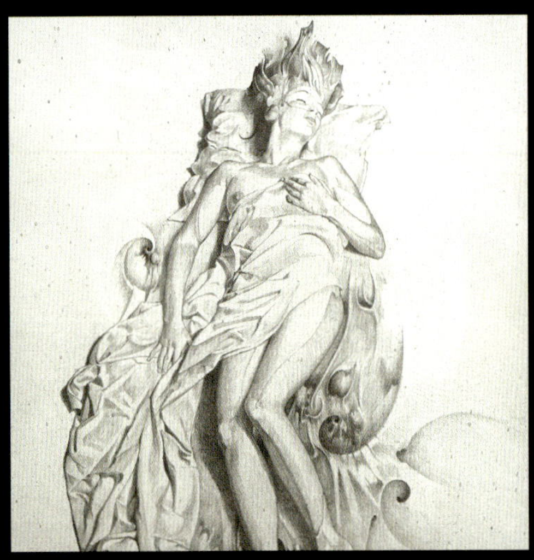

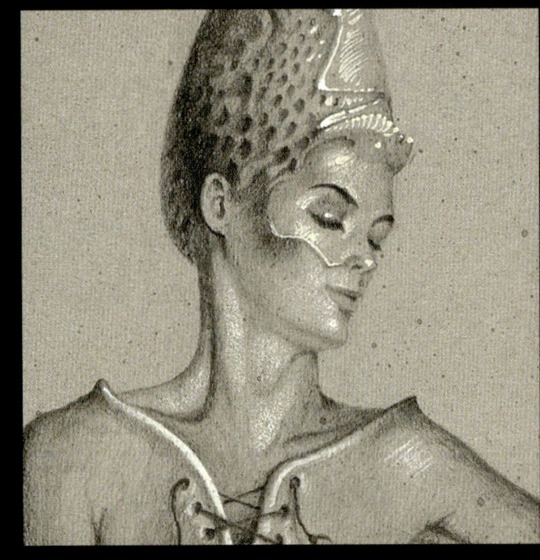

THE FEATHER

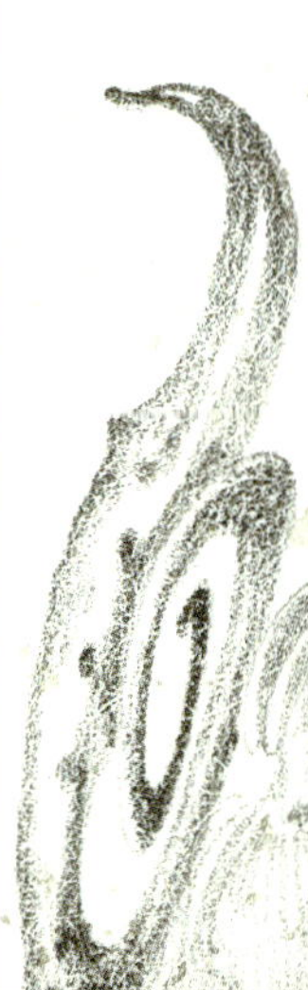

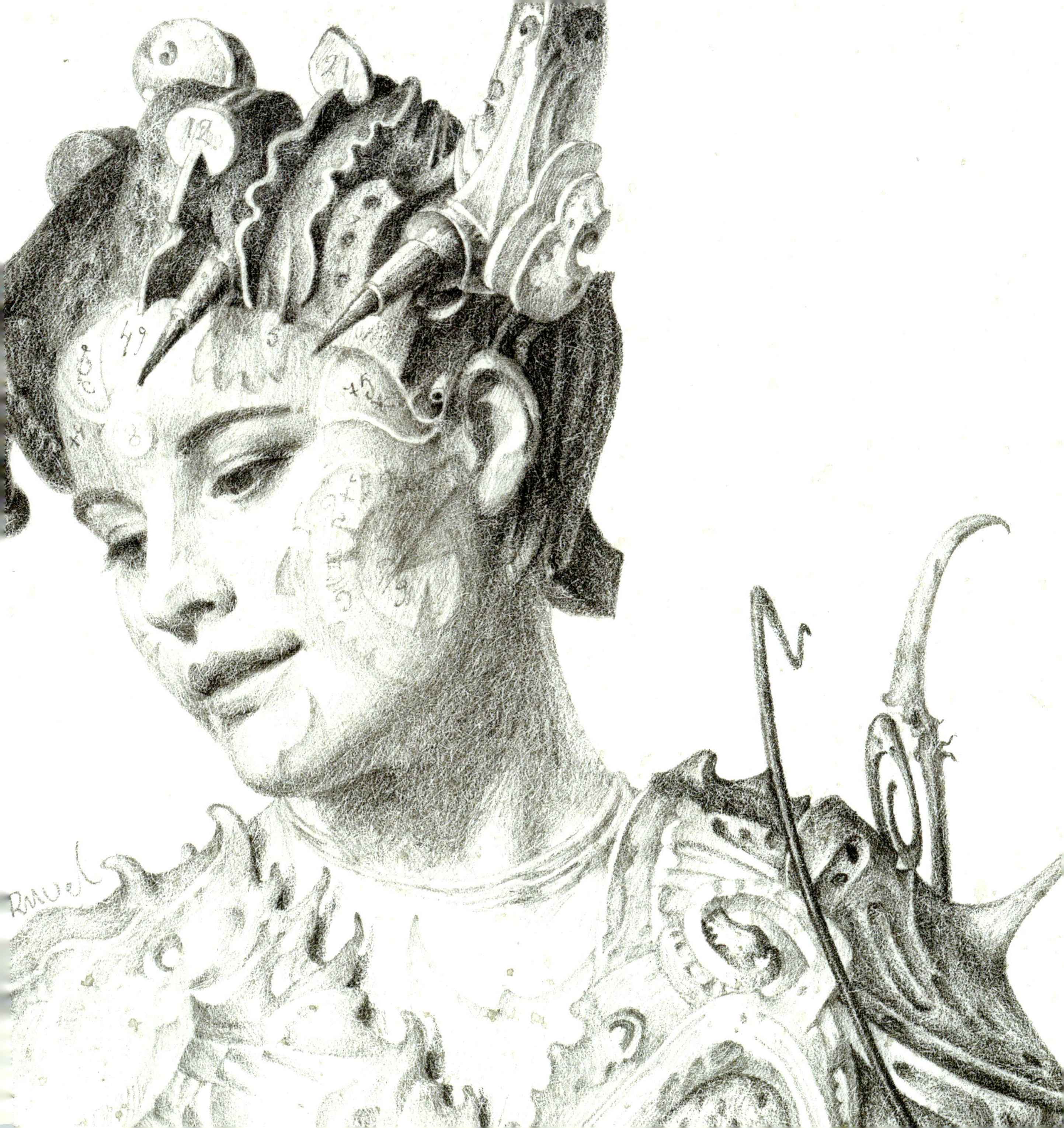

MACHINE OF ➤
PERCEPTIONS

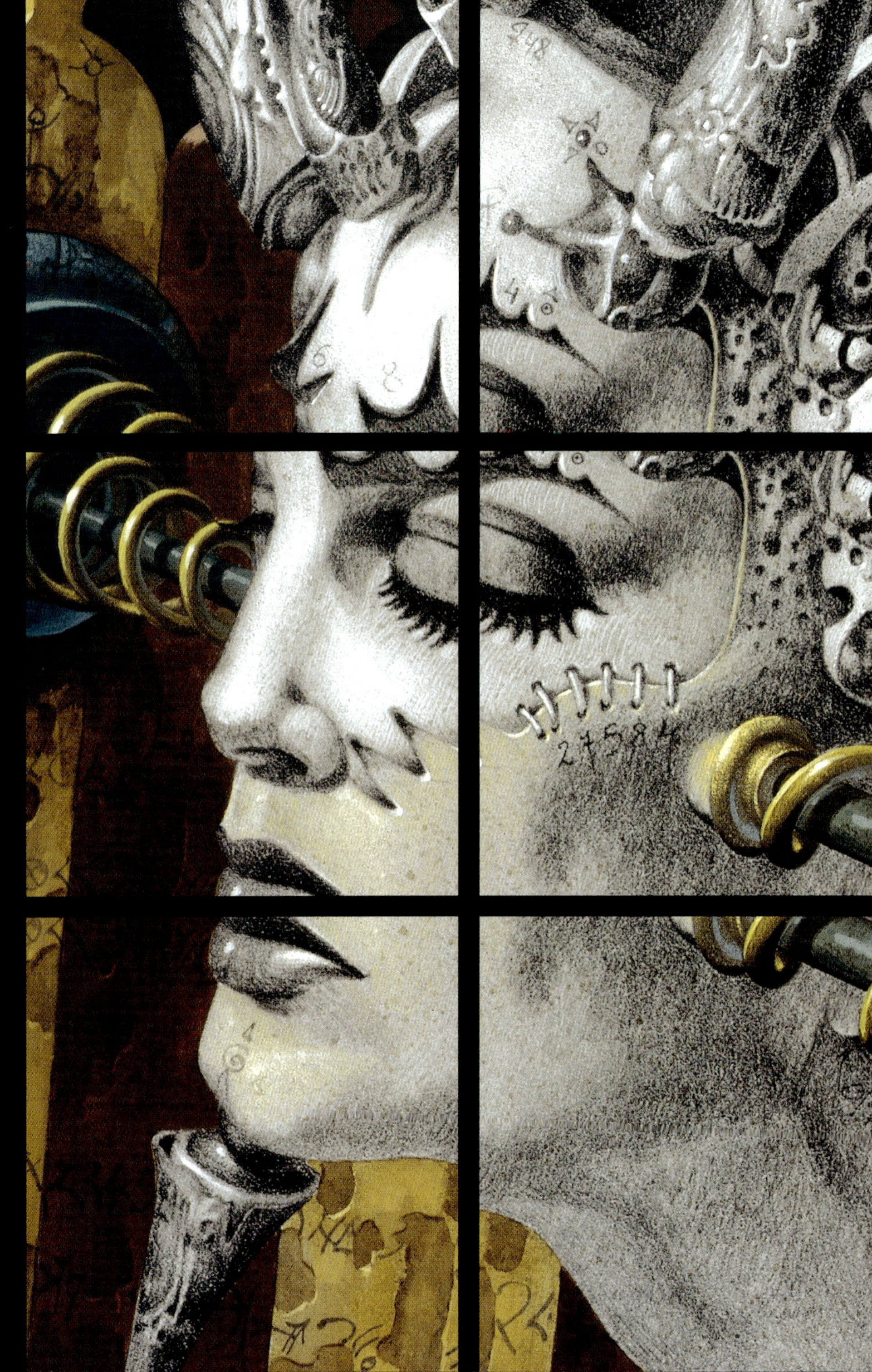

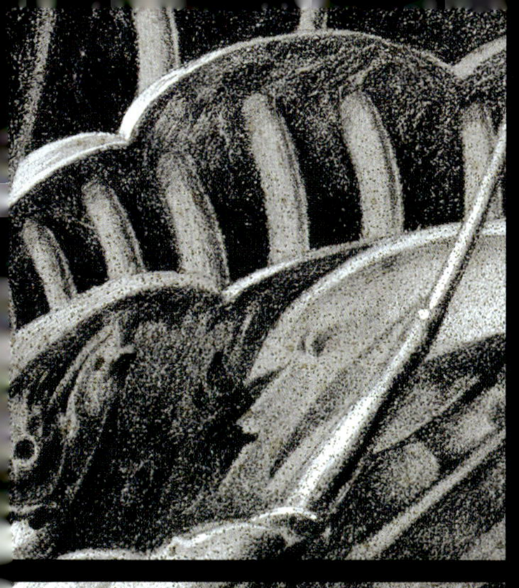

THE DAY OF APHRODITE ➤

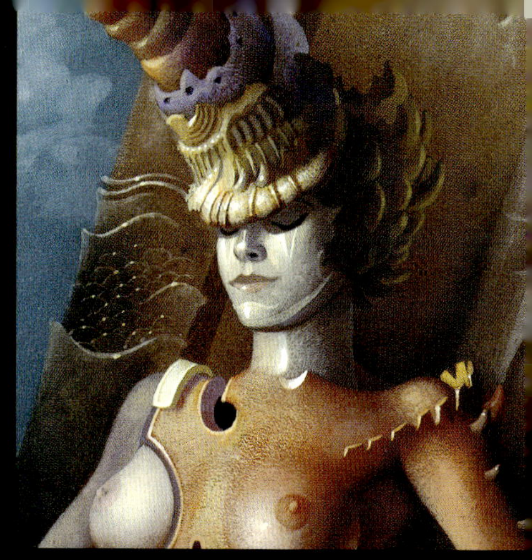

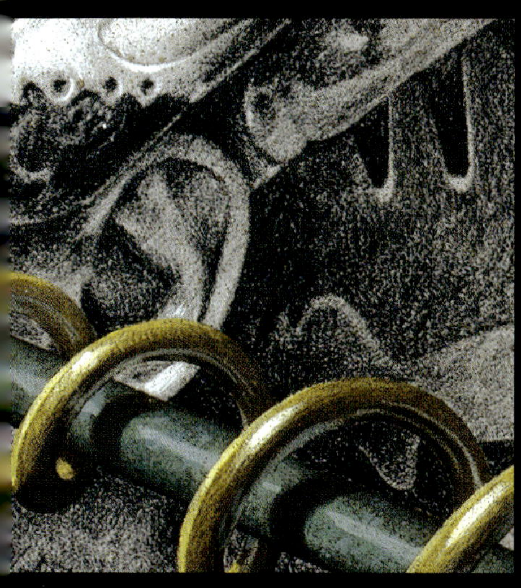

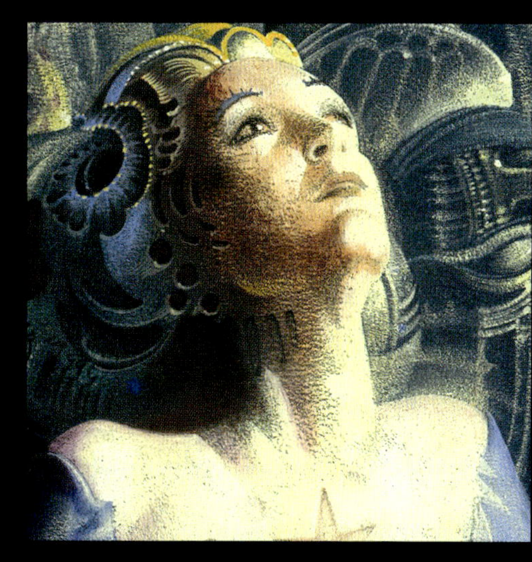

▲ MICROSCOPIC CASTAWAYS

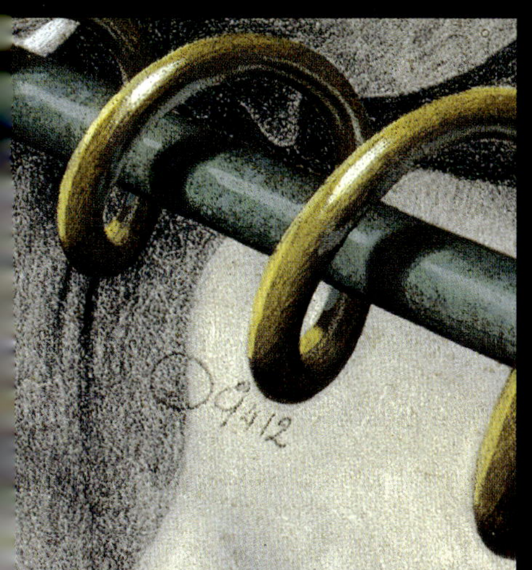

THE ARTIFICIAL SIN ➤

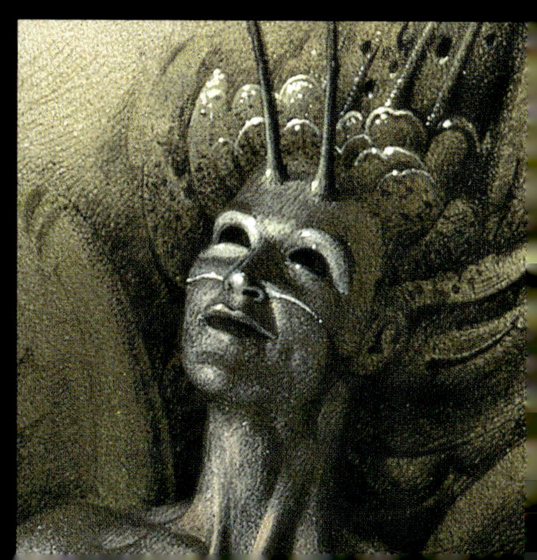

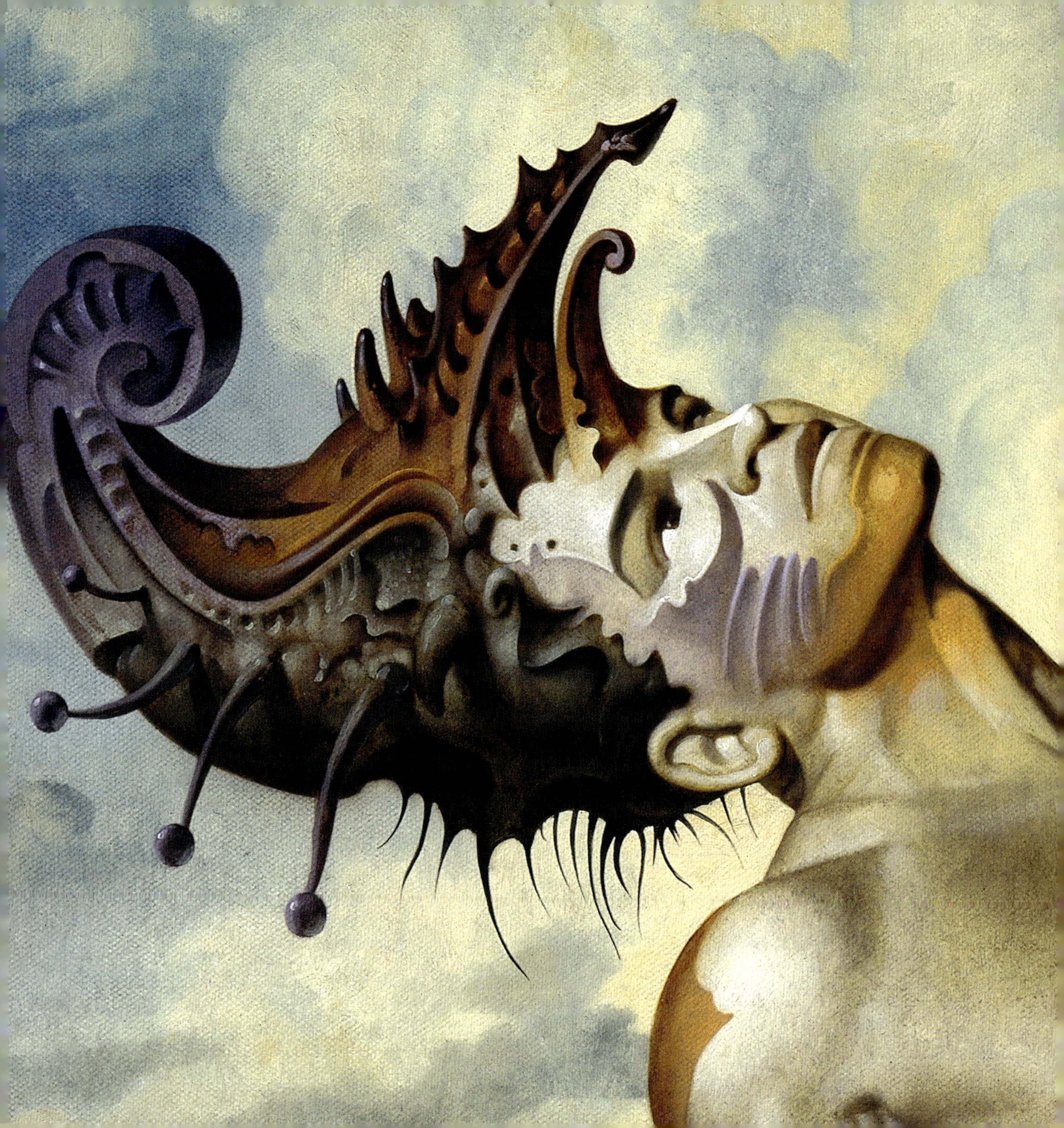

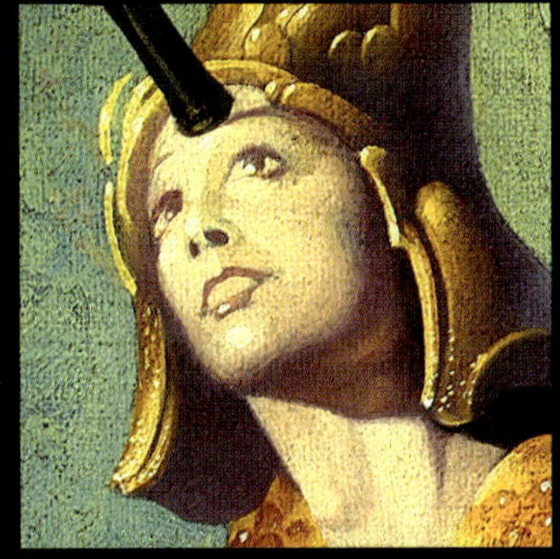

THE ASTRONOMER

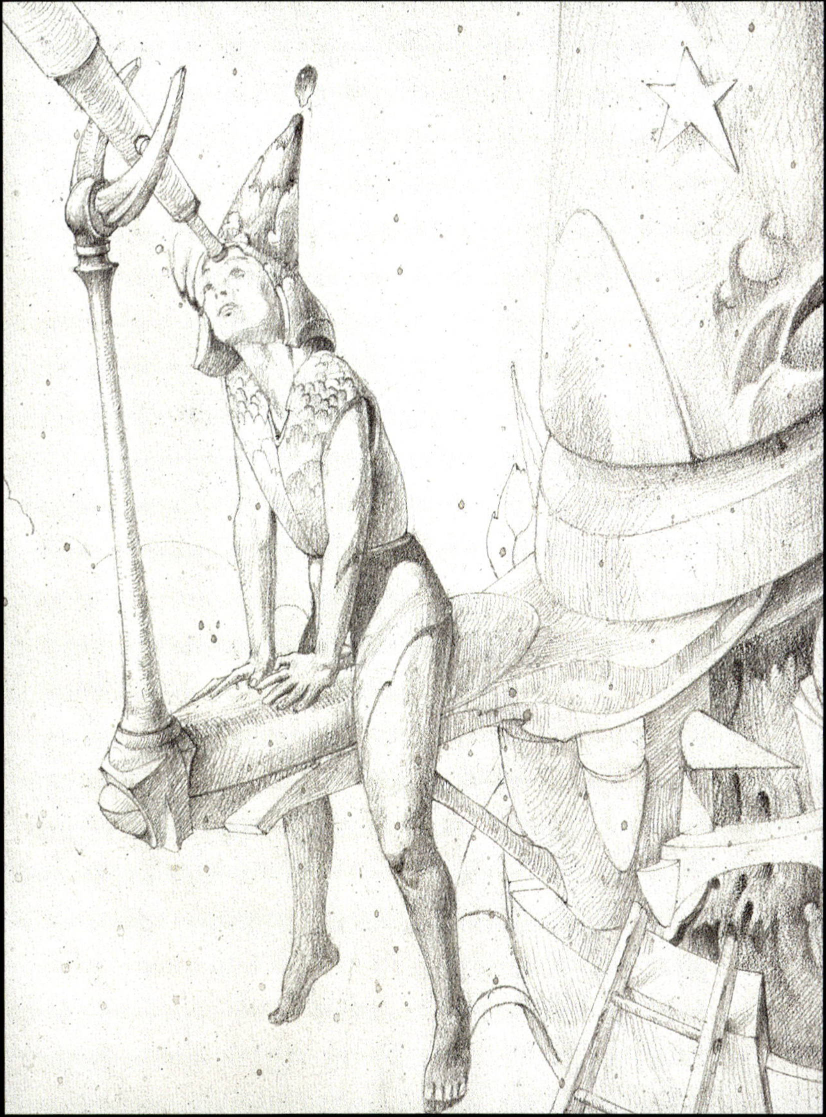

◄ THE INVISIBLE MIND

THE ASTRONOMER - study

CRAZY LOVE ➤

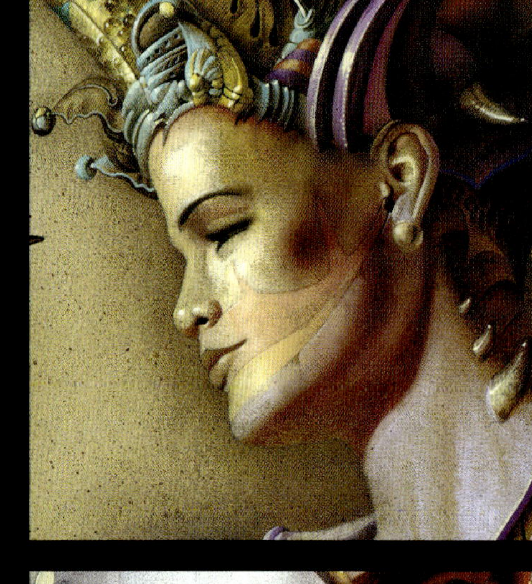

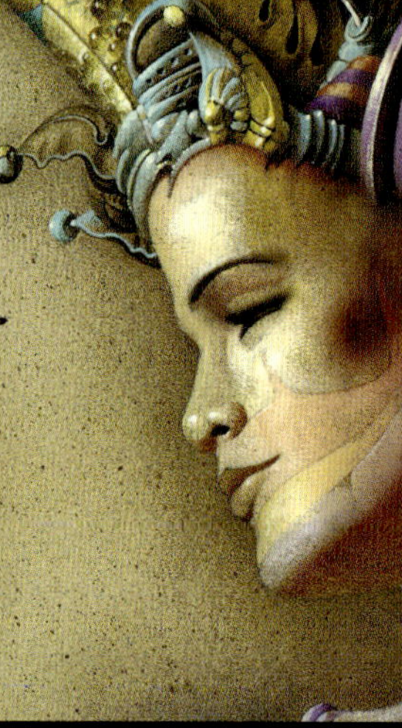

DANCE OF THE ➤
PUPPETEER

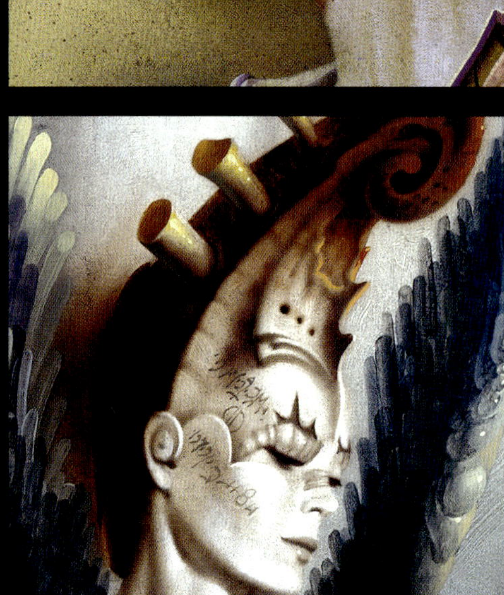

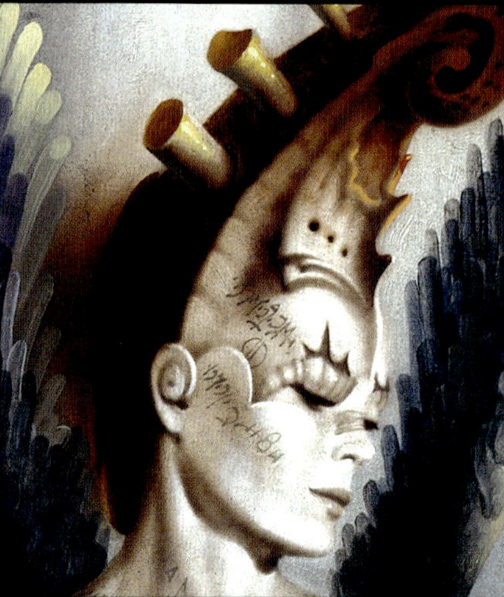

COURAGE - study ➤

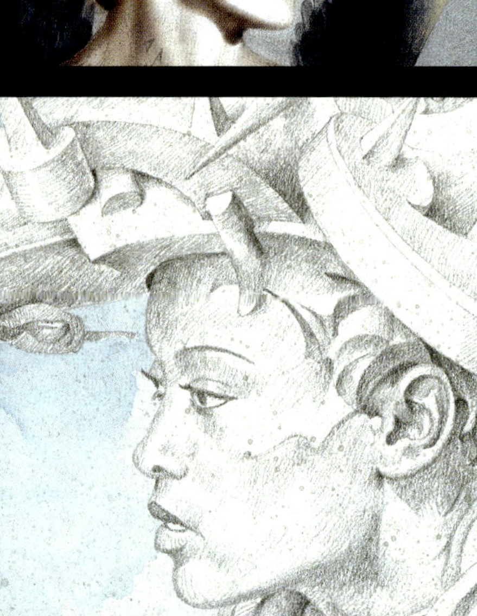

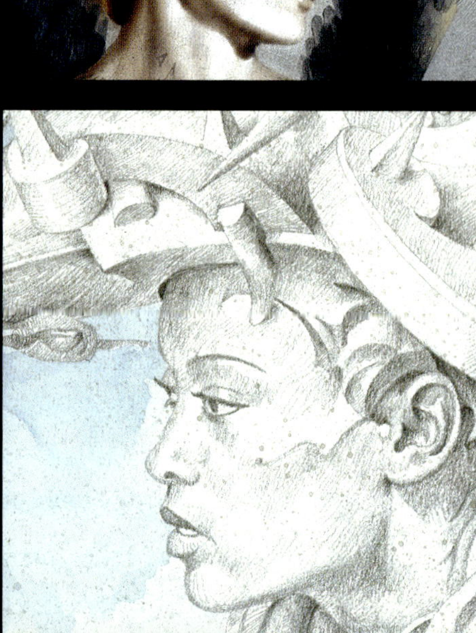

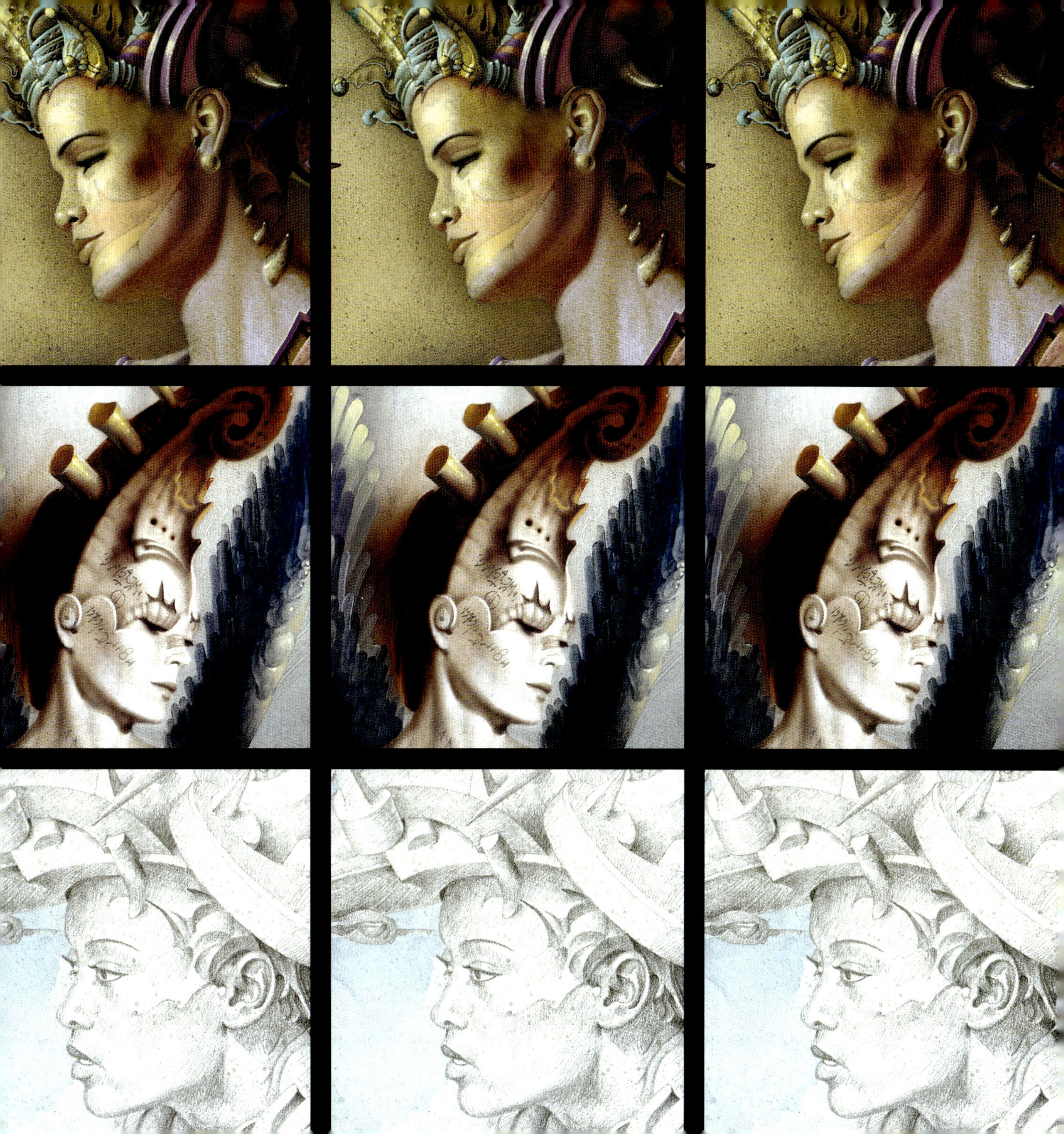

THE SONG

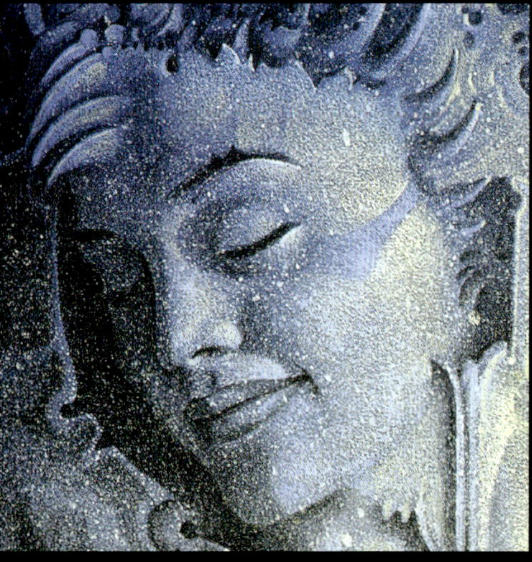

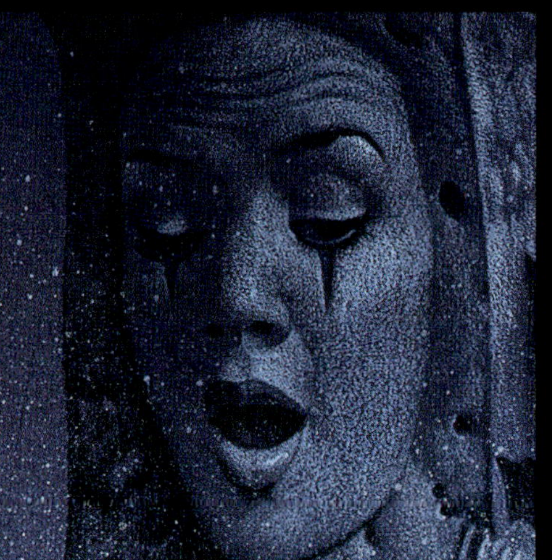

ALTER EGO

ORIGIN

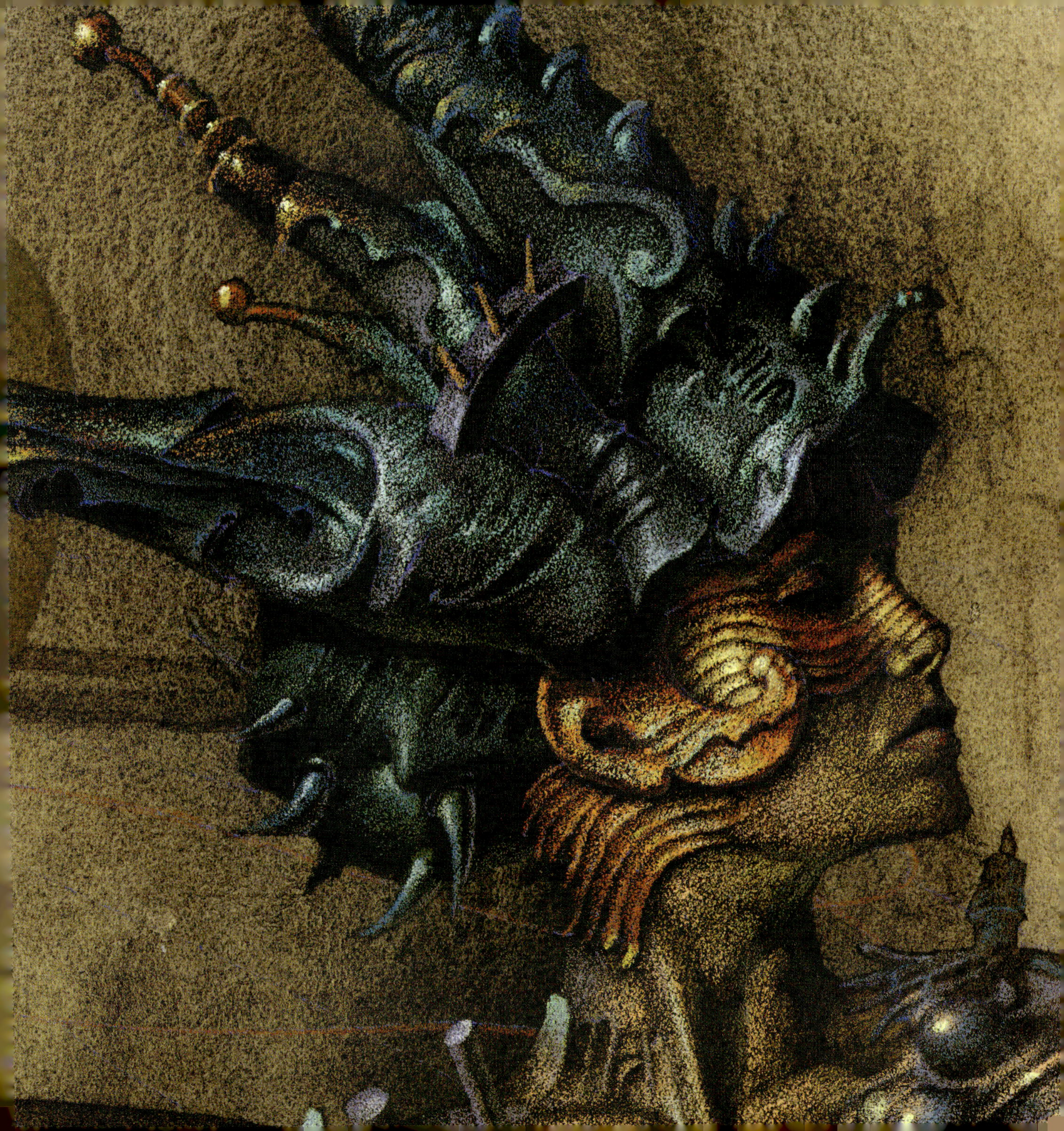

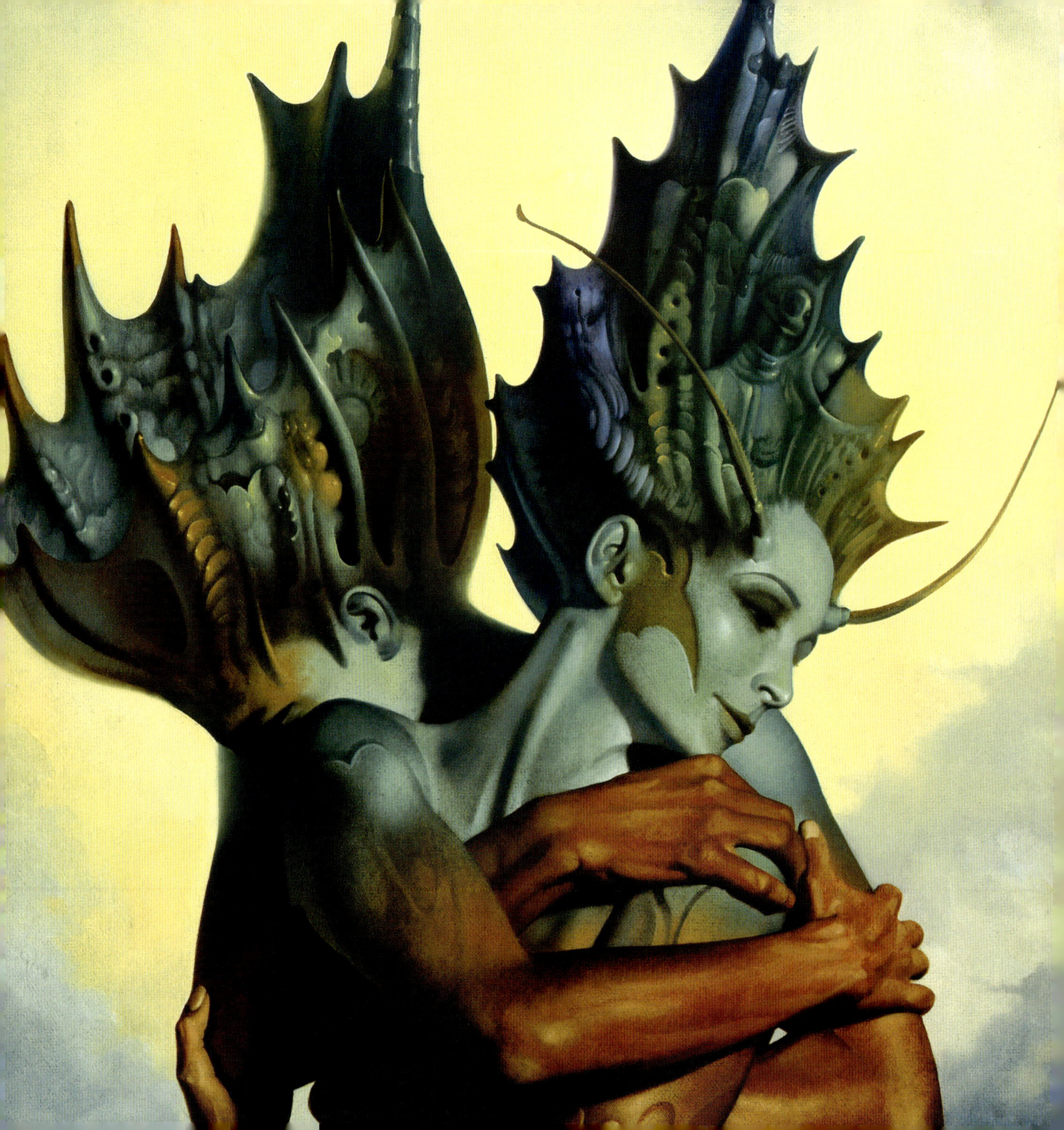

index /

index des œuvres

TUV

Gil Bruvel

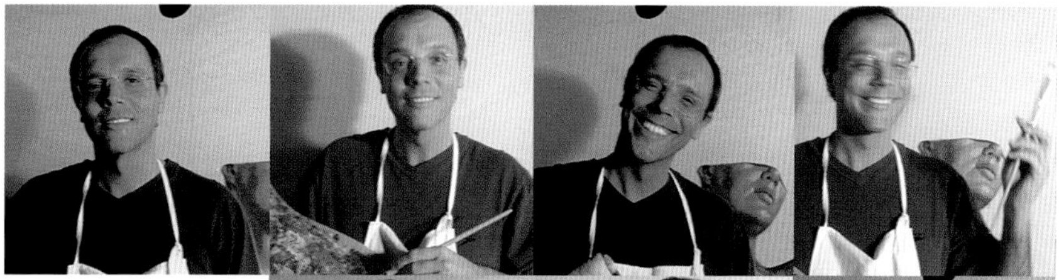

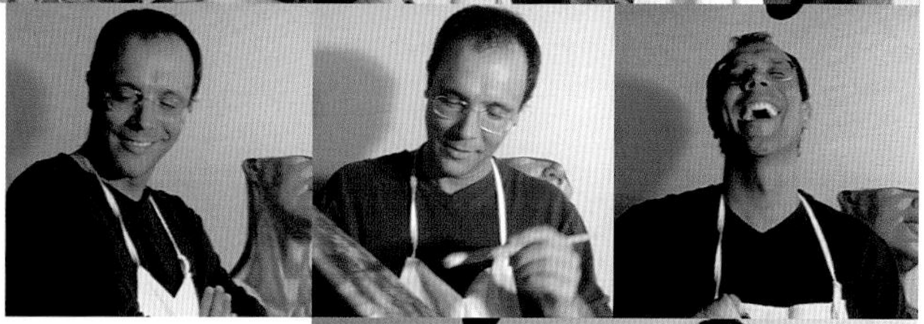

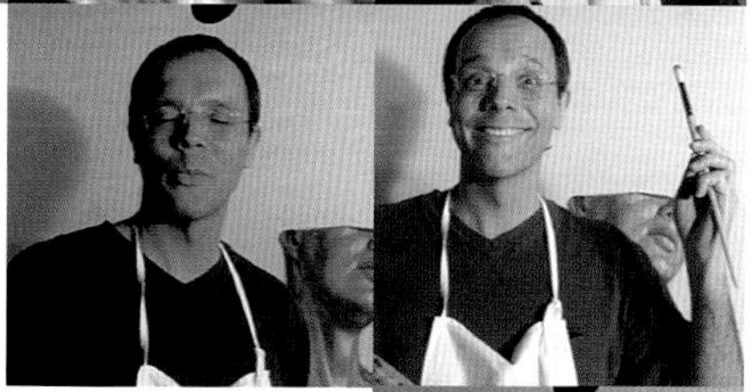

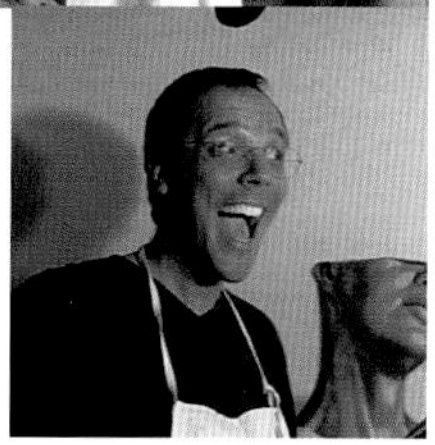

While taking drawing lessons at age 9, it became evident to me that I wanted to spend my life creating art.

Although I was born just outside of Sydney, Australia, in 1959, my French-born parents moved our family back to the small town of Istres in the south of France when I was 4 years old. There, I found myself inspired by the renowned light and landscapes in this region. As I began working with oil paint at the age of 12, this stunning environment had an enormous, lasting influence on my palette–giving me luminous colors I continue to use today. Wanting to widen my creative path, I left a traditional school in 1974 and spent the next three years in an intensive, exclusive restoration workshop, learning the techniques of the Old Masters. Ever since, I've solely dedicated my life to the pursuit of art.

I've traveled throughout Europe a great deal and many other parts of the world as well, I've also had the pleasure of living in southern California and enjoyed the captivating beauty of Maui, Hawaii, for nearly nine years. Throughout the past decade I've continued to explore my creativity by experimenting with various artistic tools, including computer graphics, and by taking on large-scale commission projects. I'm gratified to be able to share my artistic vision with collectors around the world.

In this book, I wanted to show you an intimate aspect of my creative process in which I conceive my work as a dream within a dream. This book of portraits portrays beings within their own worlds–which also offers insight into my own artistic world. I thank you for joining me on this journey.

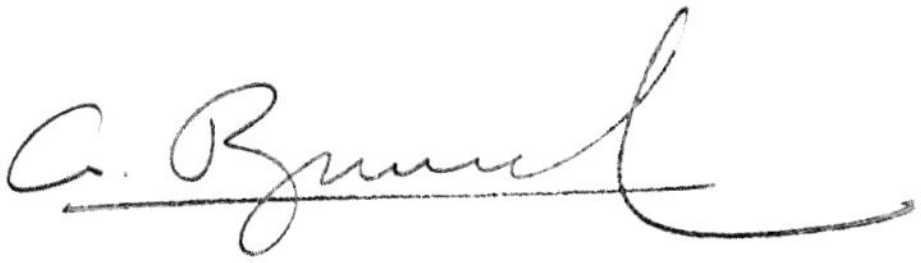

LA CONVERSATION ➤

TIME TRANSFERS ➤ ➤

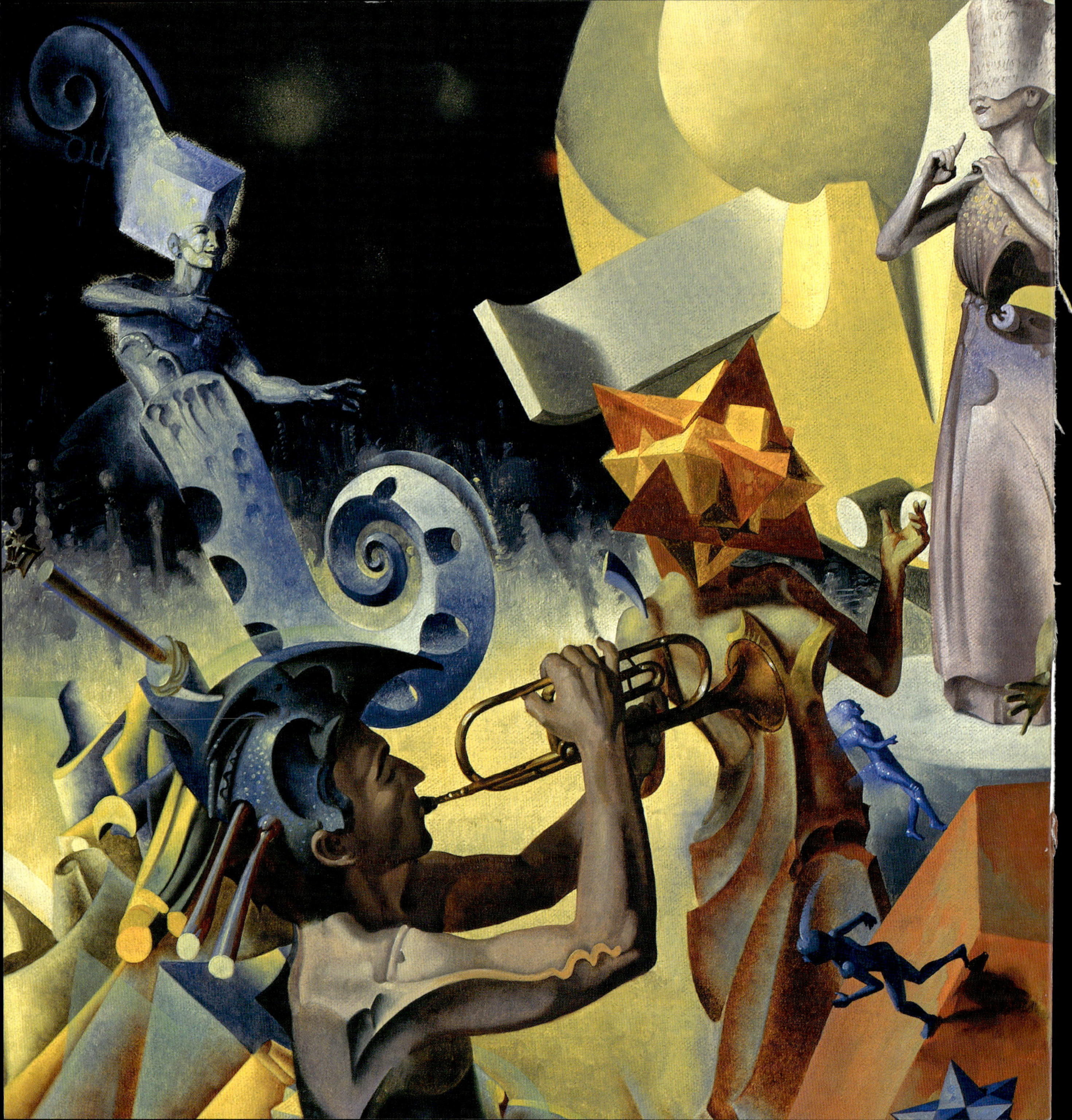

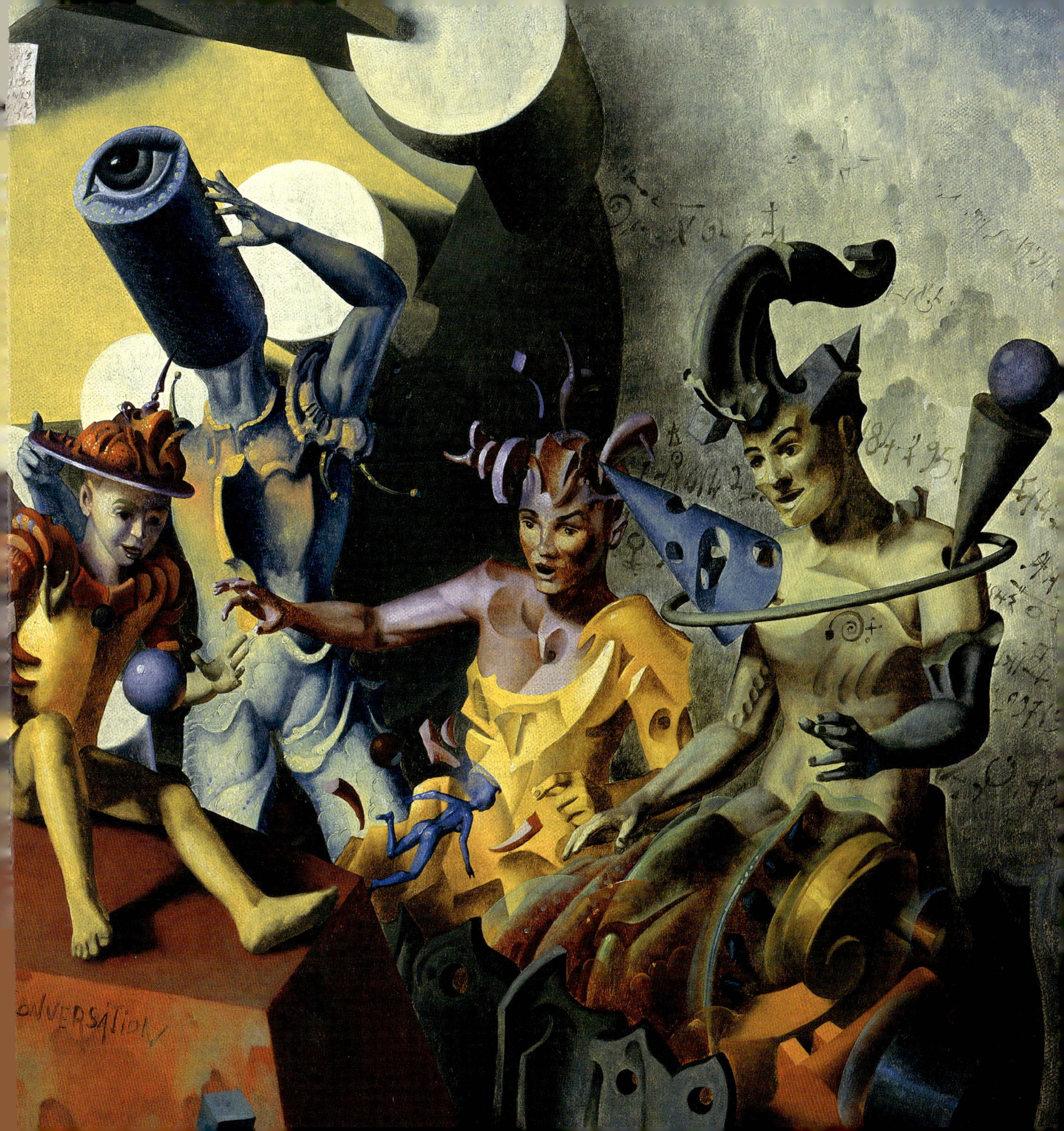
ONVERSATION

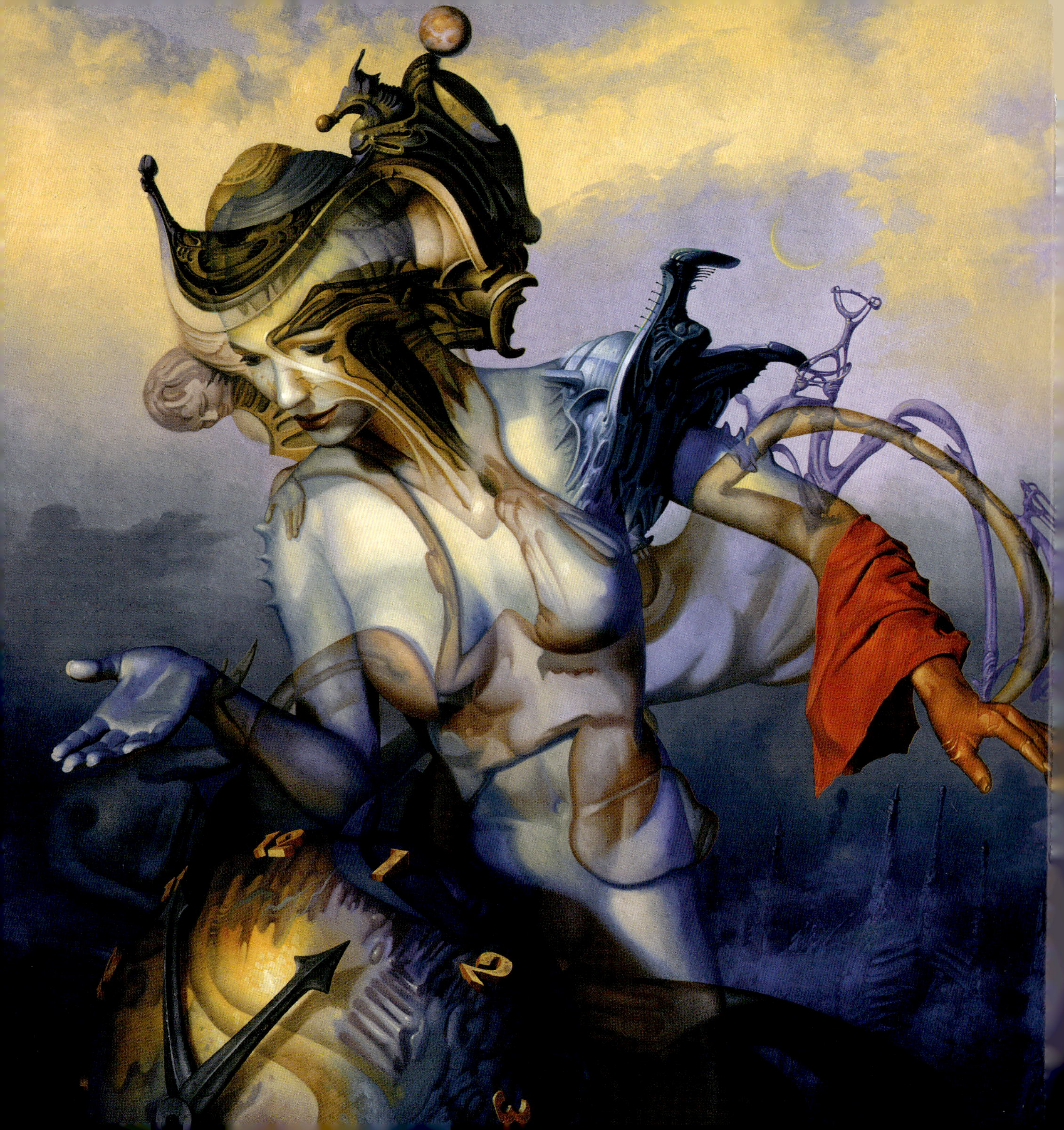